Cake

First published in 2012 by Collins
An imprint of HarperCollinsPublishers
77–85 Fulham Palace Road
London W6 8JB

www.harpercollins.co.uk

10 9 8 7 6 5 4 3 2 1

Text © Rachel Allen 2012

Photography © Philip Webb 2012

Rachel Allen asserts the moral right to be identified as the
author of this work.

A catalogue record for this book is available from the British Library.

The author and the publishers would like to thank the following for
permission to include these cakes:

Page 97, NYC crumb cake from *Baked in America* by David Lesniak
and David Muniz, Ebury Press, 2011. Page 86, Vegan chocolate
cake adapted by the kind permission of Giorgio Locatelli.

Page 54, coconut photograph © Image Source/Getty Images.

ISBN: 978-0-00-730905-4

Printed and bound by Lego, Italy

MIX
Paper from
responsible sources
FSC™ C007454

FSC™ is a non-profit international organisation established to promote the
responsible management of the world's forests. Products carrying the FSC
label are independently certified to assure consumers that they come from
forests that are managed to meet the social, economic and ecological needs
of present and future generations, and other controlled sources.

Find out more about HarperCollins and the environment at
www.harpercollins.co.uk/green

Cake

RACHEL ALLEN

Collins

Contents

Introduction

I love every type of cake, whether light and buttery or dense and fudgy. In fact, I have adored baking ever since I was a child, when I began making cakes with my mother and sister. I was transfixed by the whole process – from stirring the ingredients in a big bowl to popping the filled tin in the oven and waiting for the magic to happen. Then, hey presto, the mixture had turned into a proper cake, beautifully risen and golden and with mouth-watering smells filling the kitchen. Our finished creation was then carefully removed and decorated before being placed on a plate and proudly presented to the rest of the family or to friends.

I know I'm not alone in my passion for cakes. Indeed, I get asked for my cake recipes more than any other type of dish! This book is aimed at anyone who has ever enjoyed a slice of cake – whether baking is your favourite pastime or if you've never tried it before. My previous book, *Bake*, was dedicated to all types of baking, from pies and casseroles to puddings and biscuits. This volume focuses exclusively on cake baking, showing you how to quickly master the basics, add effortless decoration and expand your repertoire of great-looking, great-tasting cakes to give, share and enjoy.

There is always something in my diary that offers the perfect excuse to bake a cake. With this in mind, I've divided the book into sections, each with a selection of cakes for different occasions, be it a simple picnic or coffee with a friend, or an elaborate event like a wedding, birthday or special celebration. You'll find chapters devoted to fast cakes, festive cakes, classic and teatime cakes, novelty cakes for children's parties and recipes catering specifically for people with allergies or food intolerances.

The recipes in this book are all easy to follow, with no particular level of skill or experience required. Most are quick and simple to make, while a few will take a little more time and effort. The sections on cake decoration include recipes for honeycomb, chocolate squares and fondant-icing shapes, each of which will help you add that special finishing touch or real 'wow' factor. Icing and decoration are usually tailored to specific cakes, but you can experiment with mixing ideas from different recipes and be as creative as you like.

There is something in *Cake* for everyone, from the casual cook to the committed baker, and I hope you enjoy using this book as much as I've enjoyed creating the recipes for it. I believe that divine recipes are made to be shared and cake tastes best when enjoyed with friends or family. It's true that cakes are an indulgence and not something to have every day, but eaten every so often they are a genuine treat. Even a tiny sliver can really brighten your day or transform an otherwise ordinary get-together into a memorable occasion – magic not only in the making but in the eating!

Rachel x

You don't always need a special reason to bake a cake and this chapter is full of cakes that are really easy to put together. The recipes are not elaborate; there are no grand tiers or complicated icings here. The cakes are straightforward without involving too much technique or hours of labour. These cakes are the ones that I keep in a tin in the kitchen, ready for when a friend calls round or invites me over for coffee. They are also good for popping into a lunchbox or at the end of a simple supper, when you don't need a fancy dessert, just a little slice of something sweet. Easily achievable and simply delicious, these are cake recipes that you'll return to again and again.

01/ Easy

Lemon poppy-seed cake

Poppy seeds are used in cakes and many other dishes across the world, their fragrant nutty taste going especially well with the citrus flavour of lemon or orange. There is a lot of milk in this recipe, which makes the crumb very tender and soft. It's baked in a bundt tin, which gives more of a crusty outer layer, though if you don't have one, a standard round cake tin would do just as well, or you could use the mixture to make muffins (see page 12). If you like, you could decorate with candied orange slices (see page 340), placing these on the iced cake instead of sprinkling over the poppy seeds.

Prep time: **10 minutes**
Baking time: **50–70 minutes**
Ready in: **1 hour 40 minutes**
Serves: **10–14**

325g (11½oz) plain flour, plus extra
   for dusting
1½ tsp baking powder
1½ tsp salt
400g (14oz) caster sugar
25g (1oz) poppy seeds, plus
   1–2 tsp to decorate
225ml (8fl oz) sunflower or vegetable
   oil, plus extra for greasing
4 eggs
1 tsp vanilla extract
325ml (11½fl oz) milk
Finely grated zest of 1 lemon
Candied orange slices (see page 340),
   to decorate (optional)

For the icing
200g (7oz) icing sugar, sifted
3 tbsp lemon juice

2.5 litre (4⅓ pint) bundt tin (about
   23cm/9in in diameter) or 25cm (10in)
   diameter cake tin (see page 336)

Preheat the oven to 180°C (350°F), Gas mark 4, then grease the bundt tin with sunflower or vegetable oil and dust with flour. If you're using a standard type of cake tin, grease the sides and line the base with a disc of baking parchment.

Sift the flour, baking powder and salt into a large bowl, add the sugar and poppy seeds and mix together.

In a separate bowl, whisk together the remaining ingredients until combined. Tip this mixture into the dry ingredients and mix together using a wooden spoon to make a smooth batter. You may need to use a whisk briefly to get rid of any lumps of flour.

Tip into the prepared tin and bake for 50–60 minutes (60–70 minutes if using a standard cake tin). When cooked, the cake should feel springy to the touch and a skewer inserted into the centre should come out clean.

Remove the cake from the oven and allow to sit for just 2 minutes, then loosen the edges with a small, sharp knife, place a wire rack upside down on top of the cake and carefully turn it over. Gently remove the tin and allow to cool completely (see page 336).

While the cake is baking, or while it's cooling, you can make the icing. Beat the icing sugar and lemon juice together until smooth. Carefully transfer the cake to a cake stand or serving plate, then drizzle the icing backwards and forwards from the centre to the outside of the cake in a zigzig pattern. Sprinkle over the poppy seeds straight away and the candied orange slices (see page 340), if you're using them, before the icing has a chance to dry.

Recipe continued overleaf

Orange poppy-seed cake

Make the cake as in the recipe on page 10, replacing the lemon zest in the sponge with the finely grated zest of 1 orange and using orange juice instead of lemon juice in the icing.

Lemon poppy-seed muffins

Prep time: 10 minutes
Baking time: 20–25 minutes
Ready in: 1 hour
Makes: 12 muffins

215g (7½oz) plain flour
1 tsp baking powder
Pinch of salt
265g (9½oz) caster sugar
15g (½oz) poppy seeds, plus 2 tsp
   for sprinkling
150ml (5fl oz) sunflower or vegetable oil
3 eggs
½ tsp vanilla extract
215ml (7½fl oz) milk
Finely grated zest of ½ large lemon

For the icing
130g (4½oz) icing sugar, sifted
1–2 tbsp lemon juice

12-cup muffin tray and 12 muffin cases
   (see page 336)

Preheat the oven to 180°C (350°F), Gas mark 4, and line the muffin tray with the paper cases.

Mix the ingredients for the sponge following the main recipe on page 10, then divide the batter between the paper cases, filling each case three-quarters full.

Bake for 20–25 minutes or until lightly golden on top and springy to the touch. Allow to cool in the muffin tray for 5 minutes, then transfer to a wire rack to cool down fully.

Make the icing as on page 10, then drizzle it over the cooled muffins and sprinkle with the poppy seeds to finish.

Apricot, pistachio and saffron muffins

I adore the combination of the sweet juicy apricots with the exotically perfumed saffron. Use peaches (fresh or tinned) in place of the apricots if you wish. These muffins are delicious served with a spoonful of crème fraîche and a piping-hot cup of coffee or tea.

Prep time: 15 minutes
Baking time: 35 minutes
Ready in: 1 hour 15 minutes
Makes: 12 muffins

225ml (8fl oz) buttermilk
2 eggs
Pinch of saffron
300g (11oz) plain flour
2 tsp baking powder
½ tsp bicarbonate of soda
½ tsp salt
200g (7oz) caster sugar
125g (4½oz) butter, cut into
   1cm (½in) cubes
300g (11oz) fresh or tinned apricots
   (about 7 fresh apricots, stones
   removed), roughly chopped
75g (3oz) unsalted shelled pistachios,
   roughly chopped

12-cup muffin tray and 12 muffin cases
   (see page 336)

Preheat the oven to 180°C (350°F), Gas mark 4, and line the muffin tray with the paper cases.

Place the buttermilk, eggs and saffron in a bowl and whisk together until smooth.

In a separate large bowl, sift together the flour, baking powder, bicarbonate of soda and salt and mix in the sugar. Add the cubes of butter and rub in with your fingertips until the mixture resembles coarse breadcrumbs.

Add the wet ingredients and mix together, then fold in the apricots and pistachios. Spoon the batter into the muffin cases, filling each case about three-quarters full.

Bake for about 35 minutes or until golden brown on top and springy to the touch. Allow the muffins to cool for 5 minutes, then remove from the tin and place on a wire rack to finish cooling.

Pear and ginger muffins

These soft, moist muffins are flavoured with chunks of pear and the gentle heat of ginger. The riper the pears, the sweeter the muffins will be. They would be perfect for a picnic or a quick snack on the run.

Prep time: 10 minutes
Baking time: 20 minutes
Ready in: 45 minutes
Makes: 12 muffins

275g (10oz) plain flour, sifted
200g (7oz) caster sugar
2 tsp baking powder
1 tbsp ground ginger
1 tsp salt
4 eggs, beaten
150ml (5fl oz) vegetable oil
300g (11oz) pears, peeled, cored
   and cut into 1cm (½in) dice

12-cup muffin tray and 12 muffin cases
   (see page 336)

Preheat the oven to 180°C (350°F), Gas mark 4, and line the muffin tray with the paper cases.

Place all the ingredients, except the pears, in a large bowl and whisk together until smooth, then fold in the pears and divide between the muffin cases, filling each case three-quarters full. Bake for about 20 minutes or until well risen, golden and feeling springy to the touch.

Remove from the oven and allow to cool for 5 minutes, then take from the muffin tray and place on a wire rack to cool down fully.

Apple and ginger (or cinnamon) muffins

Follow the recipe above, replacing the pears with the same quantity of chopped eating apples and either keeping the ginger or replacing it with 2 teaspoons of ground cinnamon.

Coconut and lime cake

Ingredients grown together seem to go together. Just as apples and blackberries are a perfect match, so too are coconut and lime. The coconut flavour in this recipe comes from both desiccated coconut and coconut milk. The coconut milk is an unusual addition, but it is nonetheless an excellent baking ingredient that helps make the cake lovely and soft due to its high oil content. If at all possible, serve this cake outside on a summer's evening, ideally accompanied by piña coladas or margaritas!

Prep time: 20 minutes
Baking time: 30–35 minutes
Ready in: 1 hour 45 minutes
Serves: 8–12

150ml (5fl oz) coconut milk
    (see the tip below)
50g (2oz) desiccated coconut
25ml (1fl oz) milk
250g (9oz) butter, softened,
    plus extra for greasing
250g (9oz) caster sugar
3 eggs, beaten
Juice and finely grated zest of 2 limes
275g (10oz) self-raising flour
50g (2oz) coconut flakes, toasted
    (see the tip below), to decorate

For the icing
15ml (½fl oz) coconut milk
250g (9oz) icing sugar, sifted
Juice of ½–1 lime

20cm (8in) square cake tin with 5cm
    (2in) sides (see page 334)

Preheat the oven to 180°C (350°F), Gas mark 4, then butter the sides of the cake tin and line the base with a square of baking parchment. Pour the coconut milk into a saucepan and place over a high heat. As soon as it boils, remove from the heat and stir in the desiccated coconut and the milk.

Cream the butter until soft in a large bowl or in an electric food mixer. Add the sugar and beat until the mixture is light and fluffy.

Whisk the eggs together with the lime juice and zest in a small bowl, then gradually add the eggs to the creamed butter mixture, beating all the time. Sift in the flour and fold in gently to mix.

Tip the batter into the prepared tin and smooth the top with a spatula or palette knife. Place in the oven and bake for 30–35 minutes. When the cake is ready, a skewer inserted into the centre will come out very slightly sticky.

Leave to cool in the tin for 10 minutes, then use a small, sharp knife to loosen the edges and carefully remove the cake from the tin before leaving on a wire rack to finish cooling (see page 334).

As the cake cools, make the icing. In a bowl, whisk together the coconut milk, icing sugar and the juice of half a lime, adding more if the mixture seems too stiff. Carefully pour the icing over the cake, to cover it in an even layer, then sprinkle over the toasted coconut flakes.

Tip This recipe uses a small (165ml) tin of coconut milk. If you can't get a small tin, then use a larger one and store any leftover milk in the fridge, where it will keep (in an airtight container) for up to four days, or it can be frozen. Coconut flakes can be toasted in a dry, hot frying pan for a few minutes.

Apple and walnut cake

Some spices have their favourite accompaniments: cinnamon, for example, seems to prefer apple to almost anything else. The two are combined here with crunchy walnuts and muscovado (soft brown) sugar for its unrefined, caramel flavour. I've used some wholemeal flour in this recipe as I like the difference it makes, adding a little weightiness in both texture and taste. The cake makes a delicious dessert, eaten warm with whipped cream, or you could serve it in the afternoon with tea.

Prep time: **20** minutes
Baking time: **55** minutes
Ready in: **1 hour 45 minutes**
Serves: **10–12**

300g (11oz) plain flour
1 tsp ground cinnamon
2 tsp baking powder
½ tsp bicarbonate of soda
1 tsp salt
175g (6oz) wholemeal flour
225g (8oz) soft light brown sugar
175ml (6fl oz) sunflower oil, plus
    extra for greasing
3 eggs
150ml (5fl oz) milk
3 eating apples, peeled, cored and
    chopped into 1cm (½in) dice
75g (3oz) walnuts, roughly chopped

For the glaze
150g (5oz) soft light brown sugar
75g (3oz) butter

25cm (10in) diameter cake tin with
    6cm (2½in) sides (see page 334)

Preheat the oven to 170°C (325°F), Gas mark 3, then grease the sides of the cake tin with sunflower oil and line the base with a disc of baking parchment.

Sift the plain flour, cinnamon, baking powder, bicarbonate of soda and salt into a large bowl, then add the wholemeal flour and sugar and mix together.

In a separate bowl, whisk together the sunflower oil, eggs and milk, then tip these into the flour and whisk until you have a smooth batter, and stir in the apples and walnuts. Pour the mixture into the prepared tin and bake for 55 minutes or until a skewer inserted into the centre of the cake comes out clean.

About 5 minutes before the cake is due to come out, make the glaze. Put the sugar, butter and 1 tablespoon of water into a saucepan and place over a medium heat. Stir until the sugar has dissolved, then remove from the heat.

When the cake is cooked, take it out of the oven and let it sit in the tin for 10 minutes. Using a small, sharp knife, loosen around the edges and carefully remove the cake from the tin before transferring to a serving plate (see page 334).

Reheat the glaze and brush all over the cake, then allow to cool before serving. The glaze means this cake will keep for up to a week in an airtight container.

Bakewell cake

The Derbyshire town of Bakewell is responsible for the invention of the classic tart to which the town gave its name. The divine combination of raspberries and almonds makes for a gorgeous recipe – its inventor must have been someone who baked very well indeed! This cake is an evolution of the idea, using fresh or frozen raspberries rather than raspberry jam. It's a simple recipe but a perfect example of how a simple combination of flavours can be deliciously effective.

Prep time: **15 minutes**
Baking time: **50–55 minutes**
Ready in: **1 hour 45 minutes**
Serves: **6–8**

150g (5oz) butter, softened, plus extra for greasing
150g (5oz) caster sugar
2 eggs
A few drops (not more than $\frac{1}{8}$ tsp) of almond essence or extract
50ml (2fl oz) milk
150g (5oz) self-raising flour, sifted
150g (5oz) ground almonds
150g (5oz) fresh or frozen (and defrosted) raspberries
25g (1oz) flaked almonds
Icing sugar, for dusting
Softly whipped cream and fresh raspberries, to decorate

20cm (8in) diameter cake tin with 6cm (2½ in) sides (see page 334)

Preheat the oven to 180°C (350°F), Gas mark 4, then butter the sides of the cake tin and line the base with a disc of baking parchment.

Cream the butter until soft in a large bowl or in an electric food mixer. Add the sugar and beat until the mixture is light and fluffy.

Whisk the eggs and the almond essence or extract together in a small bowl for a few seconds or just until combined, then gradually add the eggs to the creamed butter mixture, beating all the time. Next beat in the milk, then add the flour and ground almonds, carefully folding these in just until they are mixed.

Next add the raspberries and fold in gently so as not to break them up too much. Tip the batter into the prepared tin, then scatter over the flaked almonds. Bake for 50–55 minutes or until a skewer inserted into the centre of the cake comes out clean.

Remove from the oven and allow to cool in the tin for 10 minutes. Use a small, sharp knife to loosen the edges, then carefully remove the cake from the tin and leave on a wire rack to cool down completely before transferring to a serving plate (see page 334).

Dust with icing sugar. Serve with softly whipped cream if you wish, or decorate with fresh raspberries.

Marbled chocolate crumble cake

I adore marbled cakes – they look so special with the different colours of sponge swirling into each other. In this recipe the crumble topping adds a contrasting crunch as well as an extra hit of chocolate. Serve on its own or after dinner with some softly whipped cream or crème fraîche.

Prep time: 25 minutes
Baking time: 50–60 minutes
Ready in: 2 hours
Serves: 6–8

225g (8oz) butter, softened, plus extra for greasing
225g (8oz) caster sugar
4 eggs
1 tsp vanilla extract
225g (8oz) plain flour
2 tsp baking powder
50ml (2fl oz) milk
25g (1oz) cocoa powder
Icing sugar, for dusting

For the crumble topping
125g (4½oz) plain flour, sifted
75g (3oz) caster sugar
75g (3oz) unsalted butter, chilled and cut into cubes
75g (3oz) dark or milk chocolate, in chips or roughly chopped into pieces

23cm (9in) diameter spring-form or loose-bottomed cake tin with 6cm (2½in) sides (see page 336)

First make the crumble topping. Using your fingertips, rub together the flour, sugar and butter in a large bowl until it resembles thick breadcrumbs, then mix in the chocolate pieces. Set aside in the fridge while you make the sponge.

Preheat the oven to 180°C (350°F), Gas mark 4, and butter the sides and the base of the cake tin. If you're using a spring-form tin, make sure the base is upside down so there's no lip and the cake can slide off easily when cooked. Cream the butter until soft in a large bowl or in an electric food mixer. Add the sugar and beat until the mixture is light and fluffy.

Whisk the eggs and vanilla extract together in a small bowl for a few seconds or just until combined, then gradually add the eggs to the creamed butter and sugar mixture, beating all the time. Sift in the flour and baking powder and fold in carefully, then add the milk and mix gently to combine. Tip half of the cake mixture into another large bowl, then sift the cocoa powder into this bowl and fold it in.

Place the two different cake mixtures in the prepared tin by alternating heaped tablespoonfuls of the vanilla batter with the chocolate one, then, with a skewer or similar implement, gently draw swirls through the cake mixture to 'marbleise' it. Try not to over-mix or you won't get that wonderful marbled effect.

Scatter the crumble mixture evenly over the top of the cake mixture and bake for 50–60 minutes or until the crumble is golden and a skewer inserted into the centre of the cake comes out clean.

Remove from the oven and allow to cool in the tin for 10 minutes, then loosen around the edges using a small, sharp knife and remove the sides of the tin (see page 336). Place the cake (sitting on the base of the tin) on a wire rack and allow to cool completely.

Use a palette knife or metal fish slice to loosen the bottom of the cake from the base of the tin, then slide the palette knife or fish slice under the cake and carefully ease it onto a plate. Dust with icing sugar to serve.

Lemon crumble cupcakes

This recipe takes lemon cupcakes to the next level. The lemon curd is easy to make (see overleaf) – though you could use a bought variety, of course – and adds a wonderfully sweet-sharp citrus softness. The crumble topping is quick to put together, meanwhile, and adds a great contrasting crunch.

Prep time: 30 minutes (excluding the lemon curd)
Baking time: 30 minutes
Ready in: 1 hour 30 minutes
Makes: 12 cupcakes

200g (7oz) butter, softened
200g (7oz) caster sugar
4 eggs
200g (7oz) self-raising flour
Juice of 1 lemon
150g (5oz) lemon curd (see page 27)

For the crumble topping
75g (3oz) plain flour
75g (3oz) caster sugar
Finely grated zest of 1 lemon
100g (3½oz) butter, chilled and cut into 1cm (½in) cubes

12-cup muffin tray and 12 muffin cases (see page 336)

Preheat the oven to 180°C (350°F), Gas mark 4, and line the muffin tray with the paper cases.

First make the crumble topping. Sift the flour into a bowl, then add the sugar and lemon zest and mix together to combine. Use your fingertips to rub the butter into the flour until the mixture forms coarse flakes and crumbs, then set aside in the fridge until needed.

To make the cupcake batter, cream the butter in a large bowl or in an electric food mixer until soft. Add the sugar and beat until the mixture is light and fluffy.

Whisk the eggs together in a small bowl for a few seconds or just until mixed, then gradually add them to the creamed butter mixture, beating all the time. Sift in the flour and add the lemon juice, then fold in gently to incorporate.

Divide half of the batter between the muffin cases, filling each about one-third full. Add roughly ½ tablespoon of lemon curd to each paper case, so that it forms a small dollop in the middle. Then divide the other half of the batter between the cases, spooning it over the lemon curd. Finally divide the lemon crumble mixture between the cupcakes.

Bake for about 30 minutes or until nice and golden on top and lightly springy to the touch in the middle. Don't worry if some of the curd bubbles over the top of the cupcakes while they cook.

Allow to cool for 10 minutes before removing from the muffin tray and placing on a wire rack to cool down completely.

Recipe continued overleaf

Lemon curd

Prep time: **10 minutes**
Cooking time: **10 minutes**
Ready in: **30 minutes**
Makes: **300g (11oz)**

75g (3oz) butter
150g (5oz) caster sugar
Juice and finely grated
  zest of 3 lemons
2 eggs
1 egg yolk

In a saucepan over a very low heat, melt the butter with the sugar, lemon zest and juice. Place the eggs and egg yolk in a bowl and beat together well, then pour into the pan.

Stir carefully over a low heat until the mixture has thickened enough to coat the back of a spoon. Take care not to let the mixture get too hot, or the eggs may scramble.

Remove from the heat and pour into a bowl or a sterilised jar (see the tip below). The lemon curd will thicken further as it cools. Stored in the fridge, it will keep for a couple of weeks.

Orange curd

Make in the same way, substituting the lemons with two oranges and reducing the amount of caster sugar to 125g (4½oz).

Tip To sterilise jars for jams and preserves, wash them in hot soapy water, then rinse and dry. Place the jars upturned on a baking tray in the oven (preheated to at least 130°C/250°F/Gas mark ½) for approximately 15 minutes or until completely dry. Leave them upturned on a clean tea towel until ready to use. Alternatively, you can put them through a hot cycle in the dishwasher.

Tropical cake

Fresh pineapple is almost reason enough to head to sunnier climes – tangy slices dripping with juice can be one of the great culinary pleasures of a holiday in the tropics. The pineapples we get here can be a little dry by comparison. For this recipe it's fine to use tinned pineapple, however, as it is more predictable in the amount of moisture and sweetness it contains. With the coconut and mango, this cake is a real celebration of tropical flavours.

Prep time: **25 minutes**
Baking time: **45 minutes**
Ready in: **2 hours**
Serves: **8–12**

250g (9oz) tinned pineapple
(drained weight of a 432g tin)
200g (7oz) soft light brown sugar
225g (8oz) butter, softened,
plus extra for greasing
3 eggs
125g (4½oz) self-raising flour,
plus extra for dusting
100g (3½oz) desiccated coconut
1 large mango, peeled and sliced,
to decorate

For the icing
250g (9oz) mascarpone
50g (2oz) icing sugar, sifted

23cm (9in) square cake tin with 5cm
(2in) sides (see page 334)

Preheat the oven to 180°C (350°F), Gas mark 4, then butter the sides of the cake tin and dust with flour and line the base with a square of baking parchment.

Place the pineapple in a food processor and whiz for a minute or two until puréed, then put into a saucepan with the sugar. Set over a low heat and cook, stirring occasionally, for about 5 minutes or until the mixture turns a light brown colour. Then set aside and allow to cool.

Beat the cooled pineapple purée with the butter in a large bowl or in an electric food mixer. Whisk the eggs together in a small bowl for just a few seconds until mixed, then gradually add the eggs to the pineapple and butter mixture, beating continuously. Sift in the flour, add the coconut and fold in gently to combine.

Tip the batter into the prepared tin, then bake in the oven for about 45 minutes or until a skewer inserted into the centre of the cake comes out clean. Allow the cake to sit in the tin for about 20 minutes, then use a small, sharp knife to loosen the edges and carefully remove the cake from the tin before leaving on a wire rack to cool down completely (see page 334).

To make the icing, whisk together the mascarpone and icing sugar, then spread over the cooled cake using a palette knife and finish by decorating with the sliced mango.

Toscatårta or Swedish almond cake

There is a banquet of baked Swedish treats, from *kanelbullar* (cinnamon buns) to *kladdkaka* (sticky chocolate cake), but one of the most well known is this relatively simple but absolutely divine almond cake – a light sponge topped with sweetened buttery almonds. Traditionally eaten at Christmas, it goes down just as well in the summer. Great on its own or with sweet, ripe strawberries.

Prep time: 15 minutes
Baking time: 45–50 minutes
Ready in: 1 hour 20 minutes
Serves: 8–10

3 eggs
150g (5oz) caster sugar
150g (5oz) plain flour, plus extra
  for dusting
1½ tsp baking powder
2 tsp vanilla extract
3 tbsp milk
75g (3oz) butter, melted, plus extra
  for greasing

For the topping
50g (2oz) butter
100g (3½oz) flaked almonds
50g (2oz) caster sugar
2 tsp plain flour
3 tbsp double or regular cream
1 tsp vanilla extract

23cm (9in) diameter spring-form or
  loose-bottomed cake tin with 6cm
  (2½in) sides (see page 336)

Preheat the oven to 180°C (350°F), Gas mark 4, then grease the base and sides of the cake tin with butter and dust with flour. If you're using a spring-form tin, make sure the base is upside down, so there's no lip and the cake can slide off easily when cooked.

Using a hand-held electric beater or an electric food mixer, whisk together the eggs and the sugar for 5–7 minutes or until thick and mousse-like.

Sift in the flour and baking powder and pour in the vanilla extract, milk and melted butter, then fold everything in until combined. Tip the mixture into the prepared tin and bake for 30–35 minutes or until a skewer inserted into the centre of the cake comes out moist but not totally clean, as the mixture will still need another 10 minutes of cooking. Increase the heat to 200°C (400°F), Gas mark 6.

Just before the 30–35 minutes are up, make the topping. Place the butter in a saucepan over a medium heat. When it has melted, add the remaining ingredients and bring to the boil, allowing the mixture to bubble away for 1 minute.

After the cake has been cooking for 30–35 minutes, remove it from the oven and spoon the almond mixture evenly over the top. Place it back in the oven and bake for about 10–15 minutes or until the topping is golden.

Leave to cool in the tin for 10 minutes. Then, using a small, sharp knife, loosen around the edges and carefully remove the sides of the tin (see page 336) before placing the cake (still on the base of the tin) on a wire rack to cool down fully.

To transfer to a plate, use a palette knife to loosen the bottom of the cake from the tin, then slide the knife under the cake and ease it onto the plate to serve.

Lemon and rosemary polenta cake

The polenta and ground almonds in this cake mean that it's already moist even before it's smothered in a rosemary-lemon syrup as it emerges from the oven. The polenta gives a slight crunch too, which contrasts with the moist crumb. If you use a gluten-free baking powder, the cake will be totally gluten free. Stored in an airtight container, it will keep for a week or so.

Prep time: **30 minutes**
Baking time: **1 hour 15 minutes–**
    1 hour 25 minutes
Ready in: **2 hours 30 minutes**
Serves: **10–12**

225g (8oz) fine polenta
1 tsp baking powder
450g (1lb) butter, softened, plus
    extra for greasing
450g (1lb) caster sugar
450g (1lb) ground almonds
6 eggs
Finely grated zest of 2 lemons
3 tsp finely chopped rosemary leaves,
    plus sprigs of rosemary to decorate

For the syrup
Juice of 2 lemons
2 large sprigs of rosemary
100g (3½oz) caster sugar

25cm (10in) diameter cake tin with
    6cm(2½in) sides (see page 334)

Preheat the oven to 170°C (325°F), Gas mark 3, then butter the sides of the cake tin and line the base with a disc of baking parchment.

Mix the polenta and baking powder together in a bowl. In a separate large bowl or in an electric food mixer, cream the butter until soft. Add the sugar and beat until the mixture is light and fluffy, then beat in the ground almonds.

Whisk the eggs together in a small bowl for a few seconds or just until mixed, then gradually add them to the creamed butter mixture, beating all the time. Add the lemon zest and chopped rosemary, then gently fold in the polenta and baking powder to combine.

Tip the batter into the prepared tin and bake on the lowest shelf of the oven for between 1 hour 15 minutes and 1 hour 25 minutes or until a skewer inserted into the centre of the cake comes out clean. The cake will cook to a deep golden-brown colour and may dip a little in the middle.

While the cake is cooking, make the syrup. Place all the ingredients in a saucepan, along with 50ml (2fl oz) of water. Place the saucepan on the hob, and bring to the boil, stirring to dissolve the sugar. Boil for 3–4 minutes until ever so slightly thickened, then remove from the heat and discard the rosemary sprigs.

When the cake is cooked, take it out of the oven and let it sit in the tin for 10 minutes. Loosen around the edges using a small, sharp knife, then carefully remove the cake from the tin and transfer to a serving plate (see page 334). Reheat the syrup and pour over the cake, then leave the cake to cool down completely before serving. I like to decorate the centre with a few flowering sprigs of rosemary.

Orange sour-cream cake

Cakes made with sour cream are especially moist and have a very slight tang to them, which here is complemented by the bittersweet marmalade glaze. That tang is nicely accentuated by serving with spoonfuls of rich, thick crème fraîche. Kept covered, this cake will keep for 3–4 days.

Prep time: 10 minutes
Baking time: 40–50 minutes
Ready in: 1 hour 30 minutes
Serves: 6–8

200g (7oz) butter, softened,
   plus extra for greasing
200g (7oz) caster sugar
2 large eggs, beaten
Finely grated zest of 1 orange
200ml (7fl oz) sour cream
300g (11oz) plain flour
2 tsp baking powder

For the glaze
Juice of 1 orange
100g (3½oz) marmalade

20cm (8in) diameter cake tin with 6cm
   (2½in) sides (see page 334)

Preheat the oven to 180°C (350°F), Gas mark 4, then butter the sides of the cake tin and line the base with a disc of baking parchment.

Cream the butter until soft in a large bowl or in an electric food mixer. Add the sugar and beat until the mixture is light and fluffy. Gradually add the eggs to the creamed butter mixture, beating all the time. Next beat in the orange zest and sour cream, then sift in the flour and baking powder and fold in to combine.

Tip the mixture into the prepared cake tin, then bake for 40–50 minutes or until a skewer inserted into the centre of the cake comes out clean.

While the cake is cooking, make the glaze. Place the orange juice and marmalade in a saucepan. About 5 minutes before the cake has finished cooking, place the pan on the hob and bring to the boil, stirring to dissolve the marmalade. Then remove from the heat.

When the cake is cooked, take it out of the oven and let it sit in the tin for just 5 minutes. Loosening around the edges using a small, sharp knife, carefully remove the cake from the tin (see page 334), peeling away the baking parchment, then transfer to a serving plate.

Straight away pour the marmalade glaze over the cake (after reheating it if it has had a chance to cool down), then allow the cake to cool down fully while soaking up the syrup.

Sometimes we need a cake quickly. It could be a last-minute panic or when there is simply too much else to fit into the day to dedicate two hours to cake making. These fast recipes are for times like that. People often assume that if you have made a cake it has taken hours of work and you must be a genius, but that isn't necessarily the case. Making a cake can take minutes rather than hours. Some of these faster cakes are made in the food processor, some are quite simple and some are not iced, but none of them take long to make. These cakes are not about delicate sugar craft or laborious preparation, they are smart recipes that make great-tasting cakes without cutting any corners.

02/ Fast

Muscovado Madeira cake

This classic English cake got its name from the sweet Madeira wine that it was traditionally served with back in the eighteenth century. Nowadays it's more often eaten with tea, although if you do have a bottle of Madeira or dessert wine, it would go perfectly with either of those. This version is flavoured with the deep molasses sweetness of muscovado (soft brown) sugar. It's a versatile recipe and you could include a handful of glacé cherries, the finely grated zest of an orange or even a teaspoon of ground cinnamon if you like, adding these at the same time as the flour. (See also the additional variations below.)

Prep time: **10 minutes**
Baking time: **40–45 minutes**
Ready in: **1 hour 15 minutes**
Serves: **6–8**

175g (6oz) butter, softened
175g (6oz) dark soft brown sugar
5 eggs
275g (10oz) self-raising flour

900g (2lb) loaf tin (see page 334)

Preheat the oven to 180°C (350°F), Gas mark 4, then line the base and sides of the loaf tin with baking parchment, with the paper coming above the sides of the tin to enable the cake to be lifted out easily.

Cream the butter until soft in a large bowl or in an electric food mixer. Add the sugar and beat until the mixture is light and fluffy.

Whisk the eggs together in a small bowl for just a few seconds until mixed, then gradually add them to the creamed butter mixture, beating all the time. Sift in the flour and fold in gently to combine. Tip the batter into the prepared tin and bake for 40–45 minutes or until a skewer inserted into the centre of the cake comes out clean.

Remove from the oven and allow to cool for 5 minutes. Carefully lift the cake out of the tin using the baking parchment, then peel away the paper and leave on a wire rack to finish cooling down.

Lemon Madeira cake

Make the cake as above, substituting caster sugar for the brown sugar and adding the finely grated zest of 1 lemon to the mixture with the eggs.

Coffee Madeira cake

Replace the brown sugar with caster sugar and mix in 3 tablespoons of coffee essence (Camp or Irel) with the eggs before adding to the batter.

Tip If any of this cake is left over, you could use it for making Cake pops (see page 220).

Winter breakfast muffins

A hint of spice and a little ginger is sometimes all I need to perk me up on a frosty winter's morning. Well, that and ten minutes standing by the Aga with a big cup of coffee! I like the plump juiciness of sultanas, but if you'd prefer you could use currants or raisins instead.

Prep time: **15 minutes**
Baking time: **30 minutes**
Ready in: **1 hour 15 minutes**
Makes: **12 muffins**

300g (11oz) plain flour
½ tsp bicarbonate of soda
½ tsp salt
2 tsp mixed spice
100g (3½oz) caster sugar
125g (4½oz) butter, cut into 1cm
    (½in) cubes
2 eggs
175ml (6fl oz) buttermilk
100g (3½oz) golden syrup
25g (1oz) stem ginger in syrup
    (drained weight), finely chopped
50g (2oz) sultanas

12-cup muffin tray and 12 muffin cases
    (see page 336)

Preheat the oven to 180°C (350°F), Gas mark 4, and line the muffin tray with the paper cases.

Sift the flour, bicarbonate of soda, salt and spice into a large bowl, then add the sugar and mix together. Add the butter and rub together with your fingertips until the mixture resembles breadcrumbs.

In another bowl, whisk together the eggs, buttermilk and golden syrup. Tip this into the flour mixture along with the chopped stem ginger and the sultanas, and beat until well mixed.

Divide the batter between the muffin cases, filling each about three-quarters full.

Bake the muffins for about 30 minutes or until well risen and springy to the touch. Allow the muffins to cool for about 5 minutes before removing them from the tin and placing on a wire rack to finish cooling.

Tip If you like, you could use some of the syrup from the stem-ginger jar to brush over the top of the muffins after they come out of the oven.

Macadamia nut and lemon cakes

This quick recipe uses a food processor to whiz up macadamia nuts before incorporating them into a lemon sponge mixture. The sharpness of the lemon contrasts so well with the rich and buttery nuts. If you can't get hold of macadamias, you can replace them with ready-ground almonds for an even speedier cake, as the almonds won't need whizzing in the food processor.

Prep time: **20 minutes**
Baking time: **15–18 minutes**
Ready in: **50 minutes**
Makes: **12 cakes**

50g (2oz) macadamia nuts
150g (5oz) self-raising flour, sifted
150g (5oz) caster sugar
3 eggs
Finely grated zest of 2 lemons
100g (3½oz) butter, melted

For the icing
200g (7oz) lemon curd (to make it yourself, see page 27)
25g (1oz) macadamia nuts (or almonds), lightly toasted (see the tip opposite) and roughly chopped

12-cup muffin tray and 12 muffin cases (see page 336)

Preheat the oven to 180°C (350°F), Gas mark 4, and line the muffin tray with the paper cases.

Place the macadamia nuts in a food processor and whiz for a minute or two until fairly fine. Add the rest of the ingredients and pulse just until combined. Divide the batter between the muffin cases, filling each up to three-quarters full.

Bake for 15–18 minutes or until the cakes spring back lightly to the touch. Take out of the oven and allow to cool for 5 minutes, then remove from the tin and place on a wire rack to cool down fully.

When the cupcakes are cool, spread generously with lemon curd, then scatter over the toasted macadamia nuts.

Tip To toast nuts, either scatter them over a baking tray in a single layer and toast them in the oven (preheated to 180°C/350°F/Gas mark 4) for 4–5 minutes or until golden brown, or place them in a frying pan and toast over a medium–low heat for a similar length of time. In either case, the nuts need to be shaken every so often to prevent them burning on one side.

Lemongrass coconut cake

Coconut and lemongrass, two quintessentially Southeast Asian ingredients, are combined here in this deliciously moist cake. The lemongrass is added to a syrup that infuses the sponge with its aromatic flavour. Found in supermarkets as well as in Asian food shops, the taste of lemongrass is certainly reminiscent of lemons but has a unique floral flavour all of its own.

Prep time: **15 minutes**
Baking time: **40–45 minutes**
Ready in: **1 hour 30 minutes**
Serves: **6–8**

4 stalks of lemongrass, base and tops trimmed, outer leaves removed but reserved for the syrup (see below)
250g (9oz) caster sugar
4 eggs
200g (7oz) butter, softened, plus extra for greasing
125g (4½oz) desiccated coconut
125g (4½oz) plain flour, plus extra for dusting
2 tsp baking powder
Greek yoghurt or crème fraîche, to serve

For the syrup
Reserved trimmings and outer leaves of the lemongrass (see above)
75g (3oz) caster sugar

23cm (9in) diameter cake tin with 6cm (2½in) sides (see page 334)

Preheat the oven to 170°C (325°F), Gas mark 3. Butter the sides of the cake tin and dust with flour, then line the base with a disc of baking parchment.

Slice the lemongrass stalks quite thinly into rounds about 3mm (⅛in) thick, then place in a food processor with the caster sugar and whiz for 1–2 minutes or until the lemongrass is finely puréed and very aromatic. Add the eggs, butter and coconut and whiz again until combined, then sift the flour and baking powder together and add to the machine, whizzing very briefly just until the ingredients come together.

Tip the mixture into the prepared tin and bake for 40–45 minutes or until a skewer inserted into the centre of the cake comes out clean.

While the cake is cooking, make the syrup. Roughly chop the lemongrass trimmings, place in a saucepan with the sugar and 75ml (3fl oz) of water and set over a high heat. Stir the mixture until the sugar is dissolved, then bring to the boil and boil for 2 minutes before removing from the heat and leaving to infuse.

When the cake has finished baking, take it out of the oven and let it sit in the tin for 10 minutes. Loosen around the edges using a small, sharp knife and carefully remove the cake from the tin before transferring to a serving plate (see page 334).

Reheat the syrup, then pierce holes all over the cake with a skewer and pour the hot syrup through a sieve onto the cake, moving the pan and sieve around as you pour so that the syrup covers the top of the cake. Allow the cake to cool down completely.

Serve with a dollop of natural Greek yoghurt or crème fraîche.

Fast cinnamon yoghurt cake

The yoghurt in this cake gives it a gentle tang and ensures it is wonderfully light. The sweetness comes mostly from honey, and being made with sunflower or vegetable oil, this cake has a deliciously soft crumb. It will keep in an airtight box for up to a week.

Prep time: 10 minutes
Baking time: **35 minutes**
Ready in: **1 hour 15 minutes**
Serves: **6–8**

225g (8oz) self-raising flour
1 tsp baking powder
1 tbsp ground cinnamon
75g (3oz) ground almonds
100g (3½oz) caster sugar
2 eggs
50g (2oz) honey
250ml (9fl oz) natural yoghurt
150ml (5fl oz) sunflower or vegetable oil, plus extra for greasing

To decorate
1 tbsp icing sugar
½ tsp ground cinnamon

23cm (9in) diameter cake tin with 6cm (2½in) sides (see page 334)

Preheat the oven to 180°C (350°F), Gas mark 4, then grease the sides of the cake tin with vegetable oil and line the base with a disc of baking parchment.

Sift the flour, baking powder and cinnamon into a large bowl, add the ground almonds and sugar and mix everything together.

In a separate bowl, whisk together the eggs, honey, yoghurt and vegetable oil. Add this mixture to the dry ingredients, then carefully fold in to combine.

Tip the batter into the prepared tin and bake for about 35 minutes or until golden on top and a skewer inserted into the centre of the cake comes out clean. Remove from the oven and allow to cool in the tin for 10 minutes. Use a small, sharp knife to loosen the edges, then carefully remove the cake from the tin and leave to cool down completely on a wire rack before transferring to a serving plate (see page 334).

Mix together the icing sugar and cinnamon and dust over the cake to serve.

Raspberry and blueberry friands

A friand is a type of cake that is very popular down under in both New Zealand and Australia. The sponge is extremely light, made with an egg-white foam and ground almonds. These will stay wonderfully moist for up to three days if kept in an airtight box.

Prep time: **10 minutes**
Baking time: **20–25 minutes**
Ready in: **1 hour**
Makes: **12 cakes**

7 egg whites (about 250ml/9fl oz)
150g (5oz) icing sugar, plus extra
    for dusting
50g (2oz) plain flour
100g (3½oz) ground almonds
100g (3½oz) butter, melted
24 fresh or frozen (and defrosted)
    raspberries
24 fresh or frozen (and defrosted)
    blueberries
Icing sugar, to dust

12-cup muffin tray and 12 muffin cases
    (see page 336)

Preheat the oven to 190°C (375°F), Gas mark 5, and line the muffin tray with the paper cases.

Whisk the egg whites in a bowl using a hand-held electric whisk or in an electric food mixer, beating until the egg whites are foamy but not holding stiff peaks. Sift in the icing sugar and flour, then add the ground almonds and melted butter and stir just to combine.

Divide the mixture between the muffin cases, filling each three-quarters full, then add two raspberries and two blueberries to the centre of each cake, pressing the fruit in lightly. Bake for 20–25 minutes or until a light golden colour and slightly springy to the touch.

Remove the friands from the oven and leave in the tin for 5 minutes, then remove from the tray and place on a wire rack to cool completely.

Arrange on a plate and dust with icing sugar to serve.

Marzipan cake

This cake is incredibly quick to make, with the food processor doing all of the work. The marzipan gives the cake a wonderfully moist texture and an intense almondy flavour. You can make your own marzipan, and I've included a recipe opposite, or, for a super-fast cake, just use shop-bought marzipan if you prefer.

Prep time: 5 minutes (excluding the marzipan)
Baking time: 50 minutes
Ready in: 1 hour 30 minutes
Serves: 8–12

125g (4½oz) caster sugar
125g (4½oz) marzipan (to make it yourself, see opposite)
100g (3½oz) butter, softened, plus extra for greasing
4 eggs
A few drops (not more than ⅛ tsp) of almond essence or extract
75g (3oz) plain flour, plus extra for dusting
¾ tsp baking powder
¼ tsp salt

20cm (8in) diameter cake tin with 6cm (2½in) sides (see page 334)

Preheat the oven to 170°C (325°F), Gas mark 3. Butter the sides of the cake tin and dust with flour, then line the base with a disc of baking parchment.

Place the sugar and marzipan in a food processor and whiz together until the marzipan is finely ground and the mixture resembles grains of sand.

Next add the butter, eggs and almond essence or extract and whiz until smooth and fluffy. Sift the flour, baking powder and salt into the machine and pulse a few times, just until all the ingredients are incorporated. (Try not to over-mix or your cake will be a little heavy.)

Scrape the batter into the prepared tin and bake the cake on a lower shelf in the oven for about 50 minutes or until the top is golden brown and a skewer inserted into the centre comes out clean.

Remove from the oven and allow to sit for 5 minutes, then use a small, sharp knife to loosen the edges of the cake tin. Allow to cool completely in the tin before carefully removing the cake and transferring to a serving plate (see page 334).

Marzipan

Prep time: **5 minutes**
Cooking time: **10 minutes**
Ready in: **30 minutes**
Makes: **450g (1lb)**

225g (8oz) caster or granulated sugar
175g (6oz) ground almonds
A few drops (not more than ⅛ tsp)
    of almond essence or extract
1 egg white, lightly beaten

Place the sugar in a heavy-based saucepan and pour in 75ml (3fl oz) of water, then continue to heat for 5–10 minutes or until a sugar thermometer reads 110–115°C (230–235°F). If you don't have a thermometer, this is the 'thread stage'. The mixture will be thick and syrupy and the last couple of drops that fall from a spoon will form a thread.

Remove the pan from the heat and stir until the syrup is cloudy. Add the ground almonds, almond essence or extract and egg white and mix well. Transfer to a bowl and allow the marzipan to cool and become pliable.

Tip Marzipan is incredibly useful for so many cakes, from icing to decoration and even as a key ingredient in the actual sponge (as in the recipe opposite). It will keep in the fridge, covered, for up to three months, and it can be frozen too.

Apple, oat and pecan bars

Eating apples are best in this recipe as they keep their shape while baking, whereas cooking apples tend to disintegrate as they cook. These bars are full of texture from the apples, and have the slight chewiness of oats and the crunch of pecans. They're good candidates for lunchboxes and will keep for 4–5 days in an airtight container.

Prep time: **10 minutes**
Baking time: **25–30 minutes**
Ready in: **1 hour 15 minutes**
Makes: **12 bars**

2 eating apples (unpeeled), cored, cut into quarters and roughly chopped
150g (5oz) butter, softened, plus extra for greasing
150g (5oz) light soft brown sugar
50g (2oz) porridge oats
2 eggs
200g (7oz) self-raising flour, sifted
50g (2oz) pecans, plus 12 to decorate

23 x 30cm (9 x 12in) Swiss roll tin

Preheat the oven to 180°C (350°F), Gas mark 4, then grease the sides of the Swiss roll tin with butter and line the base with baking parchment.

Place the prepared apples in a food processor and pulse a few times until they're in small pieces. Add the butter and sugar and cream together for 20 seconds or so, then add all the remaining ingredients and pulse just until mixed.

Tip the mixture into the prepared tin and place the pecans on top, spaced apart to form an even grid (4 x 3). Bake for 25–30 minutes or until risen and golden, then remove from the oven and leave in the tin to cool down completely.

When cool, cut into 12 bars, each with one pecan on top, and remove from the tin.

Raspberry and coconut squares

Raspberry jam and coconut are one of those combinations that seem meant for each other and they've found their way into quite a few of my recipes. This cake is simple and so fast to make – perfect as an after-school treat or a last-minute addition to finish off lunch.

Prep time: 20 minutes
Baking time: 15–20 minutes
Ready in: 1 hour
Makes: 24 squares

225g (8oz) butter, plus extra for greasing
225g (8oz) caster sugar
4 eggs
225g (8oz) self-raising flour
250g (9oz) raspberry jam
50g (2oz) desiccated coconut, to decorate

23 x 30cm (9 x 12in) Swiss roll tin

Preheat the oven to 180°C (350°F), Gas mark 4, then grease the sides of the Swiss roll tin with butter and line the base with baking parchment.

Cream the butter until soft in a large bowl or in an electric food mixer. Add the sugar and beat until the mixture is light and fluffy.

Whisk the eggs together in a small bowl for a few seconds or just until mixed, then gradually add them to the creamed butter mixture, beating all the time. Sift in the flour and fold in gently to incorporate.

Tip the batter into the prepared tin and smooth the top with a palette knife or spatula. Bake for 15–20 minutes or until golden on top and springy to the touch.

Remove from the oven and allow to cool for 5 minutes, then loosen the edges with a small, sharp knife. Place a wire rack upside down on top of the cake and carefully turn over. Remove the tin and peel off the baking parchment, then turn over again onto another wire rack so the cake is upright, and leave it to cool down completely.

Once the cake has cooled, cover with raspberry jam, then sprinkle the coconut evenly over the cake and cut into 24 squares to serve.

Crunchy peanut butter banana muffins

The combination of peanut butter and banana works so well in these muffins, which are really easy to make. They'll keep for 4–5 days in an airtight container, though when their amazing smell draws everyone into the kitchen, I can't promise they'll last more than 4–5 minutes!

Prep time: **10 minutes**
Baking time: **20–25 minutes**
Ready in: **50 minutes**
Makes: **12 muffins**

75g (3oz) butter, softened
200g (7oz) caster sugar
150g (5oz) crunchy peanut butter
2 very ripe bananas (about 200g/7oz
    when peeled), peeled and mashed
4 eggs, beaten
250g (9oz) self-raising flour

12-cup muffin tray and 12 muffin cases
    (see page 336)

Preheat the oven to 180°C (350°F), Gas mark 4, and line the muffin tray with the paper cases.

Cream the butter until soft in a large bowl or in an electric food mixer. Add the sugar, peanut butter and the mashed bananas, then beat until the mixture is light and fluffy.

Whisk the eggs together in a small bowl for a few seconds or just until mixed, then gradually add them to the creamed butter mixture, beating continuously. Sift in the flour and fold in gently to combine.

Divide the batter between the muffin cases, filling each up to three-quarters full, and bake for 20–25 minutes or until risen and golden. Place on a wire rack to cool for 5 minutes, then remove from the tin and leave on the rack to finish cooling.

Upside-down peach and saffron cake

An upside-down cake takes so little time to bring together. Here I've combined lightly caramelised peaches with that most magical of spices, saffron. If you can get good fresh peaches, then do use them, but they're quite hard to find, even in late summer. Tinned peaches work perfectly well otherwise. Delicious as a dessert, this cake would also be lovely to serve guests for afternoon tea.

Prep time: **10 minutes**
Baking time: **30–35 minutes**
Ready in: **1 hour**
Serves: **6–8**

50g (2oz) butter
175g (6oz) caster sugar
4 fresh peaches, quartered and stones removed, or 1 x 410g tin of sliced peaches
200g (7oz) plain flour
1 tsp baking powder
½ tsp bicarbonate of soda
¼ tsp salt
2 eggs
200ml (7fl oz) buttermilk
75ml (3fl oz) sunflower oil
Large pinch of saffron
Greek yoghurt or softly whipped cream, to serve

26cm (10½in) diameter ovenproof frying pan (measured across the top)

Preheat the oven to 180°C (350°F), Gas mark 4.

Place the butter in the frying pan and melt over a medium heat, then sprinkle over 50g (2oz) of the sugar and cook for 3 minutes or until light golden, stirring regularly. Remove from the heat and add the peaches in a single layer, cut side down.

Sift the flour, baking powder, bicarbonate of soda and salt into a large bowl, add the remaining caster sugar and mix together. In a separate bowl, whisk together the eggs, buttermilk, sunflower oil and saffron. Make a well in the centre of the dry ingredients, then pour in the buttermilk mixture and whisk together to form a very soft batter.

Pour the batter evenly over the peaches, taking care not to disturb them in the pan, then place in the oven and bake for 30–35 minutes or until slightly springy in the middle and a skewer inserted into the centre of the cake comes out clean.

Allow to cool for just 5 minutes before turning out by placing an inverted serving plate over the top of the pan and turning the pan and plate over together in one quick movement.

Serve warm or at room temperature with Greek yoghurt or softly whipped cream.

It seems that more and more people have food intolerances or are avoiding animal products or gluten through necessity or choice. The cakes in this chapter are geared towards people with particular allergies or intolerances and are also for people who simply would like to bake cakes that are a little better for you. For children in particular, there is just no substitute for a great cake and I am so often asked for cake recipes that are egg or gluten free. While it is tricky to make a cake with no eggs, I've included a few delicious recipes that have no eggs, but still work wonderfully. Having an intolerance or allergy should not mean having to forgo cakes completely. These recipes have been carefully crafted and don't compromise on flavour or texture, so they can be enjoyed by all.

03/ Healthy

Chocolate, rum and almond cake

Alcohol and chocolate have long been combined in desserts, the alcohol accentuating and offsetting the rich, fruity flavour of dark chocolate. It also shows how versatile chocolate can be: often associated with sweet cakes and dishes for children, here it is elegant and sophisticated, perfect for a dinner party. This will keep for 4–5 days and, as it contains no flour, has the advantage of being gluten free. For an extra impressive finishing touch why not decorate with chocolate squares (see page 344) instead of the blanched almonds?

Prep time: **15 minutes**
Baking time: **38–45 minutes**
Ready in: **1 hour 45 minutes**
Serves: **8–10**

225g (8oz) dark chocolate, in drops or broken into pieces
225g (8oz) ground almonds
250g (9oz) caster sugar
150g (5oz) butter, softened, plus extra for greasing
6 eggs, beaten
4 tbsp rum
8 blanched almonds, to decorate
Softly whipped cream or crème fraîche, to serve

For the glaze
75ml (3fl oz) double or regular cream
125g (4½oz) dark chocolate, in drops or broken into pieces
2 tbsp rum

20cm (8in) diameter spring-form cake tin with 6cm (2½in) sides (see page 336)

Preheat the oven to 180°C (350°F), Gas mark 4, then butter the sides of the cake tin and line the base with a disc of baking parchment. Make sure the base of the tin is upside down, so there's no lip and the cake can slide off easily when cooked.

Place the chocolate in a heatproof bowl and set over a saucepan of simmering water. Leave just until melted, stirring occasionally, then remove from the heat and set aside.

Place the ground almonds, sugar and butter in a food processor and whiz until well mixed. Add the eggs, rum and melted chocolate and whiz until blended.

Tip the cake mixture into the prepared tin and cook for 38–45 minutes or until puffed up and slightly cracked on the surface but still quite moist in the centre – a skewer inserted into the centre of the cake will still be slightly sticky.

Remove from the oven and allow to cool in the tin for 20 minutes, then loosen the sides using a small, sharp knife and carefully remove the cake from the tin before transferring to a wire rack to cool down fully (see page 336).

Recipe continued overleaf

While the cake is baking, or while it's cooling, make the glaze. Pour the cream into a saucepan and bring to the boil, then take off the heat, add the chocolate, stirring to melt, and mix in the rum.

Transfer the cooled cake to a serving plate and pour over the chocolate glaze (reheating if necessary), then decorate with the blanched almonds by placing these in an evenly spaced circle, with the nuts pointing inwards, around the edge of the cake. Serve in slices with softly whipped cream or crème fraîche.

Variations

I've used rum in this recipe, but you could just as easily use brandy, whiskey or even orange liqueur. The flavours will all be slightly different, but the effect will be much the same.

Sugar-free banana bread

Agave syrup is made from the agave plant, grown primarily in Mexico. The syrup is extracted from the plant and produced in concentrated form. Sticky and slightly sweeter than sugar, it's considered healthier as it has a lower GI (glycaemic index), and releases energy more steadily than pure sugar. In this recipe the agave combines with the natural sweetness of bananas for a gorgeously healthy take on banana bread. I love to eat this straight from the oven, but it keeps well for a good few days. A slice or two would be perfect for a picnic.

Prep time: **10 minutes**
Baking time: **55–65 minutes**
Ready in: **1 hour 45 minutes**
Serves: **6–10**

125g (4½oz) plain flour
¾ tsp bicarbonate of soda
½ tsp salt
150g (5oz) wholemeal flour
350g (12oz) mashed bananas
  (about 4 bananas)
3 eggs
100ml (3½fl oz) agave syrup
75ml (3fl oz) sunflower or
  extra-virgin olive oil
50ml (2fl oz) natural yoghurt
Finely grated zest of 1 lemon

900g (2lb) loaf tin (see page 334)

Preheat the oven to 180°C (350°F), Gas mark 4, and line the base and sides of the loaf tin with baking parchment, with the paper coming above the sides of the tin to enable the cake to be lifted out easily.

Sift the plain flour, bicarbonate of soda and salt into a large bowl, then mix in the wholemeal flour. In a separate bowl, whisk together the remaining ingredients.

Add this mixture to the dry ingredients, folding together to combine. Tip the batter into the prepared loaf tin, then bake for 55–65 minutes or until the top is just turning golden brown and a skewer inserted into the centre of the cake comes out clean.

Remove from the oven and allow to sit for 10 minutes. Carefully lift the cake out of the tin using the baking parchment, then peel away the paper and leave on a wire rack to finish cooling.

30-day bran and pumpkin seed muffins

These are called '30-day muffins' because the batter will keep happily in the fridge for a month! They're sugar free and you can easily make them dairy free too by using rice or soya milk. The pumpkin seeds are healthy, packed with nutrition, but they're also delicious – lightly toasted in the oven for a characteristic crunch. I like to eat these muffins still warm for breakfast, but they make a handy and healthy lunchbox treat too.

Prep time: 10 minutes
Baking time: 15–22 minutes
Ready in: 45 minutes
Makes: 12 muffins

200g (7oz) plain flour
1½ tsp bicarbonate of soda
¾ tsp salt
200g (7oz) wholemeal flour
50g (2oz) bran
50g (2oz) pumpkin seeds, plus
    25g (1oz) for sprinkling
3 eggs
200ml (7fl oz) light agave syrup
100ml (3½ fl oz) sunflower oil
50ml (2fl oz) milk or rice or soya milk

12-cup muffin tray and up to 12 muffin
    cases (see page 336)

Preheat the oven to 180°C (350°F), Gas mark 4, and line the muffin tray with the paper cases (or fewer if you prefer – see the tip below).

Sift the plain flour, bicarbonate of soda and salt into a large bowl and mix in the wholemeal flour, bran and pumpkin seeds.

In a separate bowl, whisk together the remaining ingredients. Make a well in the centre of the flour and pumpkin seed mixture and pour in the wet ingredients, whisking together to incorporate fully.

Fill each of the muffin cases three-quarters full, then scatter with the additional pumpkin seeds and cook for 15–22 minutes or until springy to the touch. Allow to cool in the tin for 5 minutes, then remove from the tin and place on a wire rack to finish cooling.

Fruity bran and pumpkin seed muffins

I often add a small handful or so of dried fruit to the batter, such as raisins, chopped dried apricots or dates. Make up the recipe as above, adding the fruit to the fully mixed batter before filling the muffin cases.

Tip If you'd like to make fewer than 12 muffins, cover the remaining batter and place in the fridge, where it will keep for up to a month. It will thicken over time, so thin slightly by whisking in a little more milk or water – the mixture should be quite sloppy.

Tahini honey cake

I love tahini, the peanut butter-like paste made from sesame seeds. Tahini is ubiquitous in Middle Eastern cooking, used in all sorts of salads and sauces. It also finds its way into many sweet dishes and desserts, usually sweetened with honey. This recipe combines these flavours with the citrus tang of oranges and a touch of cinnamon to make a cake that would be ideal served after a big, generous Middle Eastern meal or perfect with a cup of coffee. The cake also has the advantage of being vegan (for those vegans who choose to eat honey).

Prep time: 10 minutes
Baking time: 30–35 minutes
Ready in: 1 hour
Serves: 6–8

Sunflower oil, for greasing

75g (3oz) wholemeal flour

1 tsp bicarbonate of soda, sifted

1 tsp ground cinnamon

Pinch of salt

100g (3½oz) fresh or frozen white breadcrumbs

125g (4½oz) honey, plus 1 tsp for drizzling

100ml (3½fl oz) light tahini

Juice and finely grated zest of 2 oranges

20cm (8in) diameter cake tin with 6cm (2½in) sides (see page 334)

Preheat the oven to 180°C (350°F), Gas mark 4, then grease the sides of the cake tin with sunflower oil and line the base with a disc of baking parchment.

Place the flour in a food processor with the bicarbonate of soda, cinnamon, salt and breadcrumbs and whiz for about 30 seconds or until fine.

In a bowl, mix together the 125g (4½oz) of honey, along with the remaining ingredients. Add to the food processor with the dry ingredients and whiz together for about 20 seconds or until it just comes together. Tip the batter into the prepared tin and bake for 30–35 minutes or until a skewer inserted into the centre of the cake comes out clean.

When the cake is cooked, take it out of the oven and let it sit in the tin for 5 minutes. Loosen around the edges using a small, sharp knife, then carefully remove the cake from the tin and transfer to a serving plate (see page 334).

Drizzle over the remaining honey and allow to cool down completely before serving.

Gluten- and dairy-free pecan brownies

You'll be amazed at how gorgeously fudgy these brownies are despite not containing a hint of dairy or gluten. The pecans aren't essential but I love the crunchy contrast they provide with the softness of the brownies.

Prep time: 10 minutes
Baking time: 45 minutes
Ready in: 2 hours
Makes: 12 brownies

125g (4½oz) dark chocolate, in drops or broken into pieces

225g (8oz) soft dark brown sugar

125ml (4½fl oz) sunflower oil, plus extra for greasing

½ tsp vanilla extract

2 eggs

75g (3oz) ground almonds

25g (1oz) rice flour

½ tsp salt

½ tsp baking powder or gluten-free baking powder

75g (3oz) pecans, chopped, plus 12 whole (shelled) pecans to decorate

20cm (8in) square cake tin with 5cm (2in) sides (see page 334)

Preheat the oven to 180°C (350°F), Gas mark 4. If the cake tin has a removable base, grease the sides of the tin with sunflower oil and line the base with a square of baking parchment, otherwise line the base and sides of the tin.

Place the chocolate in a heatproof bowl and set over a saucepan of gently simmering water. Leave just until melted, stirring occasionally, then remove from the heat and add the sugar, sunflower oil, vanilla extract and eggs and whisk together well. Next add the ground almonds, rice flour, salt, baking powder and chopped pecans and fold in until well mixed.

Tip into the prepared tin, then place the 12 whole pecans in an even grid on top. Bake for about 45 minutes or until the middle of the cake still wobbles slightly when you gently shake the tin – a skewer inserted into the centre should come out with a little moisture on it.

Remove from the oven, place on a wire rack and allow to cool in the tin for at least an hour before carefully removing the cake (see page 334) and cutting into 12 squares (each with a pecan in the middle) to serve.

Vegan frosted lemon cake

Whether you're vegan by choice or intolerant to dairy foods and eggs, finding cakes that both work and taste good can be tricky. It's certainly not impossible, though, as this cake proves with its intense lemony flavour and a soft, light crumb that is just as good as anything made with butter or eggs. For the icing I've used a soya spread, which works wonderfully when sweetened and thickened with the icing sugar. You could use any other citrus fruits to flavour this cake as well (see the variations opposite).

Prep time: **20 minutes**
Baking time: **45–50 minutes**
Ready in: **1 hour 45 minutes**
Serves: **8–12**

450g (1lb) plain flour, plus extra
    for dusting
2 tsp baking powder
1 tsp bicarbonate of soda
300g (11oz) caster sugar
125ml (4½fl oz) sunflower oil,
    plus extra for greasing
Finely grated zest of 3 lemons
Juice of 3 lemons plus enough
    water to make 300ml (½ pint)

For the frosting
175g (6oz) soya spread
500g (1lb 2oz) icing sugar, sifted
Pinch of salt
Finely grated zest of 1 lemon
1 tsp lemon juice

23cm (9in) diameter cake tin with
    6cm (2½in) sides (see page 334)

Preheat the oven to 170°C (325°F), Gas mark 3. Grease the sides of the cake tin with sunflower oil and dust with flour, then line the base with a disc of baking parchment.

Sift the flour, baking powder and bicarbonate of soda into a large bowl and mix in the sugar. In a separate bowl, mix together all the remaining ingredients. Add these to the dry ingredients and stir well until the mixture comes together.

Pour the batter into the prepared tin and bake for 45–50 minutes or until springy to the touch and a skewer inserted into the centre of the cake comes out clean.

Remove from the oven and allow to cool in the tin for 10 minutes. Using a small, sharp knife, loosen around the edges, then carefully remove the cake from the tin and leave on a wire rack to finish cooling (see page 334).

As the cake cools, make the frosting. Place all the ingredients in a large bowl or in an electric food mixer. Using either a hand-held electric beater or the food mixer, whisk on full speed for 2–3 minutes or until light and fluffy.

Once the cake is cool, use a bread knife to slice it horizontally in half. Place the bottom half of the cake, cut side up, on a cake plate or stand, then spread over some of the frosting, to about 5mm ($\frac{1}{4}$ in) thick. Place the top half of the cake on top, cut side down, then spread the remaining frosting over the top and sides of the cake.

Vegan frosted orange cake

Make up the cake in the same way, substituting the lemons with the zest and juice of three oranges (with the juice topped up to 300ml/$\frac{1}{2}$ pint with water, if necessary) and reducing the sugar to 275g (10oz).

Vegan frosted lime cake

Follow the recipe as above, substituting the lemons with the zest and juice of four limes (with the juice topped up to 300ml/$\frac{1}{2}$ pint with water, if necessary).

Dairy-free blueberry crumble cake

This dairy-free cake has a divinely thick, sticky crumble topping. Naturally sweet blueberries are dotted throughout the cake and scattered on top where they burst during baking and ooze their syrupy juices into the topping. If you're intolerant to eggs, this cake works well with an egg replacer, which you can buy from health-food shops. Of course, you can use real eggs otherwise.

Prep time: **20 minutes**
Baking time: **50–60 minutes**
Ready in: **2 hours**
Serves: **8–12**

225g (8oz) plain flour
2 tsp baking powder
1 tsp bicarbonate of soda
½ tsp salt
50g (2oz) caster sugar
50g (2oz) wholemeal flour
150ml (5fl oz) soya or rice milk
50ml (2fl oz) vegetable oil
1 tbsp cider vinegar
2 tsp vanilla extract
3 eggs, beaten (or 3 tsp egg replacer mixed with 6 tsp water)
250g (9oz) fresh or frozen (and defrosted) blueberries

For the crumble topping
50g (2oz) plain flour
½ tsp ground cinnamon
150g (5oz) soft dark brown sugar
2 tbsp soya spread

20cm (8in) square cake tin with 5cm (2in) sides (see page 334)

Preheat the oven to 180°C (350°F), Gas mark 4, then line the base and sides of the cake tin with baking parchment, with the paper coming above the sides of the tin to enable the cake to be lifted out easily.

First make the topping. Sift the flour and cinnamon into a large bowl, add the sugar and mix together. Using your fingers, rub in the soya spread until the mixture forms a crumbly topping.

Sift the plain flour, baking powder, bicarbonate of soda and salt into a separate bowl and mix in the sugar and wholemeal flour. In another bowl, whisk together the soya or rice milk, vegetable oil, vinegar and vanilla extract until well combined.

Add the beaten eggs, or egg replacer mixture, to the wet ingredients, then gradually pour them into the flour mixture and mix just until combined.

Fold in about half of the blueberries, then pour the batter into the prepared tin. Scatter the remaining blueberries over the top of the cake and then sprinkle the crumble topping evenly over the top of the batter.

Bake for 50–60 minutes or until a skewer inserted into the centre of the cake comes out clean. The top will be golden brown and look uneven, but don't worry as that's part of its charm.

Allow the cake to sit in the tin for 20 minutes before lifting out using the baking parchment, then carefully peel away the paper and allow to cool down fully on a wire rack.

Cut into squares and arrange on a plate to serve.

Date and almond honey cake

This fantastically dense, moist cake has echoes of sticky toffee pudding. It contains no refined sugar, all the sweetness coming from the honey and dates, while the wholemeal flour imparts its lovely nutty flavour.

Prep time: **15 minutes**
Baking time: **45–50 minutes**
Ready in: **2 hours**
Serves: **6–8**

100g (3½oz) chopped dates
200g (7oz) butter, softened, plus extra for greasing
200g (7oz) honey, plus 2 tbsp for drizzling
3 eggs
100g (3½oz) ground almonds
125g (4½oz) wholemeal flour
1½ tsp baking powder
25g (1oz) flaked almonds

20cm (8in) diameter cake tin with 6cm (2½in) sides (see page 334)

Preheat the oven to 180°C (350°F), Gas mark 4, then butter the sides of the cake tin and line the base with a disc of baking parchment. Place the tin on a baking sheet, as some butter may seep out during cooking if you are using a spring-form cake tin.

Place the dates in a saucepan and pour in 50ml (2fl oz) of water. Set over a high heat and cook for 2–3 minutes or until soft, then remove from the heat and set aside.

Cream the butter and the 200g (7oz) of honey until soft in a large bowl or in an electric food mixer. Whisk the eggs together in a small bowl for a few seconds until just mixed, then gradually add them to the creamed butter and honey mixture, beating all the time.

Stir in the cooked dates, along with any remaining cooking liquid, followed by the ground almonds, then add the flour and baking powder and fold in gently to incorporate. Tip the mixture into the prepared tin, smoothing the surface gently with a palette knife, then scatter the flaked almonds evenly over the top.

Place in the oven and bake for 45–50 minutes or until a skewer inserted into the centre of the cake comes out clean. It will be quite dark-looking, but don't worry – the cake will be perfectly moist inside.

Remove from the oven and allow to cool in the tin for 10 minutes. Loosen the sides using a small, sharp knife and carefully remove the cake from the tin before transferring to a cake stand or plate (see page 334).

Use a skewer to pierce a few holes in the top of the cake, then drizzle over the 2 tablespoons of honey and allow to cool before cutting into slices to serve.

Dairy- and egg-free vanilla cupcakes

Even if you can eat dairy products or eggs, you'll love these simple vanilla cupcakes. The extra raising agents and vinegar really lift these, making them especially light and airy. The vanilla icing uses soya spread, which works just as butter does to form a rich sweet icing. If you don't have a dairy intolerance, however, you could simply replace the soya spread with softened butter.

Prep time: 15 minutes
Baking time: 15–20 minutes
Ready in: 1 hour
Makes: 12 cupcakes

1 tbsp white wine vinegar or cider vinegar
275ml (9½fl oz) soya or rice milk
75ml (3fl oz) sunflower or vegetable oil
1 tsp vanilla extract
225g (8oz) self-raising flour
¾ tsp baking powder
½ tsp bicarbonate of soda
¼ tsp salt
200g (7oz) caster sugar

For the icing
125g (4½oz) soya spread
350g (12oz) icing sugar, sifted
Pinch of salt
2 tsp vanilla extract or seeds scraped from ½ vanilla pod

12-cup bun tray and 12 bun cases (see page 336)
Piping bag with a 4 or 5mm (¼in) star-shaped nozzle or a freezer bag with 4 or 5mm (¼in) cut from one corner (optional)

Preheat the oven to 180°C (350°F), Gas mark 4, and line the bun tray with the paper cases.

In a bowl, mix together the vinegar, soya or rice milk, sunflower or vegetable oil and vanilla extract. In a separate bowl, sift together the flour, baking powder, bicarbonate of soda and salt, then mix in the sugar. Add the wet ingredients to the flour mixture and whisk to combine completely – this may take a minute or so.

Divide the batter between the paper cases, filling each case three-quarters full. Bake in the oven for 15–20 minutes or until golden brown and springy to the touch. Allow to cool in the tin for 5 minutes, then remove from the tray and place on a wire rack to cool down completely.

As the cupcakes cool, make the icing. Whisk all the ingredients together (this is easiest using an electric food mixer or a hand-held electric beater) until soft and light.

Using a palette knife, the back of a spoon or a piping bag (see page 340), spread the icing over the top of each cupcake before placing on a plate to serve.

Wholemeal chocolate cake

A distinctive cake that's really worth trying. Wholemeal flour contains all of the wheat grain and is high in fibre, proteins and minerals. It's not just that it's healthier, but it tastes fantastic too, with the nutty flavour complementing the dark chocolate and brown sugar.

Prep time: 15 minutes
Baking time: 20–25 minutes
Ready in: 1 hour
Serves: 6–10

125g (4½oz) wholemeal flour
1 tsp bicarbonate of soda
¼ tsp salt
50g (2oz) dark chocolate, in drops
    or broken into pieces
50g (2oz) butter, softened, plus
    extra for greasing
200g (7oz) soft light or dark
    brown sugar
2 eggs
1 tsp vanilla extract
150ml (5fl oz) sour cream
Cocoa powder, for dusting

23cm (9in) diameter cake tin with 6cm
    (2½in) sides (see page 334)

Preheat the oven to 180°C (350°F), Gas mark 4, then butter the sides of the tin and line the base with a disc of baking parchment.

Sift the flour, bicarbonate of soda and salt into a bowl and set aside. Some of the bran will be left in the sieve – you can return it to the flour bag.

Place the chocolate in a heatproof bowl and set over a saucepan of just simmering water. Leave just until the chocolate has melted, stirring from time to time, then remove from the heat and set aside.

Cream the butter until soft in a large bowl or electric food mixer. Add the sugar and beat until the mixture is light and fluffy. Whisk the eggs together in a small bowl for a few seconds or just until mixed, then gradually add them to the creamed butter mixture, beating all the time.

Beat in the vanilla extract and the melted chocolate, then gradually stir in the flour mixture along with the sour cream. Mix just until combined, then pour the batter into the prepared tin.

Bake for 20–25 minutes or until a skewer inserted into the centre of the cake comes out clean. Remove from the oven and allow to cool in the tin for 10 minutes. Loosen around the edges with a small, sharp knife, then carefully remove the cake from the tin and leave on a wire rack to finish cooling (see page 334).

Once cool, transfer to a cake plate or stand and dust with cocoa powder to serve.

Vegan raspberry muffins

These don't have a great deal of sugar in them, as much of the sweetness comes from the raspberries. For that reason, if you'd like to replace the raspberries with blackberries – which would make a great substitute – do taste the blackberries first and if they're quite sour then increase the sugar in the recipe.

Prep time: 10 minutes
Baking time: 15–20 minutes
Ready in: 1 hour
Makes: 10 muffins

225g (8oz) plain flour
3 tsp baking powder
1 tsp bicarbonate of soda
¼ tsp salt
75g (3oz) caster sugar
Finely grated zest of 1 orange
150g (5oz) fresh or frozen
    (and defrosted) raspberries
225ml (8fl oz) soya or rice milk
50ml (2fl oz) sunflower oil
1 tbsp cider vinegar
1 tsp vanilla extract

12-cup muffin tray and 10 muffin cases
    (see page 336)

Preheat the oven to 180°C (350°F), Gas mark 4, and line the muffin tray with the paper cases.

Sift the flour, baking powder, bicarbonate of soda and salt into a large bowl, then mix in the sugar and orange zest. Carefully fold in the raspberries and set aside.

In a separate bowl, whisk together the remaining ingredients, then add these to the flour mixture, folding in to combine.

Divide the batter between the muffin cases, filling each three-quarters full, then bake for 15–20 minutes or until golden on top and springy to the touch.

Remove from the oven and allow to cool in the tray for 5 minutes, then take the muffins out of the tray and place on a wire rack to cool down completely.

Sweet potato muffins

The aptly named sweet potato provides these muffins with natural sweetness and gives a divinely moist crumb. The sweetness is given a little boost with agave syrup, making these delicious treats surprisingly healthy.

Prep time: 10 minutes (excluding cooking the sweet potato)
Baking time: 30–35 minutes
Ready in: 1 hour
Makes: 12 muffins

2 sweet potatoes (unpeeled) (about 400g/14oz)
50g (2oz) butter, softened
75ml (3fl oz) buttermilk
175ml (6fl oz) natural yoghurt
100ml (3½fl oz) light agave syrup
1 egg
125g (4½oz) plain flour
1 tsp baking powder
½ tsp bicarbonate of soda
½ tsp ground or grated nutmeg
1 tbsp ground cinnamon
1 tsp ground ginger
100g (3½oz) wholemeal flour

12-cup muffin tray and 12 muffin cases (see page 336)

Preheat the oven to 200°C (400°F), Gas mark 6.

To cook the sweet potatoes, place on a baking tray and bake for about 1 hour or until tender when pierced with a fork. Cut open and scoop out the flesh and discard the skins. Place the flesh in a bowl to cool – you'll need 300g (11oz) of the cooked flesh in total. Alternatively, cook the sweet potatoes in a microwave: pierce each potato a few times with a fork, then cook on a high heat for 10–15 minutes, turning over halfway through. When cooked the sweet potatoes will be tender to the touch and soft all the way through.

Turn down the oven to 180°C (350°F), Gas mark 4, and line the muffin tray with the paper cases.

In a bowl, beat the butter with the cooked flesh of the sweet potato. In a separate bowl, whisk together the buttermilk, yoghurt, agave syrup and egg. Then add to the sweet potato mixture and beat in until well mixed.

Sift the plain flour, baking powder, bicarbonate of soda and spices into a separate bowl, then mix in the wholemeal flour. Add the dry ingredients to the sweet potato mixture and fold everything together to combine.

Divide the batter between the muffin cases, filling each three-quarters full. Bake for 30–35 minutes or until lightly springy to the touch. Allow to cool for 5 minutes before removing from the tin and placing on a wire rack to cool down fully.

Vegan chocolate cake

This cake is inspired by a recipe by Giorgio Locatelli that is a favourite of his daughter Dita, who is allergic to eggs. I have added a chocolate frosting to it to make it even more indulgent. Everyone, whether allergic to eggs or not, will love this cake.

Prep time: 45 minutes
Baking time: 45–50 minutes
Ready in: 2 hours 30 minutes
Serves: 12–16

450g (1lb) plain flour, plus extra
   for dusting
50g (2oz) cocoa powder
2 tsp baking powder
2 tsp bicarbonate of soda
300g (11oz) caster sugar
125ml (4½fl oz) sunflower oil,
   plus extra for greasing
2 tbsp white wine vinegar or cider
   vinegar
2 tsp vanilla extract

For the frosting
125g (4½oz) soya spread
300g (11oz) icing sugar, sifted
50g (2oz) cocoa powder, sifted
1 tbsp vanilla extract
Pinch of salt

23cm (9in) diameter cake tin with 6cm
   (2½in) sides (see page 334)

Preheat the oven to 170°C (325°F), Gas mark 3. Grease the sides of the cake tin with sunflower oil and dust them with flour, then line the base of the tin with a disc of baking parchment.

Sift the flour into a large bowl with the cocoa powder, baking powder and bicarbonate of soda and mix in the sugar. In a separate bowl, mix together the remaining ingredients with 300ml (½ pint) of water.

Add the wet ingredients to the flour mixture, stirring well to combine, then tip the batter into the prepared tin. Bake for 45–50 minutes or until springy to the touch and a skewer inserted into the centre of the cake comes out clean.

Remove from the oven and allow to cool in the tin for 10 minutes. Then loosen around the edges using a small, sharp knife and carefully remove the cake from the tin before leaving on a wire rack to finish cooling (see page 334).

While the cake is cooling, make the frosting. Using a hand-held electric beater or an electric food mixer, whisk all the ingredients together on full speed for 4–5 minutes or until light and thick.

Once the cake is cold to the touch, use a bread knife to cut it horizontally in two. Place the bottom half on a cake plate or stand, then spread over some of the frosting. Sandwich together with the top half, spreading the remaining frosting over the top and sides of the cake. Place in the fridge for about 20 minutes to allow it to set before serving.

Apple and blackberry oat muffins

This has to be my favourite partnership of fruit flavours, and it's serendipitous that they come into season at exactly the same time. This recipe uses eating apples rather than cookers because they're sweeter, though they will need puréeing first as they don't break down as easily when cooked.

Prep time: 15 minutes
Baking time: 25–30 minutes
Ready in: 1 hour 15 minutes
Makes: 12 muffins

425g (15oz) eating apples, peeled, cored and roughly chopped (400g (14oz) once peeled and cored)
200g (7oz) soft light brown sugar
100ml (3½fl oz) sunflower oil
75g (3oz) porridge oats
225g (8oz) plain flour, sifted
3 tsp baking powder
36 fresh or frozen (and defrosted) blackberries (about 125g/4½oz)

12-cup muffin tray and 12 muffin cases (see page 336)

Preheat the oven to 180°C (350°F), Gas mark 4, and line the muffin tray with the paper cases.

Place the apples and sugar in a saucepan and add 3 tablespoons of water, then cover with a lid and bring to a simmer. Continue to simmer for 10 minutes, stirring occasionally, then tip into a food processor or blender and whiz for a minute or until smooth.

Pour the apple purée into a bowl and stir in the sunflower oil and oats. Sift in the flour and baking powder and stir in just until mixed. Divide the batter between the muffin cases, filling each case three-quarters full, then lightly press three or four blackberries into each muffin.

Bake for 25–30 minutes or until golden brown and lightly springy to the touch in the middle. Remove from the oven and leave in the tin to cool for 5 minutes, then remove the muffins from the tin and place on a wire rack to cool down completely.

Classic cakes have withstood the test of time. They remain firm favourites not only because they taste so good, but because we hold a special affection for them. Classic cake recipes often bring back childhood memories, making them one of the most comforting foods. As these cakes are so well loved, for the most part I haven't strayed too far from the original recipes. Sometimes, though, I've added a different flavour or changed a classic shape, to put a new spin on an old favourite. Each cake is a classic from a particular place. Lamingtons are an institution in Australia and the French Brittany butter cake is the perfect showcase for Brittany's famous butter. If you are new to some of the recipes, I urge you to try them, as these cakes are classics for a reason.

04/ Classic

Baked Alaska with hot chocolate sauce

A warm crisp meringue surrounding frozen ice cream atop a delicate chocolate sponge – a temperature contrast that is always impressive. The key to this culinary feat lies in the meringue, which acts as an effective insulator so the ice cream remains frozen even in the heat of the oven. A really fun dessert for a special occasion, either served on its own or topped with this extremely moreish hot chocolate sauce (see page 93).

Prep time: **45 minutes**
Baking time: **30–35 minutes**
Ready in: **1 hour 45 minutes**
Serves: **8–10**

1 litre (1¾ pints) vanilla, coffee
   or chocolate ice cream

For the sponge base

50g (2oz) dark chocolate, in drops
   or broken into pieces
125g (4½oz) butter, softened,
   plus extra for greasing
125g (4½oz) caster sugar
2 eggs, beaten
125g (4½oz) self-raising flour, sifted

For the meringue

3 egg whites
200g (7oz) caster sugar
Pinch of cream of tartar

1 litre (1¾ pint) pudding basin
   (20cm/8in in diameter)
20cm (8in) diameter cake tin (see
   page 334)

Line the pudding basin with a double layer of cling film, leaving enough hanging over the edge to cover the sides of the basin. Place the ice cream in the basin (you may need to allow it to soften for a few minutes, but don't let it melt). Press down to get a smooth surface (giving it a few gentle bangs to help remove any air holes), then cover the top with the cling film and return it to the freezer.

Preheat the oven to 180°C (350°F), Gas mark 4, then butter the sides of the cake tin and line the base with a disc of baking parchment.

Place the chocolate in a heatproof bowl and set over a pan of gently simmering water. Leave until just melted, stirring occasionally, then remove from the heat and set aside.

Cream the butter until soft in a large bowl or in an electric food mixer. Add the sugar and beat until the mixture is light and fluffy. Gradually add the eggs to the creamed butter mixture, beating all the time. Beat in the melted chocolate, then gently fold in the flour to combine.

Tip into the prepared cake tin and bake for 25–30 minutes or until a skewer inserted into the centre of the cake comes out clean.

Remove the cake from the oven and turn the temperature up to 220°C (425°F), Gas mark 7, if cooking the meringue straight away.

Allow the cake to cool down in the tin for 10 minutes, then loosen around the edges with a small, sharp knife and carefully remove the cake before leaving on a wire rack to cool down fully (see page 334).

Recipe continued overleaf

Meanwhile, make the meringue. In a large, spotlessly clean bowl, whisk the egg whites until they form soft peaks. Add half the caster sugar and the cream of tartar and whisk until stiff peaks form and the meringue is satiny and glossy. Fold in the remaining sugar with a metal spoon or spatula.

Once it has cooled, place the cake base in the middle of a baking sheet (one that is completely flat, with no 'lip', so that the baked Alaska can be removed easily). Take the ice cream out of the freezer. With the help of the cling film, remove the ice cream from the pudding bowl and place it upside down onto the cake, removing all the cling film.

Quickly spoon over the meringue, spreading it thickly and in peaks over the ice cream and the sides of the cake, down to the baking sheet. You can cook the baked Alaska immediately or you can return it to the freezer for up to 1 hour. It will take an extra 3–4 minutes in the oven if cooking from frozen. To cook, place in the centre of the hot oven for 3–4 minutes or until the meringue is set on the outside and golden in colour.

Carefully transfer the baked Alaska to a serving plate, using a palette knife dipped in hot water to help you slide and push it onto the plate. Serve straight away on its own or with chocolate sauce (see below).

Variation

If you prefer, you can make this dish using a plain version of the sponge. Follow the recipe as above but simply omit the chocolate from the mixture.

Hot chocolate sauce

Prep time: **5 minutes**
Cooking time: **5 minutes**
Ready in: **10 minutes**
Makes: **about 400ml (14fl oz)**

200ml (7fl oz) double or regular cream
200g (7oz) dark chocolate, in drops
    or chopped into pieces
1–2 tbsp rum or brandy (optional)

To make the hot chocolate sauce, place the cream in a saucepan and bring to the boil. Add the chocolate and stir until just melted, then add the rum or brandy (if using). Reheat the sauce gently when needed.

Chocolate orange sauce

Add 1–2 tablespoons of orange liqueur (such as Cointreau or Grand Marnier) and 1 teaspoon of finely grated orange zest to the basic chocolate sauce.

Carrot cake

Carrot cake is a classic. Carrots were originally added to cakes to sweeten them when sugar was rare and expensive. Despite sugar being readily available today, carrot cake remains universally popular, the carrots adding not just sweetness but moisture and a lightly resistant texture. Here are three different types of carrot cake. This first one is cooked in a loaf tin where the cream-cheese icing has just a hint of orange. Then there are some cupcakes (see page 96), which are infused with ginger – both ground and crystallised. These are followed by a layer cake (see page 96), where the icing is laden with the caramel flavour of dulce de leche.

Prep time: **20 minutes**
Baking time: **1 hour–1 hour 15 minutes**
Ready in: **2 hours**
Serves: **8–10**

2 eggs
150ml (5fl oz) sunflower or
    vegetable oil
200g (7oz) soft light brown sugar
300g (11oz) peeled and grated
    carrots (weight when grated)
75g (3oz) pecans or walnuts,
    chopped (optional)
175g (6oz) self-raising flour
½ tsp bicarbonate of soda
1 tsp ground cinnamon
1 tsp mixed spice
Pinch of salt

For the icing
100g (3½oz) cream cheese
Finely grated zest of 1 orange
200g (7oz) icing sugar, sifted

900g (2lb) loaf tin (see page 334)

Preheat the oven to 150°C (300°F), Gas mark 2, and line the base and sides of the loaf tin with baking parchment, with the paper coming above the sides of the tin to enable the cake to be lifted out easily.

Whisk the eggs in a large bowl to break them up, then whisk in the oil, sugar, grated carrots and chopped nuts. Sift in the remaining ingredients and bring the mixture together using a wooden or large metal spoon.

Pour the mixture into the prepared loaf tin, smoothing the surface with a palette knife, and bake in the oven for between 1 hour and 1 hour 15 minutes or until a skewer inserted into the centre of the cake comes out clean.

Allow to cool in the tin for about 5 minutes, then carefully lift the cake out of the tin with the lining paper. Peel away the baking parchment and place on a wire rack to cool down fully before you ice it.

While the cake is cooling, make the icing. Beat all the ingredients together, then use a palette knife to spread evenly over the cake.

Tip Try to use a serrated knife to cut this cake into slices, as it is dense but quite crumbly.

Carrot cakes continued overleaf

Ginger carrot cupcakes

Prep time: **20 minutes**
Baking time: **20–25 minutes**
Ready in: **1 hour**
Makes: **12 cupcakes**

For adding to the cake batter
50g (2oz) crystallised ginger,
finely chopped

For the icing
200g (7oz) cream cheese
200g (7oz) icing sugar, sifted
½ tsp ground ginger

To decorate
75g (3oz) crystallised ginger,
finely chopped

12-cup muffin tray and 12 muffin cases
(see page 336)

Preheat the oven to 180°C (350°F), Gas mark 4, and line the muffin tray with the paper cases.

Mix together the ingredients for the cake batter following the second paragraph of the Carrot cake method (see page 94), omitting the nuts and adding the crystallised ginger instead, then divide the mixture between the muffin cases, filling each case three-quarters full.

Bake for 20–25 minutes or until well risen and springy to the touch, then remove from the oven and allow to cool for 5 minutes before removing from the tin and placing on a wire rack to cool down fully.

Meanwhile, make the icing. Whisk all the ingredients together in a bowl, then use a palette knife to spread evenly over each cupcake.

As a final touch, sprinkle over the chopped crystallised ginger to decorate.

Caramel carrot cake

Prep time: **20 minutes**
Baking time: **30–35 minutes**
Ready in: **2 hours**
Serves: **8–10**

For the icing
200g (7oz) icing sugar, sifted
200g (7oz) cream cheese
3 tbsp dulce de leche (see the tip
on page 168)

To decorate
Walnut or pecan halves (optional)

Two 20cm (8in) diameter cake tins
(see page 334)

Preheat the oven to 160°C (325°F), Gas mark 3, then grease the cake tins with oil and line each base with baking parchment.

Mix the ingredients for the sponge following the second paragraph of the Carrot cake method (see page 94), then divide the batter between the two prepared tins and bake for 30–35 minutes or until lightly browned on top and springy to the touch.

Remove the cakes from the oven and allow to sit in the tins for 10 minutes, then use a small, sharp knife to loosen the edges and carefully remove each cake from its tin before transferring to a wire rack to cool down completely (see page 334).

While the cakes are baking, or cooling, make the icing. Place all the ingredients in a mixing bowl and beat together until well mixed. To assemble the cake, place one layer upside down on a serving plate and spread half the icing on the top. Add the second layer, placing it right side up, then spread the rest of the icing over the top. You might like to decorate the top of the cake with walnut or pecan halves.

Classic NYC crumb cake

New York's melting pot of cultures has produced a city of amazing culinary diversity. Central to this have been the bakeries, with the Polish, Jewish and German ones being especially prominent. The classic New York City crumb cake derives from the German *Krümelkuchen*. The cake here is adapted from a recipe in *Baked in America* by David Lesniak and David Muniz, two wonderful American bakers who run a fabulous café and bakery in London called Outsider Tart, where they make some of the most delicious baked treats this side of the Atlantic. Delicious eaten as a snack, or served to friends and family, the cake will keep for 2–3 days.

Prep time: **20 minutes**
Baking time: **45–55 minutes**
Ready in: **1 hour 45 minutes**
Makes: **about 24 squares**

225g (8oz) butter, softened
350g (12oz) caster sugar
2 tsp vanilla extract
4 eggs, beaten
350ml (12fl oz) sour cream
525g (1lb 2½oz) plain flour
1 tsp baking powder
½ tsp bicarbonate of soda
1 tsp salt

For the crumb topping
150g (5oz) butter, melted
300g (11oz) plain flour
1 tbsp ground cinnamon
225g (8oz) soft dark brown sugar
¼ tsp salt

25 x 35cm (10 x 14in) roasting tin with 5cm (2in) sides (approximate size)

Preheat the oven to 180°C (350°F), Gas mark 4, then line the base and sides of the roasting tin with baking parchment, with the paper coming just above the sides of the tin to enable the cake to be lifted out easily.

First make the crumb. Pour the melted butter into a large bowl or into an electric food mixer. Sift in the flour and cinnamon and add the remaining ingredients, then mix briefly – for just 30–60 seconds if using a food mixer – until coarse and crumbly.

To make the cake batter, first cream the butter until soft in a separate large bowl or in the food mixer. Pour in the sugar and beat until the mixture is light and fluffy. Add the vanilla extract and gradually mix in the eggs. Add the sour cream, then (with the mixer on a low speed, if you're using it) sift in the remaining ingredients, and fold in to combine.

Tip the batter into the prepared tin and smooth the surface with a spatula or the back of a spoon. Sprinkle over the crumb mixture, making sure it covers the batter completely.

Bake on the lower shelf in the oven for 45–55 minutes or until golden brown on top and a skewer inserted into the centre of the cake comes out clean. Check the cake after 30 minutes and if the top is already a rich golden brown, cover the tin with foil (to prevent the cake from burning) and continue to cook for the remaining time.

Remove the cake from the oven and allow to cool in the tin completely. Then lift the cake out using the baking parchment, peel away the paper and cut into squares to serve.

St Clement's drizzle cake

The St Clement's combination of oranges and lemons is a real classic, named of course after the bells in the famous nursery rhyme. This drizzle cake is different from other syrup cakes: rather than dissolving the sugar in a hot syrup first, it's simply mixed with the citrus juices before being drizzled over the cake. The undissolved sugar crystals are essential in this recipe for their slight crunch.

Prep time: **10 minutes**
Baking time: **45 minutes**
Ready in: **1 hour 30 minutes**
Serves: **6–10**

175g (6oz) butter, softened
175g (6oz) caster sugar
2 eggs
Juice and finely grated zest of 1 lemon
Juice and finely grated zest of 1 orange
50ml (2fl oz) milk
175g (6oz) self-raising flour, sifted
100g (3½oz) granulated sugar

900g (2lb) loaf tin (see page 334)

Preheat the oven to 180°C (350°F), Gas mark 4, and line the base and sides of the loaf tin with baking parchment, with the paper coming above the sides of the tin to enable the cake to be lifted out easily.

Cream the butter until soft in a large bowl or in an electric food mixer. Add the caster sugar and beat until the mixture is light and fluffy.

Whisk the eggs together in a small bowl for a few seconds or just until mixed, then gradually add them to the creamed butter mixture, beating all the time. Beat in the lemon and orange zest, followed by the milk.

Fold in the flour until combined, then tip the mixture into the prepared loaf tin. Bake for about 45 minutes or until nice and golden on top and a skewer inserted into the centre of the cake comes out clean.

While the cake is cooking, pour the lemon and orange juice into a bowl and mix in the granulated sugar.

When the cake comes out of the oven, prick it with a skewer a few times, then drizzle the sugary juices all over the cake, allowing them to soak in. Leave the cake to cool completely in the tin, then carefully lift it out with the lining paper. Peel away the baking parchment and leave on a wire rack to finish cooling down.

Place on a plate or board and cut into slices to serve.

Dark treacly gingerbread squares

The strong, almost bitter, flavour of treacle goes so well with the equally strong taste of ginger. The bitterness is mellowed with the brown sugar, while the treacle, along with the milk, makes this cake lovely and moist. The finished squares will keep for up to 10 days if stored in an airtight container.

Prep time: 15 minutes
Baking time: 20–25 minutes
Ready in: 1 hour
Makes: 16 large or 25 smaller squares

75g (3oz) butter, plus extra for greasing
100g (3½oz) soft dark brown sugar
175g (6oz) black treacle
150ml (5fl oz) milk
1 egg
225g (8oz) plain flour
2 tsp ground ginger
1 tsp baking powder
¼ tsp bicarbonate of soda
½ tsp salt

20cm (8in) square cake tin with 5cm (2in) sides (see page 334)

Preheat the oven to 180°C (350°F), Gas mark 4. If the cake tin has a removable base, butter the sides and line the base with a square of baking parchment, otherwise line the base and sides of the tin.

Place the butter, brown sugar and treacle in a saucepan over a medium heat. Stir together until melted and combined, then remove from the heat and whisk in the milk, followed by the egg. Set aside while you prepare the other ingredients.

Sift the flour, ground ginger, baking powder, bicarbonate of soda and salt into a large bowl. Make a well in the centre, then pour in the wet ingredients and mix together thoroughly, beating the mixture with a wooden spoon just until it comes together, and making sure there are no lumps of flour.

Tip the batter into the tin and bake for 20–25 minutes or until a skewer inserted into the centre of the cake comes out clean.

Remove from the oven and allow to cool in the tin for 10 minutes, then carefully remove the cake and leave on a wire rack to cool down fully (see page 334) before placing on a chopping board and cutting into either 16 large squares or 25 smaller ones.

Dark treacly gingerbread loaf

Line the base and sides of a 900g (2lb) loaf tin with baking parchment before tipping in the cake mixture. Baked like this, the cake will take about an hour to cook. Once cooled, cut into slices and spread with butter to serve.

Angel food cake

Angel food cake is a classic American dessert, especially popular in the South. Its name derives from it being almost magically light, making it seem like the 'food of the angels'. Once the cake is made, you can cover it with rose-water or lavender icing (see page 103), if you wish. Iced or plain, this cake is delicious served with summer berries and whipped cream, to which you could add a dash of rose or orange-blossom water or a few drops of lavender essence for a refreshing, floral note.

Prep time: **20 minutes (excluding the icing)**
Baking time: **20–28 minutes**
Ready in: **1 hour 15 minutes**
Serves: **6–8**

Butter, for greasing
125g (4½oz) plain flour, plus extra for dusting
Pinch of salt
175g (6oz) caster sugar
½ tsp cream of tartar, sifted
8 egg whites (250ml/9fl oz)
2 tsp vanilla extract

23cm (9in) diameter cake tin with 6cm (2½in) sides (see page 334)

Preheat the oven to 180°C (350°F), Gas mark 4. Butter the sides of the cake tin and dust with flour, then line the base with a disc of baking parchment.

Sift the flour and salt into a bowl and mix in 150g (5oz) of the caster sugar. In a separate bowl, mix together the remaining sugar with the cream of tartar.

Tip the egg whites into a large, spotlessly clean bowl or in an electric food mixer. Using a hand-held electric beater or the food mixer, whisk the egg whites for about 20 seconds or until they begin to turn cloudy and frothy. With the beater or mixer still running, add the mixed sugar and cream of tartar, then continue to whisk until the mixture is glossy and forms stiff peaks.

Carefully fold in the vanilla extract, followed by the dry ingredients, adding these a quarter at a time and folding in very lightly, so as not to knock any air out of the mixture.

Tip the mixture into the prepared tin and bake for 20–28 minutes or until golden on top and a skewer inserted into the centre of the cake comes out clean.

Remove from the oven and allow to cool in the tin for 15 minutes. Using a small, sharp knife to loosen the edges, carefully remove the cake from the tin and leave on a wire rack to finish cooling before transferring to a plate to serve (see page 334).

While the cake is cooling, make the icing (see page 103), if using, and decorate the cake following the instructions given in the individual recipes.

Recipe continued overleaf

Variation

Instead of icing the cake, you could serve it with softly whipped cream and berries such as raspberries, blueberries, strawberries or blackberries, or a mixture. You could either top the cake with about 450ml (16fl oz) of softly whipped cream and a generous scattering of berries, or alternatively you could simply serve each slice with cream and berries.

Tip Being a delicate, fat-free sponge, it needs to be cut very carefully with a serrated knife.

Rose-water icing with pistachios

Prep time: **5 minutes**
Makes: **enough for 1 large cake**

1–2 tbsp rose water
250g (9oz) icing sugar, sifted

To decorate
75g (3oz) unsalted shelled pistachios,
   roughly chopped
Fresh or crystallised rose petals
   (see page 345) (optional)

Stir together 1 tablespoon of the rose water with the icing sugar until well mixed and runny enough for drizzling – adding a few more drops of rose water if it seems too stiff. Use a spoon to drizzle all over the cake in zigzags, then, before the icing has a chance to dry, quickly sprinkle the pistachios all over the cake and scatter with the fresh or crystallised rose petals, if using.

Lavender icing

Prep time: **5 minutes**
Makes: **enough for 1 large cake**

¼ tsp lavender essence
1–2 tbsp boiling water
250g (9oz) icing sugar, sifted

To decorate
About 8 lavender flowers (optional)

In a small bowl, mix together the lavender essence with 1 tablespoon of boiling water. Sift the icing sugar into a separate bowl, then add the lavender mixture and stir together until well mixed and runny enough for drizzling – add a few more drops of hot water if it seems too stiff. Use a spoon to drizzle all over the cake in a zigzag pattern, and scatter with the lavender flowers, if using.

Lamingtons

Lamingtons are an Aussie favourite, eaten all over the country. While their exact origins are disputed, it's generally agreed that they were named after Lord Lamington, Governor of Queensland in the late nineteenth century. Some claim the cakes are so called because they resemble the homburg hats Lamington liked to wear. Others suggest that the name came about after the governor's cook accidentally dropped some sponge cake in melted chocolate and found it was delicious when rolled in coconut. Whatever the case, these cakes are loved down under for a reason – they're not difficult to make and they look fabulous. Perfect for picnics or as an after-school treat.

Prep time: **30 minutes**
Baking time: **30 minutes**
Ready in: **1 hour 30 minutes**
Makes: **16 squares**

6 eggs
150g (5oz) caster sugar
¼ tsp salt
175g (6oz) self-raising flour
1 tsp vanilla extract
75g (3oz) butter, melted
200g (7oz) desiccated coconut,
   to decorate

For the icing
175g (6oz) milk chocolate, in drops
   or broken into pieces
50g (2oz) butter
175ml (6fl oz) milk
200g (7oz) icing sugar
50g (2oz) cocoa powder

20cm (8in) square cake tin with 6cm
   (2½in) sides (see page 334)

Preheat the oven to 180°C (350°F), Gas mark 4. If the cake tin has a removable base, butter the sides and line the base with a square of baking parchment, otherwise line the base and sides of the tin.

Place the eggs, sugar and salt in a large bowl or in an electric food mixer. Using a hand-held electric whisk or the food mixer, whisk for 6–8 minutes or until the mixture is light and thick. To test if it's thick enough, lift the whisk out and draw a figure of eight in the bowl – the '8' should remain visible for a couple of seconds.

Sift in the flour and fold it into the batter, along with the vanilla extract and melted butter. Tip the mixture into the prepared cake tin and bake for 30 minutes or until the cake begins to pull away from the sides of the tin and a skewer inserted into the centre comes out clean.

Remove from the oven and allow to cool in the tin for 5 minutes before carefully removing the cake and leaving on a wire rack to cool down fully (see page 334).

While the cake is cooking or cooling, make the icing. Place the chocolate, butter and milk in a heatproof bowl and set over a saucepan of just simmering water. Allow the butter and chocolate to melt, stirring from time to time, then remove from the heat. Sift together the icing sugar and cocoa powder and whisk into the melted chocolate, then transfer to a large bowl and set aside to cool.

Recipe continued overleaf

When the cake has finished cooling, place it on a chopping board and cut into 16 squares.

Place the coconut in a shallow bowl and put it next to the bowl of chocolate icing. Dip each sponge square into the chocolate icing, ensuring each side is just covered in the mixture and allowing any excess to drip off, then gently roll in the coconut. Transfer to a wire rack to allow the icing to set, then repeat with the rest of the squares.

Orange lamingtons or lemingtons

Replace the chocolate icing with 400g (14oz) of orange or lemon curd (see page 27) and instead of the desiccated coconut use the same quantity of toasted chopped almonds.

Jamingtons

Replace the chocolate icing with 400g (14oz) of raspberry or strawberry jam.

Battenberg cake

I remember eating Battenberg cake after school one day at my friend's house when I was about eight. I had never seen such a beautiful cake in all my life: the pink-and-white chequerboard sponge wrapped in rich almondy marzipan was to me the height of sophistication. Even now, I can't eat it without being transported back to that time. The recipe may look long, but it really isn't complicated – just follow it step by step.

Prep time: **30 minutes**
Baking time: **25–30 minutes**
Ready in: **2 hours**
Serves: **8–10**

175g (6oz) butter, softened, plus
    extra for greasing
175g (6oz) caster sugar
3 eggs, beaten
2 tbsp milk
175g (6oz) self-raising flour
Pink food colouring
150g (5oz) apricot jam
350g (12oz) marzipan (to make
    it yourself, see page 51)

20cm (8in) square cake tin with 5cm
    (2in) sides (see page 334)

Preheat the oven to 180°C (350°F), Gas mark 4, then butter the sides of the cake tin and line the base with a square of baking parchment.

Cut out another square of baking parchment the same size as the base of the tin (using the tin as a template to draw around). Fold in one side by 3cm (1¼in) to form a flap, then fold the opposite side by the same amount to make a second flap. Fold the paper in half parallel to the folds for the flaps, folding over the middle section so that there is a flap on each side and, viewed from the side, the folded shape looks like an upside-down letter 'T'. This will be used as a partition to separate the two different coloured sponges.

Cream the butter until soft in a large bowl or in an electric food mixer. Add the sugar and beat until the mixture is light and fluffy. Gradually add the eggs, beating all the time, then beat in the milk and sift in the flour, folding it in to combine.

Divide the mixture between two bowls, adding a few drops of the pink food colouring to one of the bowls and mixing in.

Place the paper shape in the centre of the tin so that it stands upright with the central fold uppermost and the flaps facing down, flat against the base of the tin. You'll see that the paper now forms a partition with a compartment on either side. Supporting the paper with one hand, pour one of the batters into one compartment. Continuing to hold the paper so that it doesn't cave in under the weight of the first batter, pour the second bowlful of batter into the other compartment. You can then take your hand off the paper as it should now be held upright by the batter pressing in on either side. (You might want to ask someone to hold the paper 'wall' steady while you pour in the batter.)

Recipe continued overleaf

Place the filled cake tin in the oven (with the partition in place) and bake for 25–30 minutes or until well risen and a skewer inserted into the centre of each section of cake comes out clean.

Remove from the oven and leave on a wire rack to cool for 10 minutes, then, loosening round the edges using a small, sharp knife, carefully remove the cake from the tin and place on the wire rack to cool down completely (see page 334).

When the cake is cool, divide it in half so you have a rectangle in each colour. Then cut each section in half lengthways so you have two rectangles in each colour. Trim all the edges so each rectangle has the same dimensions. The cross section should be a square, with the width the same as the depth. Push the jam through a sieve and, using a palette knife, spread the jam over two adjoining sides of each rectangle of cake, then stick them together along the jammed sides to form a chequerboard pattern (when viewed from the end of the cake).

Next roll out the marzipan on a work surface lightly dusted with icing sugar. It should be rolled out into a rectangle the same length as the cake and four times the width, with any excess trimmed away. Spread the remaining jam over the marzipan, then place the cake along one edge so that cake and marzipan align lengthways, and roll up the cake in the marzipan. Cut off each end of the cake to neaten, then cut into slices to serve.

Dundee cake

Dundee cake is a traditional Scottish fruitcake. It looks gorgeous with its characteristic rings of blanched almonds on top. Unlike many fruitcakes, it doesn't have any spices, the flavour coming from the wonderful array of dried fruit it contains. It will keep for weeks, and it's worth waiting a few days before cutting into it, in order to allow the flavours to develop properly.

Prep time: **20 minutes**
Baking time: **2 hours–2 hours 30 minutes**
Ready in: **4 hours**
Serves: **8–12**

150g (5oz) butter, softened
150g (5oz) caster sugar
4 eggs
225g (8oz) plain flour, sifted
1 tsp baking powder
100g (3½oz) currants
100g (3½oz) sultanas
50g (2oz) glacé cherries, cut in half
50g (2oz) whole mixed candied peel, finely chopped
50g (2oz) ground almonds
Finely grated zest of 1 orange
Finely grated zest of 1 lemon
50g (2oz) whole blanched almonds

20cm (8in) diameter cake tin with 6cm (2½in) sides (see page 334)

Preheat the oven to 150°C (300°F), Gas mark 2. Line the base and sides of the cake tin with baking parchment and wrap a collar of parchment or foil around the outside of the tin to prevent the cake from drying out during cooking.

Cream the butter until soft in a large bowl or in an electric food mixer. Add the sugar and beat until the mixture is light and fluffy.

Whisk the eggs together in a small bowl for a few seconds or until just mixed, then gradually add them to the creamed butter mixture, beating all the time.

In a separate bowl, mix together all the remaining ingredients apart from the whole almonds, then stir into the cake batter. Mix well, then tip into the prepared tin. Carefully arrange the whole almonds in concentric circles on top of the mixture, laying them lightly on top without pressing in.

Bake on the lowest shelf in the oven for between 2 hours and 2 hours 30 minutes or until springy to the touch and a skewer inserted into the centre of the cake comes out clean. It's best to check the cake halfway through cooking: if it's a deep golden brown already, place a sheet of baking parchment or foil over the top to stop it browning any further.

Remove from the oven and place on a wire rack to cool for about 30 minutes. Remove the collar of paper or foil and, using a small, sharp knife to loosen the edges, carefully remove the cake from the tin and leave on a wire rack to finish cooling before transferring to a serving plate (see page 334).

Madeleines

Madeleines are the quintessential delicate treat. The airy batter is baked in the traditional shell-shaped moulds to make a cake that is just crisp on the outside and elegantly light in the middle. This recipe is quick and easy to make, but there are many twists you can give to the basic cake (see pages 114–15), which are all delicious variations on a classic theme.

Prep time: **20 minutes (excluding any icing)**
Baking time: **12–15 minutes**
Ready in: **50 minutes**
Makes: **12 madeleines**

1 egg
50g (2oz) caster sugar
50g (2oz) plain flour, plus extra for dusting
¼ tsp baking powder
50g (2oz) butter, melted, plus extra for greasing
½ tsp vanilla extract
Icing sugar, for dusting

12-hole madeleine tray

Preheat the oven to 180°C (350°F), Gas mark 4. Brush a little melted butter over the madeleine moulds (making sure to coat every ridge) and dust a little flour into each one, tapping out any excess.

Place the egg and sugar in a large bowl or in an electric food mixer. Using a hand-held electric beater or the food mixer with its whisk attachment, whisk on a high speed for about 5 minutes or until the mixture is pale, thick and mousse-like and has grown almost three times in volume.

Sift the flour and baking powder into the whisked egg and sugar and carefully fold in, then fold in the melted butter and vanilla extract, taking care not to over-mix. Either pouring the batter directly from the bowl or using a tablespoon to spoon it in, divide the batter between the madeleine moulds, filling each almost to the top.

Bake for 12–15 minutes or until golden and lightly springy to the touch. (Try not to overcook them or they will be dry.) Remove from the oven and carefully remove each madeleine from its mould using a palette knife, then place on a wire rack to cool, if you must, as there are few things more delicious than warm madeleines served straight from the oven with nothing more than a light dusting of icing sugar.

Madeleines continued overleaf

Chocolate-dipped madeleines

Prep time: **30 minutes**
Baking time: **12–15 minutes**
Ready in: **1 hour 15 minutes**
Makes: enough **for 12 cakes**

For the chocolate coating

100g (3½oz) dark or white chocolate, in drops or broken into pieces

Prepare and bake the madeleines as on page 112 and while they are cooling, prepare the chocolate. Place the chocolate in a heatproof bowl and set over a pan of simmering water. Leave just until melted, stirring occasionally, then remove from the heat.

Holding one of the madeleines by one end, dip it into the chocolate so that it comes about a third of the way up. Remove from the chocolate, shaking off any excess into the bowl, then place on a sheet of baking parchment to set. Repeat with the rest of the madeleines until all of them are dipped.

Double chocolate madeleines

Make up the madeleines as in the main recipe on page 112, adding 1 tablespoon of cocoa powder at the same stage as the flour, then dip in the melted chocolate and leave to set.

Chocolate almond madeleines

Follow the basic madeleine recipe (see page 112), but rather than vanilla extract, add a few drops (not more than ⅛ tsp) of almond essence. Dip in the melted chocolate and then roll in 125g (4½oz) of toasted nibbed (chopped) almonds (see the tip on page 125) before leaving to set.

Madelamingtons

Follow the basic madeleine recipe (see page 112), adding 25g (1oz) of desiccated coconut at the same stage as the flour. Dip in the melted chocolate and then roll in 100g (3½oz) of desiccated coconut before leaving to set.

Lemon-striped madeleines

Prep time: **30 minutes**
Baking time: **12–15 minutes**
Ready in: **1 hour 15 minutes**
Makes: **enough for 12 cakes**

For adding to the sponge
Finely grated zest of 1 lemon

For the icing
100g (3½oz) icing, sifted
1–2 tbsp lemon juice

To the basic recipe (see page 112), add the lemon zest along with the flour. Bake the madeleines as in the main recipe, then remove from the oven and allow to cool.

When the cakes are cool, make the icing. In a bowl, mix together the icing sugar with 1 tablespoon of lemon juice. You want the icing to be thick enough to set but just liquid enough to drizzle. If it seems too thick, you may need to add a few more drops of lemon juice to get the right consistency.

Place the madeleines, ridged side up, on a plate. Set the bowl of icing close to the madeleines, then dip a spoon into the icing and lift it out again, allowing some of the icing to drip off so there isn't too much on the spoon. Holding the spoon over one of the madeleines, carefully drizzle over the icing in stripes or zigzags. Repeat with all of the madeleines, dipping the spoon back into the icing as needed.

Victoria sponge

The classic sponge cake was named after Queen Victoria, who enjoyed a slice of it with her tea. In its traditional form, it consists of two layers of cake with a raspberry jam and cream filling and dusted with icing or caster sugar. I've provided a version of it here as it's a classic, but it's a seriously versatile recipe with lots of variations that you can try – see the five different filling ideas on page 120.

Prep time: 10 minutes (excluding any filling)
Baking time: 18–25 minutes
Ready in: 1 hour
Serves: 6–8

175g (6oz) butter, softened, plus extra for greasing

175g (6oz) caster sugar

3 eggs

175g (6oz) plain flour, plus extra for dusting

1 tsp baking powder

1 tbsp milk

Icing or caster sugar, for sprinkling

Two 18cm (7in) diameter sandwich tins (see page 336)

Preheat the oven to 180°C (350°F), Gas mark 4, then butter and flour the sides of each tin and line the base with a disc of baking parchment.

Cream the butter until soft in a large bowl or in an electric food mixer. Add the sugar and beat until the mixture is light and fluffy.

Whisk the eggs together in a small bowl for a few seconds until just mixed, then gradually add them to the butter mixture, beating all the time. Sift in the flour and baking powder, then add the milk and fold in gently to incorporate.

Divide the mixture between the two tins and make a slight hollow in the centre of each cake so that when it rises it doesn't peak too much in the centre, making it difficult to sandwich together with the other half.

Place in the centre of the oven and bake for 18–25 minutes or until golden on top and springy to the touch.

Remove from the oven and allow to cool in the tins for 10 minutes, then loosen around the edges of each cake using a small, sharp knife and carefully remove from the tins before leaving on a wire rack to cool down completely (see page 336).

Once cool you can sandwich the cakes together using one of the fillings detailed on page 120. To assemble the Victoria sponge, place one cake upside down on a plate and spread over your chosen filling. Place the second cake on top, right side up, then sprinkle over the icing or caster sugar to finish.

Chocolate Victoria sponge

Make up the cake batter as in the recipe above, adding 25g (1oz) of cocoa powder with the flour for a chocolate sponge and sandwiching together with chocolate buttercream (see page 186 – using a quarter of the quantities specified).

Recipe continued overleaf

Orange or lemon Victoria sponge

Add the finely grated zest of a lemon or orange with the flour. For an orange-flavoured sponge, you could sandwich the sponge layers together with the orange and mascarpone filling (see below). For a lemon-flavoured version of this filling – to go with a lemon sponge – you could substitute the orange curd with lemon curd (see page 27) instead.

Fillings

Jam and cream or jam only

Spread 3–4 rounded tablespoons of jam, such as raspberry, strawberry or blackberry, over the first cake, followed by a layer of 125ml (4½ fl oz) of double or regular cream, whipped until almost stiff. This is best eaten on the day it's made. If you want the cake to last for a few days (without putting it in the fridge), omit the cream and use just jam in the centre; this will keep in an airtight box for 2–3 days.

Fresh fruit and cream

Substitute the jam with 200g (7oz) of fresh soft fruit, such as raspberries, blueberries (slightly mashed first) or sliced strawberries, adding these to the top of the whipped cream.

Rhubarb and cream

Place 100g (3½ oz) of sliced rhubarb in a saucepan with 50g (2oz) of caster sugar and a splash of water, cover with a lid and cook over a gentle heat for 10 minutes or until the rhubarb is soft. Bring to the boil, then take off the lid and boil, stirring continuously, until thickened. Pour into a bowl and allow to cool, then fold 125ml (4½ fl oz) of double or regular cream, whipped until almost stiff, into the cooked rhubarb and spread over the first cake.

Elderflower and strawberry

Fold 2 tablespoons of elderflower cordial into 125ml (4½ fl oz) of double or regular cream, whipped until almost stiff, and spread over the first cake, then add 175g (6oz) of sliced strawberries in an even layer on top of the cream. Sprinkle the finished cake with icing or caster sugar or, if you prefer, use elderflower sugar (see page 346).

Orange and mascarpone

Whisk 100g (3½ oz) of orange curd (see page 27) into 150g (5oz) of mascarpone and spread over the first cake. Once the cake is assembled, decorate the top with candied orange slices (see page 340) and sprinkle with caster sugar.

Brittany butter cake

This cake is a pure expression of the butter for which Brittany is famous. With so few ingredients, the flavour of the butter has nowhere to hide; the sugar is only there to sweeten the cake and the flour to give structure. Delicious eaten on its own, it also goes perfectly with strawberries and cream.

Prep time: 20 minutes
Baking time: 30 minutes
Ready in: 1 hour 10 minutes
Serves: 8–12

1 egg yolk, for the glaze
225g (8oz) plain flour, sifted
225g (8oz) caster sugar
225g (8oz) butter, softened,
    plus extra for greasing
6 egg yolks

25cm (10in) diameter cake tin
    (see page 334)

Preheat the oven to 180°C (350°F), Gas mark 4. Butter the sides of the cake tin and line the base with a disc of baking parchment.

Whisk together the egg yolk with 2 teaspoons of water for the glaze and set aside.

Either in a large bowl using a wooden spoon or in an electric food mixer using the paddle beater, mix together the flour and sugar, then add the butter and egg yolks and beat together until the mixture resembles a stiff dough.

Press into the prepared tin, and flatten with a spatula. Brush with the glaze, then decorate by drawing a fork across the cake in a criss-cross pattern of lines, each set of lines roughly 5cm (2in) apart in a sort of chequerboard design, following the traditional style for the cake.

Bake for 30 minutes or until it is a deep golden colour and a skewer inserted into the centre of the cake comes out clean.

Remove from the oven and allow to cool in the tin for 10 minutes, then loosen the edges using a small, sharp knife and carefully remove the cake from the tin before placing on a wire rack to cool down completely (see page 334).

Variation

If you like, you can add a tablespoon of rum or brandy to the dough, at the same time as the egg yolks, for another note of flavour.

Chocolate hazelnut cheesecake

Light this is not, but if you're craving something rich and indulgent, this American-style baked cheesecake, with its fabulous creamy topping and crisp buttery base, will certainly fit the bill. The cream cheese topping is loaded with chocolate and melted butter, offset by the delicate tang of sour cream. The toasted hazelnuts, roughly chopped, add another layer of texture to this divine dessert.

Prep time: **30 minutes**
Baking time: **1 hour 30 minutes**
Ready in: **4 hours**
Serves: **10–12**

100g (3½oz) butter, plus extra for greasing
350g (12oz) dark chocolate, in drops or broken into pieces
450g (1lb) cream cheese
100ml (3½fl oz) sour cream
3 eggs
175g (6oz) caster sugar
150g (5oz) hazelnuts, toasted, skinned and roughly chopped (see the tip opposite)

For the biscuit base
375g (13oz) dark chocolate digestive biscuits
3 tbsp double or regular cream
75g (3oz) butter, melted

25cm (10in) diameter spring-form cake tin with 6cm (2½in) sides (see page 336)

Preheat the oven to 170°C (325°F), Gas mark 3, and grease the sides of the cake tin with butter. Make sure the base of the cake tin is upside down, so there's no lip and the cake can slide off easily when cooked.

First make the biscuit base. Place the biscuits in a food processor and whiz until they form coarse crumbs. Alternatively, place the biscuits in a plastic bag and crush them using a rolling pin until finely broken down with only a few coarse pieces remaining. Tip the biscuit crumbs into a large bowl and mix with the cream and melted butter, then place in the cake tin, pushing the mixture down into the base to cover it as evenly as possible. Chill in the fridge while you make the topping.

Place the butter and chocolate in a large heatproof bowl and set over a saucepan of just simmering water, stirring occasionally until melted and combined. When melted, remove from the heat and whisk in the cream cheese until smooth, then whisk in the sour cream.

In a separate bowl using a hand-held electric beater or in an electric food mixer, whisk together the eggs and sugar for 2–3 minutes or until mousse-like in consistency, then turn off the machine and fold in the chocolate mixture along with the chopped hazelnuts.

Add the mixture to the chilled biscuit base, spreading it in an even layer, then bake for 1 hour 30 minutes or until almost set. It should wobble a little if you gently shake the tin, while the top will be slightly cracked.

Allow to cool in the tin on a rack for an hour, then chill, still in the tin, in the fridge for at least an hour before serving. Loosen around the edges using a small, sharp knife and unclip and remove the sides of the tin (see page 336). Then use a long, sharp knife to loosen the bottom of the cake from the base and a palette knife or metal fish slice to slide the cake onto a plate. (If you don't feel brave enough to slide it off the base, just leave it on and place it like this on the plate.)

Tip You can buy toasted hazelnuts, but for the best flavour you should toast your own. To toast them, spread them out on a baking tray and cook in the oven (preheated to 200°C/400°F/Gas mark 6) for 7–10 minutes or until their skins have darkened (rub the skin off one or two to check that the nuts are golden). Wrap the nuts in a clean tea towel (this slightly stains the tea towel, so don't use your favourite one!) and rub them for a few seconds to remove the skins, which should come off easily. Pour the skinned nuts back onto the baking tray, then either place the tray outside and let the skins just blow away (you can speed up the process by blowing gently on the hazelnuts) or just pick the hazelnuts out from the skins. Next use a knife to roughly chop the nuts, leaving some larger pieces.

'There are few hours in life more agreeable than the hour dedicated to the ceremony known as afternoon tea.'
— *The Portrait of a Lady*, Henry James

Few and far between are the days in which I don't drink tea. There is no drink that I find more comforting or calming. I will happily drink tea in the afternoon by itself, but even a small piece of cake transforms a five-minute break from work or chores into a real treat. There is no rule as to what makes a cake good with tea (or indeed with coffee). Sometimes I like a spiced fruitcake, a rich chocolate cake or a fluffy, nutty muffin. But nothing too advanced or complicated, and usually without too much icing. Here are my favourite cakes that are the perfect partners to a soothing cup of comfort.

05/ Teatime

Cheesecake brownies

I adore the effect of pale cheesecake swirled through dark sponge in these brownies. They look fabulous and the rich, strong flavour of the chocolate is nicely complemented by the slight tang of the cream cheese. These are perfect for those times when a standard brownie just doesn't seem indulgent enough.

Prep time: **20 minutes**
Baking time: **30–35 minutes**
Ready in: **1 hour 30 minutes**
Makes: **16 brownies**

100g (3½oz) butter, cut into cubes
100g (3½oz) dark chocolate, in drops or broken into pieces
125g (4½oz) caster sugar
Pinch of salt
3 eggs, beaten
75g (3oz) self-raising flour
1 tbsp cocoa powder
100g (3½oz) dark chocolate, in chips or chopped into pieces

For the cheesecake mixture
200g (7oz) cream cheese
2 egg yolks
75g (3oz) caster sugar

20cm (8in) square cake tin with 5cm (2in) sides (see page 334)

Preheat the oven to 180°C (350°F), Gas mark 4. If the cake tin has a removable base, butter the sides and line the base with a square of baking parchment, otherwise line the base and sides of the tin.

Place the butter and chocolate in a saucepan and melt over a low heat. Stir just until smooth, then remove from the heat and beat in the sugar and salt, followed by the eggs. Sift in the flour and cocoa powder, add the chocolate chips and stir in. Tip the batter into the prepared tin and spread out using a spatula.

In a clean bowl, beat all the ingredients for the cheesecake mixture together until smooth. Dot heaped teaspoonfuls of this mixture across the top of the brownie batter in the tin, then use a skewer or knife to swirl the two mixtures together, right across the tin and up to the edges.

Bake for 30–35 minutes or until the middle of the cake still wobbles slightly when you gently shake the tin – a skewer inserted into the centre should come out with a little moisture on it. Remove from the oven, place on a wire rack and allow to cool completely in the tin before carefully removing the cake (see page 334) and cutting into squares to serve.

Banoffee blondies

Blondies, with their white chocolate vanilla flavour, are a close relation of the brownie (see page 128). I like to mix additional ingredients into blondies and I love the classic 'banoffee' combination of banana and toffee when mixed with white chocolate. These blondies take a little extra effort, but it's well worth it. The almond praline adds a lovely toffee-almond crunch to contrast with the soft sweetness of the bananas. Eat either with vanilla ice cream, while the cakes are still warm, or as a picnic treat.

Prep time: **20 minutes**
Baking time: **30–35 minutes**
Ready in: **1 hour 15 minutes**
Makes: **16 blondies**

100g (3½oz) butter
225g (8oz) white chocolate, in drops
  or broken into pieces
175g (6oz) soft light brown sugar
1 egg, beaten
200g (7oz) peeled very ripe bananas
  (about 2), mashed
2 tsp vanilla extract
225g (8oz) plain flour
1 tsp baking powder
¼ tsp salt

For the almond praline
100g (3½oz) caster sugar
100g (3½oz) whole almonds
  (skin still on)

20cm (8in) square cake tin with 5cm
  (2in) sides (see page 334)

First make the almond praline. Place the caster sugar in a frying pan (preferably non-stick if you have one), spreading it over the base of the pan, then scatter over the almonds. Cook on a medium heat until the sugar turns a deep golden caramel. (You may swirl the pan once the sugar starts caramelising, but do not stir it.) Tip out onto a baking tray lined with baking parchment and allow to cool and set, then chop until the consistency of very coarse breadcrumbs, or pulse in a food processor.

Preheat the oven to 180°C (350°F), Gas mark 4. If the cake tin has a removable base, butter the sides and line the base with a square of baking parchment, otherwise line the base and sides of the tin.

Place the butter and white chocolate in a saucepan and set over a low heat. When the butter has melted, remove from the heat and stir to melt the chocolate. Pour into a large bowl and beat in the sugar, egg, mashed bananas and vanilla extract, then stir in the almond praline.

Sift in the remaining ingredients and fold in thoroughly to mix, then spoon the mixture into the prepared tin and bake for 30–35 minutes or until just set and golden on top.

Either allow to cool completely in the tin or allow to cool in the tin for 5–10 minutes and serve while still warm. Carefully remove the cake from the tin (see page 334) and cut into squares for serving.

Cappuccino squares

A light and fluffy buttercream icing mimics the layer of frothy milk in these playful, cappuccino-style cakes. Unsurprisingly, these squares go especially well with coffee, or indeed cappuccino.

Prep time: **20 minutes**
Baking time: **40 minutes**
Ready in: **1 hour 45 minutes**
Makes: **16 squares**

200g (7oz) butter, softened,
    plus extra for greasing
200g (7oz) caster sugar
3 eggs
325g (11½oz) plain flour, sifted
3 tsp baking powder
150ml (5fl oz) milk
2 tbsp coffee essence (ideally
    Camp or Irel)

For the vanilla buttercream icing
200g (7oz) butter, softened
150g (5oz) icing sugar, sifted
2 tsp vanilla extract
3 tbsp milk

To decorate
1 tbsp cocoa powder, for dusting
16 chocolate-covered coffee beans
    (see page 341) (optional)

20cm (8in) square cake tin with 5cm
    (2in) sides (see page 334)

Preheat the oven to 180°C (350°F), Gas mark 4. If the cake tin has a removable base, butter the sides and line the base with a square of baking parchment, otherwise line the base and sides of the tin.

Place all the ingredients for the sponge in a food processor and whiz for 10–20 seconds or just until combined. Alternatively, cream the butter until soft using a hand-held electric beater, then beat in the sugar, whisk in the eggs one at a time and fold in the remaining ingredients.

Tip the mixture into the prepared tin, smooth over the top with a palette knife and bake in the oven for 40 minutes or until a skewer inserted into the centre of the cake comes out clean.

Remove from the oven and allow to cool in the tin for 10 minutes before carefully removing the cake from the tin and leaving on a wire rack to finish cooling (see page 334).

While the cake is in the oven, or while it's cooling, make the vanilla buttercream icing. Place all the ingredients in the food processor, having cleaned the bowl and mixer blade, and whiz until light and fluffy. Alternatively, cream the butter until soft using the electric beater, then beat in the remaining ingredients.

Transfer the cake to a plate and spread the icing over the top using a palette knife, dust with cocoa powder then cut into squares to serve. As a finishing touch, you could decorate the tops with chocolate-covered coffee beans (see page 341), adding several beans to the centre of each square.

Ras el hanout spiced fruitcake

Ras el hanout refers to a Moroccan blend of spices. It doesn't refer to a specific blend, however: ras el hanout just means 'top of the shop' in Arabic, indicating a mix of the very best spices a market stall or shop may have to offer. This recipe uses a blend of spices that may be a little unusual for a cake but convey all the exotic aromas of a Marrakech market. Interestingly, this cake has no fat, the large amount of dried fruit doing the job instead, keeping it lovely and moist. Stored in an airtight container, it will keep for a few weeks.

Prep time: **15 minutes**
Baking time: **45 minutes**
Ready in: **1 hour 30 minutes**
Serves: **6–8**

Butter, for greasing
75g (3oz) raisins
75g (3oz) dried apricots, chopped
75g (3oz) dried blueberries or dried cranberries (or use raisins)
75g (3oz) sultanas
75g (3oz) currants
250ml (9fl oz) hot black tea
½ tsp ground cinnamon
Pinch of ground cloves
Pinch of chilli powder
½ tsp ground cardamom
¼ tsp ground coriander
¼ tsp ground cumin
¼ tsp turmeric
½ tsp ground nutmeg
225g (8oz) self-raising flour
150g (5oz) soft light brown sugar
1 egg, lightly beaten

20cm (8in) diameter cake tin with 6cm (2½in) sides (see page 334)

Preheat the oven to 180°C (350°F), Gas mark 4, then butter the sides of the cake tin and line the base with a disc of baking parchment.

Put all the dried fruit in a heatproof bowl and pour over the hot tea. Stir thoroughly, then add the ground spices and leave to cool for 10 minutes.

Sift the flour into a large bowl and mix in the sugar, then add the soaked fruit mixture and the beaten egg and stir until all the ingredients are completely incorporated.

Tip the mixture into the prepared cake tin and bake for about 45 minutes or until well risen and springy to the touch – a skewer inserted into the centre should come out clean.

Remove from the oven and allow to cool for 10 minutes. Using a small, sharp knife to loosen the edges, carefully remove the cake from the tin and leave on a wire rack to cool down fully before transferring to a serving plate (see page 334).

Chocolate and pecan muffins with maple glaze

Half muffin, half cupcake, these aren't quite as indulgent as a fully fledged cupcake but a bit of a treat nonetheless. I like the speckled appearance created by the chocolate chips as well as the contrast in texture when combined with the crunchy pecans.

Prep time: 10 minutes
Baking time: 25 minutes
Ready in: 1 hour
Makes: 12 muffins

200g (7oz) butter
200g (7oz) caster sugar
4 eggs
100g (3½oz) milk or dark chocolate, in drops or broken into pieces
75g (3oz) pecans, roughly chopped
200g (7oz) self-raising flour
25ml (1fl oz) maple syrup, for the glaze

12-cup muffin tray and 12 muffin cases (see page 336)

Preheat the oven to 180°C (350°F), Gas mark 4, and line the muffin tray with the paper cases.

Cream the butter until soft in a large bowl or in an electric food mixer. Add the sugar and beat until the mixture is light and fluffy. Beat in the eggs one at a time, then tip in the chocolate and pecans and fold in with the flour to combine.

Divide the batter between the muffin cases, filling each case three-quarters full. Bake for about 25 minutes or until golden on top and lightly springy to the touch. Transfer the tin to a wire rack and brush each muffin with some of the maple syrup. Allow to cool for 5 minutes, then remove from the tin and place on the wire rack to finish cooling.

Coffee mascarpone cake

The rich creamy mascarpone provides the perfect foil to this simple coffee sponge. The coffee essence is very useful because it provides coffee flavour without adding too much liquid to your cake mixture. If you can't get hold of it, you can always substitute the same quantity of very strong coffee for the essence. The cocoa isn't just for decoration: it's essential to this recipe, with its magic mocha twist.

Prep time: 20 minutes
Baking time: 20 minutes
Ready in: 1 hour
Serves: 8–12

175g (6oz) butter, softened, plus extra for greasing
175g (6oz) caster sugar
3 eggs, beaten
2 tbsp coffee essence (ideally Camp or Irel)
175g (6oz) self-raising flour, plus extra for dusting
Cocoa powder, for dusting

For the filling and icing
250g (9oz) mascarpone
3 tbsp icing sugar, sifted
1 tbsp coffee essence (ideally Camp or Irel)

Two 18cm (7in) diameter cake tins (see page 334)

Preheat the oven to 180°C (350°F), Gas mark 4, then butter the sides of the cake tins, dusting them lightly with flour, and line the base of each tin with a disc of baking parchment.

Cream the butter until soft in a large bowl or in an electric food mixer. Add the sugar and beat until the mixture is light and fluffy. Gradually add the eggs and coffee essence to the creamed butter mixture, beating all the time. Sift in the flour and fold in gently to mix.

Divide the batter between the two prepared tins, making a slight hollow in the centre so they will rise with a flat top. Place in the oven and bake for about 20 minutes or until well risen, golden brown and springy to the touch.

Remove from the oven and allow to sit in the tins for 10 minutes. Loosen round the edges of each cake using a small, sharp knife, then carefully remove from the tins and leave on a wire rack to cool down completely (see page 334).

Meanwhile, make the icing. Place the mascarpone in a bowl, and mix in the icing sugar along with the coffee essence.

Place one of the cakes upside down on a plate, then spread over half the icing. Place the other cake, right side up, on top of the filling, then spread with the rest of the icing and dust with the cocoa powder.

Ginger golden syrup loaf

I love stem ginger – little pieces of peeled young ginger preserved in a jar of sweet sugary syrup. It keeps its flavour and spiciness well, making it ideal for chopping up for use in a cake, as in this recipe, or spooned over vanilla ice cream. The sweet syrup is just divine – I like to use it in cocktails or, as here, drizzled over the cake while it's still hot so it really soaks up that gorgeous ginger taste.

Prep time: **10 minutes**
Baking time: **50–60 minutes**
Ready in: **1 hour 30 minutes**
Serves: **6–10**

225g (8oz) golden syrup
100g (3½oz) butter
100g (3½oz) caster sugar
75g (3oz) stem ginger in syrup
   (drained), chopped, reserving
   3 tbsp of syrup for the glaze
200ml (7fl oz) milk
2 eggs, beaten
225g (8oz) self-raising flour
1 tbsp ground ginger
1 tsp bicarbonate of soda
1 tsp salt

900g (2lb) loaf tin (see page 334)

Preheat the oven to 180°C (350°F), Gas mark 4, then line the base and sides of the loaf tin with baking parchment, with the paper coming above the sides of the tin to enable the cake to be lifted out easily.

Place the golden syrup, butter and sugar in a saucepan and stir over a medium–low heat until the butter has melted and the mixture is smooth. Set aside and allow to cool, then mix in the ginger, milk and eggs.

Meanwhile, sift the remaining ingredients into a large bowl. Make a well in the centre, then pour in the wet ingredients and mix thoroughly.

Tip the mixture – which will be quite runny – into the prepared loaf tin and bake in the centre of the oven for 50–60 minutes or until a skewer inserted into the centre of the cake comes out clean.

Remove from the oven and drizzle or brush the reserved stem ginger syrup over the loaf while it's still hot.

Allow to cool for 10 minutes in the tin, then carefully lift the cake out of the tin with the lining paper and place on a wire rack. Peel away the baking parchment and leave to cool down fully.

Banana, almond and honey muffins

The honey in these muffins brings out the natural sweetness of the ripe bananas. When baking it's best to try and use the ripest bananas you can – the darker the better. As a banana darkens it converts more of its starch to sugar and will make these muffins moist and even sweeter.

Prep time: **10 minutes**
Baking time: **25 minutes**
Ready in: **1 hour**
Makes: **12 muffins**

125g (4½oz) plain flour

2 tsp baking powder

½ tsp salt

175g (6oz) wholemeal flour

350g (12oz) peeled very ripe bananas
   (3–4 in total), mashed

2 eggs

75ml (3fl oz) sunflower oil

150g (5oz) honey

175g (6oz) almonds (skin still on),
   chopped

12-cup muffin tray and 12 muffin cases
   (see page 336)

Preheat the oven to 180°C (350°F), Gas mark 4, and line the muffin tray with the paper cases.

Sift the plain flour into a large bowl with the baking powder and salt and mix in the wholemeal flour. Place the bananas in a separate bowl with the eggs, sunflower oil and honey and whisk to combine. Tip into the dry ingredients and beat until smooth, adding the almonds just as the mixture is coming together.

Divide the batter between the muffin cases – they should each be about three-quarters full – then bake for about 25 minutes or until golden on top and springy to the touch.

Remove the tray from the oven and allow the muffins to cool for 5 minutes, then take them from the tray and place on a wire rack to finish cooling.

Boiled fruitcake

In researching this book I found so many places in which the traditional cake was really just another variation of a fruitcake. The fruits and spices change from place to place, but the basic formula is similar. My recipe for fruitcake isn't tied to any specific place; it's a combination of ideas from different regions. The dates when boiled and cooked add their divine toffee taste. The golden syrup is the only sugar here, which makes the cake especially moist.

Prep time: 15 minutes
Baking time: 1 hour 30 minutes–2 hours
Ready in: 3 hours
Serves: 6–8

150g (5oz) butter, plus extra for greasing
200g (7oz) golden syrup
225g (8oz) raisins
225g (8oz) currants
100g (3½oz) sultanas
100g (3½oz) pitted dates, chopped
100g (3½oz) whole mixed candied peel, chopped
150ml (5fl oz) milk
225g (8oz) plain flour
1 tsp mixed spice
½ tsp grated nutmeg
½ tsp bicarbonate of soda
Pinch of salt
2 eggs, beaten

20cm (8in) diameter cake tin with 6cm (2½in) sides (see page 334)

Preheat the oven to 150°C (300°F), Gas mark 2. Butter the sides of the cake tin and line the base with a disc of baking parchment. Double wrap the outside of the cake tin with extra baking parchment or foil, which will help prevent the cake from drying out.

Place the butter in a saucepan with the golden syrup, dried fruit, mixed peel and milk. Set over a low heat and stir until the butter has melted, then increase the heat to a simmer. Simmer for 5 minutes, stirring occasionally, then remove from the heat and set aside.

In a large bowl, sift together the flour, mixed spice, nutmeg, bicarbonate of soda and salt. Add the cooled fruit mixture to the dry ingredients, along with the beaten eggs, and mix together thoroughly.

Tip the mixture into the prepared tin and bake on the lowest shelf in the oven for between 1 hour 30 minutes and 2 hours or until a skewer inserted into the centre of the cake comes out clean. Check the cake after an hour (without taking it out of the oven) and if it is browning too much on top, cover with baking parchment or a sheet of foil for the remainder of the cooking time. When cooked, remove from the oven and place on a wire rack to cool completely in the tin.

When completely cool, loosen around the edges with a small, sharp knife and carefully remove the cake from the tin (see page 334). You can cut the cake into slices now, if you like, or leave for a few days in an airtight container to let the flavours develop. Stored like this, it will keep for a few weeks.

Nutty toffee cake

Here, the sweetness of dates and maple syrup combines with the glorious crunchiness and rich flavour of three different types of nut – almonds, walnuts and brazils. You could use just one type of nut if you'd prefer. Arranging them in a ring around the outside of the cake is best: not only does it look good, but it also prevents the centre of the cake from sinking a little under their weight.

Prep time: **10 minutes**
Baking time: **40 minutes**
Ready in: **1 hour 15 minutes**
Serves: **8–10**

225g (8oz) mixed whole almonds, brazil nuts and walnuts (see the tip below), or 225g (8oz) one type of nut (almonds, brazil nuts or walnuts)
200g (7oz) butter, softened, plus extra for greasing
200g (7oz) soft brown sugar
4 eggs
150g (5oz) pitted dates, chopped
150g (5oz) self-raising flour, plus extra for dusting
50ml (2fl oz) maple syrup

23cm (9in) spring-form or loose-bottomed cake tin with 6cm (2½in) sides (see page 336)

Preheat the oven to 180°C (350°F), Gas mark 4, then butter the sides and base of the cake tin and dust with flour. If you're using a spring-form tin, make sure the base is upside down, so there's no lip and the cake can slide off easily when cooked.

Tip 100g (3½oz) of the nuts into a food processor and whiz for a couple of minutes until fine. Add the butter and sugar, then whiz briefly until the mixture is soft and fluffy. Add the eggs one at time, pulsing just to combine, then add the dates and pulse a few times to combine.

Tip the mixture into a large bowl, then sift in the flour, folding in just until combined. Pour the batter into the prepared tin, then carefully arrange the remaining nuts in a circle or band about 5cm (2in) wide around the edge of the cake, leaving the centre free of nuts otherwise they'd weigh down the centre of the cake.

Bake for about 40 minutes or until golden brown on top and well risen – a skewer inserted into the centre of the cake should come out clean. Remove from the oven and immediately brush the nuts and top of the cake with the maple syrup.

Allow to cool for 20 minutes, then loosen around the edges using a small, sharp knife and carefully remove the sides of the cake tin (see page 336). Place on a wire rack to cool down fully, then use a palette knife or metal fish slice to loosen the bottom of the cake from the base of the tin and, with the help of the knife or fish slice, ease the cake onto a plate to serve.

Tip When using walnuts, make sure to taste them before you add them to a cake, as if they are rancid or bitter they will affect the cake's flavour.

Cardamom yoghurt cake

Cardamom is one of my favourite spices and it surprisingly works just as well in cakes as in curries. Its floral fragrance is enhanced here with just a little orange zest. You can buy ready-ground cardamom, which will work well in this cake. For the best flavour, use whole cardamom pods, which you can peel and grind yourself (see the tip below).

Prep time: **25 minutes**
Baking time: **50–55 minutes**
Ready in: **2 hours**
Serves: **10–12**

250g (9oz) butter, softened, plus extra for greasing
225g (8oz) caster sugar
Juice and finely grated zest of ½ large or 1 small orange
1 tsp freshly ground cardamom seeds (from about 12–14 pods) (see the tip below) or 1 tsp ready-ground cardamom
4 eggs
225ml (8fl oz) natural yoghurt
350g (12oz) plain flour
1½ tsp baking powder
¼ tsp salt
75g (3oz) fresh raspberries, to decorate

For the icing
225g (8oz) icing sugar, sifted
¼ tsp ready-ground cardamom or the ground seeds of 5 cardamom pods (see the tip below)
25–30ml (1–1¼fl oz) natural yoghurt

2.5 litre (4⅓ pint) bundt tin (about 23cm/9in in diameter) or 25cm (10in) diameter cake tin with 6cm (2½in) sides (see pages 334–6)

Preheat the oven to 180°C (350°F), Gas mark 4, and butter the bundt tin. If you're using a standard type of cake tin, butter the sides and line the base with a disc of baking parchment.

Cream the butter until soft in a large bowl or in an electric food mixer. Add the sugar and beat until the mixture is light and fluffy. Next beat in the orange juice and zest and the ground cardamom.

Add the eggs one at a time, beating well between each addition, then mix in the yoghurt. Next sift in the flour, baking powder and salt, folding in just until combined.

Tip the batter into the prepared tin and smooth the top with a spatula or palette knife. Bake the cake for 50–55 minutes or until a skewer inserted into the centre of the cake comes out clean. Allow to cool for just 5 minutes, then, if using a bundt tin, place a wire rack on the top and invert the cake so it is upside down, then remove the tin, turn upright again and leave to cool on the wire rack. For removing a standard type of cake tin, follow the instructions on page 334 before leaving to cool.

As the cake cools, make the icing. Beat together the icing sugar, cardamom and 25ml (1fl oz) of the yoghurt, adding a tiny bit more yoghurt if the mixture seems too stiff. (It should be a thick drizzling consistency: too thin and the icing will slide off the cake – too thick and you won't be able to drizzle it.) Place the cake on a cake stand or serving plate, then drizzle the icing backwards and forwards from the centre to the outside of the cake in a zigzag pattern (or in zigzags across the top if it's been made in a standard tin). Decorate with the raspberries immediately while the icing is still wet so they stick to the icing.

Tip To remove the seeds from cardamom pods, lightly crush the pods, then pick out the black seeds and discard the husks. Crush the black seeds using a pestle and mortar or place in a plastic bag and use a rolling pin.

Ginger peach muffins

Sweet peaches are given a boost here with some slightly spicy ginger, both fresh and ground. The wholemeal flour provides these muffins with a hint of nuttiness, and a general feeling that they must be healthy for you, as well as tasting good. They would be welcome at any time of the day, but especially as a mid-morning or mid-afternoon snack.

Prep time: 10 minutes
Baking time: 25–30 minutes
Ready in: 1 hour
Makes: 12 muffins

200g (7oz) plain flour
1 tsp baking powder
1 tsp bicarbonate of soda
1 tsp ground ginger
½ tsp salt
100g (3½oz) wholemeal flour
100g (3½oz) soft light brown sugar
75g (3oz) butter, melted
150ml (5fl oz) buttermilk
1 egg
50g (2oz) peeled root ginger, finely grated
200g (7oz) fresh or tinned sliced peaches (drained), cut into 1–2cm (½–¾in) chunks

12-cup muffin tray and 12 muffin cases (see page 336)

Preheat the oven to 180°C (350°F), Gas mark 4, and line the muffin tray with the paper cases.

Sift the plain flour into a large bowl with the baking powder, bicarbonate of soda, ground ginger and salt, and mix in the wholemeal flour and brown sugar. In a separate bowl, whisk together the melted butter, buttermilk, egg and grated ginger. Pour the wet ingredients into the flour mixture and mix together until well combined, then fold in the peaches.

Divide the batter between the muffin cases, filling each about three-quarters full, then bake for 25–30 minutes or until well risen and golden. Remove from the oven and allow to cool in the tin for 5 minutes before transferring from the tin onto a wire rack to cool down fully.

Pear crumble cake

Each of the layers in this cake is essential to the finished dish. The bottom layer consists of soft sponge. Next comes a layer of moist pears flavoured with a little cinnamon and lightly caramelised sugar, while on top is a layer of crumble enhanced by the texture and flavour of hazelnuts and brown sugar. It's absolutely worth the little extra effort it takes to make.

Prep time: 25 minutes
Baking time: 45 minutes
Ready in: 1 hour 40 minutes
Serves: 6–10

225g (8oz) butter, softened, plus extra for greasing
225g (8oz) caster sugar
4 eggs
225g (8oz) self-raising flour
Double or regular cream, whipped, to serve

For the cooked pears
400g (14oz) peeled and cored pears, chopped
1 tsp cinnamon
50g (2oz) butter
50g (2oz) caster sugar

For the crumble topping
100g (3½oz) butter
150g (5oz) plain flour, sifted
100g (3½oz) demerara or light soft brown sugar
100g (3½oz) hazelnuts, toasted, skinned and roughly chopped (see the tip on page 125)

23cm (9in) diameter spring-form or loose-bottomed cake tin with 6cm (2½in) sides (see page 336)

Preheat the oven to 170°C (325°F), Gas mark 3, and butter the sides and base of the cake tin. If you're using a spring-form tin, make sure the base is upside down, so there's no lip and the cake can slide off easily when cooked.

First cook the pears. Place the chopped fruit in a saucepan with the cinnamon, butter and sugar and set over a medium heat, then cook, uncovered and stirring every now and again, for 5–10 minutes or until most of the liquid has evaporated. Remove from the heat and set aside.

To make the crumble topping, melt the butter gently in a saucepan, then add the flour, sugar and chopped, toasted hazelnuts. Stir to mix and then set aside while you make the sponge.

Cream the butter until soft in a large bowl or in an electric food mixer. Add the sugar and beat until the mixture is light and fluffy.

Whisk the eggs together in a small bowl for a few seconds until just mixed, then gradually add the eggs to the creamed butter mixture, beating all the time. Sift in the flour and fold in gently until mixed, then tip the batter into the prepared tin.

Add the cooked pears to the tin, spreading them out in an even layer over the mixture. Sprinkle the crumble evenly over the pears, then bake for about 45 minutes or until well risen and deep golden in colour.

Remove from the oven and allow to cool in the tin for 10 minutes. Loosening around the edges using a small, sharp knife, carefully remove the sides of the tin (see page 336) and place the cake on a wire rack to cool down, unless you'd prefer to serve it warm.

When you're ready to serve, use a palette knife or fish slice to loosen the bottom of the cake from the base of the tin, then slide the knife under the cake and carefully ease it onto a plate. Cut the cake into slices and serve warm or cold with softly whipped cream, to which you could add a little icing sugar and a splash of brandy or pear liqueur.

Double chocolate peanut butter brownies

Fudgy, sticky and unapologetically rich, these brownies bring together two quintessentially American treats – brownies and peanut butter. For me, crunchy peanut butter is essential, as the chunks of peanut break up the softness of the brownie. I like to serve these with coffee, but they're so good I'll happily eat them regardless of whether I've a cup to hand!

Prep time: **15 minutes**
Baking time: **30–35 minutes**
Ready in: **1 hour**
Makes: **16 brownies**

225g (8oz) dark chocolate, in drops or broken into pieces
225g (8oz) butter
300g (11oz) caster sugar
3 eggs, beaten
75g (3oz) plain flour
1 tsp baking powder
100g (3½oz) white chocolate, in chips or chopped into pieces
200g (7oz) crunchy peanut butter

20cm (8in) square cake tin with 5cm (2in) sides (see page 334)

Preheat the oven 180°C (350°F), Gas mark 4, then line the base and sides of the baking tin with parchment paper. If the cake tin has a removable base, butter the sides and line the base with a square of baking parchment, otherwise line the base and sides of the tin.

Place the chocolate and butter in a heatproof bowl and set over a saucepan of simmering water. Stir occasionally just until melted, then set aside.

In a separate large bowl using a hand-held electric beater or using an electric food mixer, whisk together the sugar and eggs for a few minutes or until pale and light. Pour in the melted chocolate and continue to whisk until thickened, then sift in the flour and the baking powder, folding in just to combine.

Pour the mixture into the prepared tin, then scatter over the white chocolate chips or pieces. Using a teaspoon, dot the peanut butter in heaped teaspoonfuls across the batter, swirling them in with the back of your spoon.

Bake in the oven for 30–35 minutes or until softly set in the centre – the cake should wobble slightly in the middle when you gently shake the tin. Remove from the oven and set on a wire rack to cool completely in the tin before carefully removing (see page 334) and cutting into squares to serve.

Tip Do let the cooked brownie mixture cool completely in the tin before cutting up and serving, as when warm the brownies have a tendency to fall apart.

Cake may be my favourite dessert. There are few more satisfying ways to finish a meal than a forkful (or five) of a moist tender cake accompanied perhaps by its own special sauce or some whipped cream. One of the advantages of serving cake for dessert is that cake can be made ahead, either hours or a day beforehand, leaving you free to enjoy spending time with your friends without having to worry about making dessert. Rather than an icing topping, many of these cakes have a sauce that can be served warm and gently drizzled over individual slices as a sophisticated end to an evening meal. These cakes work wonderfully well with a liqueur or dessert wine. And if there are any leftovers they are lovely the next day with a cup of coffee. Whichever recipe you choose to make, these cakes are all worth saving room for!

06/ Dessert

Marmalade steamed pudding

A steamed pudding is essentially a cake that has been steamed rather than baked. As you'd expect, the result is moist and dense rather than light and airy. It's a type of dish that I find supremely comforting – there's just something about dipping a spoon into a thick soft pudding soaked with syrup. Marmalade works particularly well, with a citrus tang that offsets the rich sponge to perfection.

Prep time: 15 minutes
Cooking time: 1 hour
Ready in: 1 hour 15 minutes
Serves: 8–10

200g (7oz) butter, softened, plus extra for greasing
200g (7oz) caster sugar
3 eggs, lightly beaten
250g (9oz) plain flour
1 tsp baking powder
½ tsp bicarbonate of soda
50ml (2fl oz) milk
125ml (4½fl oz) marmalade
Double or regular cream, whipped, or orange crème anglaise (see page 157), to serve

1.2 litre (2 pint) heatproof pudding basin

Lightly butter the pudding basin. Cream the butter until soft in a large bowl or an electric food mixer. Add the sugar and beat until the mixture is light and fluffy. Whisk the eggs together in a small bowl for a few seconds or just until mixed, then gradually add them to the butter mixture, beating all the time. Sift in the flour, baking powder and bicarbonate of soda and fold into the batter until just incorporated, then mix in the milk. Spoon the marmalade into the base of the prepared pudding basin and tip in the sponge batter.

To prepare the pudding for steaming, first cut out a piece of foil and a disc of baking parchment at least 6cm (2½in) wider in circumference than the top of the basin, and secure the disc over the lip of the basin by tying a piece of string around it.

Select a saucepan not much larger than the basin. Place the pudding in the saucepan and carefully pour in enough hot water to come no higher than three-quarters of the way up the basin.

Cover the pan with a lid and simmer for approximately 1 hour or until it feels springy to the touch and a skewer inserted into the centre of the pudding comes out clean. Keep the water topped up in the saucepan during cooking, otherwise it may boil dry, burning the pudding.

Carefully remove the basin from the pan and turn out onto a warmed serving plate, allowing the marmalade to ooze down the sides. Serve with softly whipped cream or orange crème anglaise (see page 157).

Jam steamed pudding

Replace the marmalade with the same quantity of jam, such as strawberry, raspberry or plum.

Banana cake with butterscotch sauce

I adore the way bananas work in cakes. Soft and sweet, their flavour permeates the sponge, adding moisture to make a lovely soft crumb. This cake is ideal for adding to lunchboxes but if you're eating it for dessert, try it with a spoonful of vanilla ice cream and this delicious butterscotch sauce (see opposite) drizzled over the top.

Prep time: 15 minutes
Baking time: 40–45 minutes
Ready in: 1 hour 30 minutes
Serves: 6–8

250g (9oz) plain flour
2 tsp baking powder
½ tsp bicarbonate of soda
250g (9oz) caster sugar
150ml (5fl oz) sunflower oil, plus
    extra for greasing
250g (9oz) peeled ripe bananas
    (2–3 in total), mashed
2 eggs
50ml (2fl oz) natural yoghurt
1 tsp vanilla extract
Vanilla ice cream or butterscotch sauce
    (see opposite), to serve

23cm (9in) diameter cake tin with 6cm
    (2½in) sides (see page 334)

Preheat the oven to 180°C (350°F), Gas mark 4, then grease the cake tin with sunflower oil and line the base with a disc of baking parchment.

In a large bowl, sift together the flour, baking powder and bicarbonate of soda, then mix in the sugar. Using a separate bowl, whisk together the remaining ingredients until they are fully combined.

Pour the wet ingredients into the flour mixture and stir to mix together. Tip the batter into the prepared tin and cook for 40–45 minutes or until a skewer inserted into the centre of the cake comes out with just a small amount of moisture left on it.

Remove from the oven and allow to cool in the tin for 10 minutes, then use a small, sharp knife to loosen the edges and carefully remove the cake from the tin before leaving on a wire rack to cool down completely (see page 334), unless you'd prefer to eat it warm.

Serve in slices on its own or with vanilla ice cream and butterscotch sauce (see opposite).

Butterscotch sauce

Prep time: **5** minutes

Cooking time: **3** minutes

Ready in: **10** minutes

Makes: **500ml (18fl oz)**

100g (3½oz) butter

250g (9oz) golden syrup

100g (3½oz) soft dark brown sugar

200ml (7fl oz) double or regular cream

1 tsp vanilla extract

¼ tsp salt

Place all the ingredients in a saucepan and set over a medium heat. Bring to the boil and continue to boil, stirring occasionally, for 3 minutes, then remove from the heat. This sauce can be reheated and it will keep very well in an airtight container in the fridge for up to six months.

Walnut and orange cake

Walnut and orange go surprisingly well together, the slight crunch of the nuts contrasting with the soft, citrusy sponge. Walnuts are better the fresher they are – left too long they can go a little bitter. If you can't get good ones, use pecans instead. The orange crème anglaise (see opposite) isn't essential to this recipe, but it goes so well with this cake, making the perfect end to a meal.

Prep time: 10 minutes
Baking time: 45 minutes
Ready in: 1 hour 20 minutes
Serves: 8–10

225g (8oz) butter, softened, plus extra for greasing
225g (8oz) caster sugar
4 eggs
Juice and finely grated zest of 1 orange
225g (8oz) plain flour, sifted
2 tsp baking powder
200g (7oz) walnuts, chopped
Orange crème anglaise (see opposite), to serve

23cm (9in) diameter cake tin with 6cm (2½ in) sides (see page 334)

Preheat the oven to 180°C (350°F), Gas mark 4, then butter the sides of the cake tin and line the base with a disc of baking parchment.

Cream the butter until soft in a large bowl or in an electric food mixer. Add the sugar and beat until the mixture is light and fluffy.

Whisk the eggs together in a small bowl for a few seconds or just until mixed, then gradually add them to the butter and sugar mixture, beating all the time. Next beat in the orange juice and zest, then gently fold in the flour, baking powder and walnuts until fully incorporated.

Tip the batter into the prepared tin and bake for about 45 minutes or until well risen and golden brown on top, and a skewer inserted into the centre of the cake comes out clean.

Remove from the oven and allow to cool in the tin for 10 minutes, then loosen around the edges using a small sharp knife and carefully remove the cake from the tin before leaving on a wire rack to finish cooling down (see page 334), unless you're serving it warm.

Place on a cake plate and serve either warm with the orange crème anglaise (see opposite), if you wish, or cooled down as a snack with a cup of tea or coffee.

Orange crème anglaise

Prep time: 15 minutes
Cooking time: 5–8 minutes
Ready in: 25 minutes
Makes: 600ml (1 pint)

500ml (18fl oz) milk
5 egg yolks
100g (3½oz) caster sugar
Pinch of salt
1 tsp finely grated orange zest

Pour the milk into a saucepan and bring to the boil. Meanwhile, whisk the egg yolks, sugar and salt together in a large bowl for a few minutes until pale and thick. Gradually whisk the hot milk into the beaten eggs and sugar and pour the whole mixture back into the saucepan, adding the orange zest.

Return to a low heat and cook gently for 5–8 minutes, stirring all the time, until the custard thickens slightly (enough to just coat the back of the spoon). If it boils it will scramble, so just keep it at a bare simmer. Once it's cooked, remove from the heat and pour into a warm jug to serve. If reheating, do so very gently on a low heat so that the eggs don't scramble.

Chocolate fudge cake

There are times when I don't want chocolate to be diluted or compromised by any other ingredient – I want a full-on onslaught of chocolate! At times like these, I turn to this cake. Here, every ingredient lives to serve the chocolate, giving it texture, moisture and fudginess. This cake makes an ideal dessert, especially when served with a spoonful of lightly whipped cream.

Prep time: 20 minutes
Baking time: 1 hour
Ready in: 2 hours 15 minutes
Serves: 10–12

225g (8oz) dark chocolate, in drops
 or broken into pieces
225g (8oz) butter, plus extra
 for greasing
325g (11½oz) caster sugar
6 eggs, separated
200g (7oz) ground almonds
75g (3oz) plain flour, sifted
1 tsp baking powder
2 tsp vanilla extract
Pinch of salt

For the icing
275g (10oz) icing sugar
100g (3½oz) cocoa powder
125g (4½oz) butter
175g (6oz) caster sugar

25cm (10in) diameter spring-form or
 loose-bottomed cake tin with 6cm
 (2½in) sides (see page 336)

Preheat the oven to 160°C (325°F), Gas mark 3, then butter the sides of the cake tin and line the base with a disc of baking parchment. If you're using a spring-form tin, make sure the base is upside down, so there's no lip and the cake can slide off easily when cooked.

Place the chocolate in a heatproof bowl set over a pan of simmering water. Leave just until melted, stirring occasionally, then set aside.

Either in a large bowl using a wooden spoon or in the bowl of an electric mixer using the paddle beater, cream the butter until soft. Add the sugar and beat until the mixture is light and fluffy. Add the egg yolks one at a time, beating well between each addition. Mix in the ground almonds and the melted chocolate, followed by the flour, baking powder and vanilla extract.

Tip the egg whites into a separate bowl, add a pinch of salt, and beat until stiff but still smooth in appearance – do not over-beat. Fold the egg whites into the cake mixture and then pour the mixture into the prepared tin.

Bake for about 1 hour or until a skewer inserted into the centre of the cake comes out clean but moist. Leave in the tin for 20 minutes, then loosen the edges of the cake using a small, sharp knife and remove the sides of the tin before carefully transferring to a serving plate to cool down fully (see page 336).

While the cake is cooling, make the icing. Sift the icing sugar and cocoa powder into a mixing bowl. Place the butter, caster sugar and 100ml (3½fl oz) of water in a saucepan and set over a medium heat. Stir all the ingredients together until the butter is melted and the sugar has dissolved, then pour into the dry ingredients and mix together well.

When the cake has cooled, pour over the icing, allowing it to drizzle down the sides.

Irish coffee cups

Warm coffee cakes served in teacups, with a whiskey sauce and whipped cream, make a smart and playful dessert dish. The perfect pudding to serve at a dinner party, in fact, as both the cakes and sauce can be made ahead of time. The cakes are better if made on the same day, but the sauce can be made up to a couple of days ahead. Reheat the sauce in a saucepan and reheat the cakes in the oven (preheated to 130°C/250°F/Gas mark ½) for 10 minutes or just until warmed through.

Prep time: **30 minutes**
Baking time: **25–30 minutes**
Ready in: **1 hour**
Makes: **4 cakes**

125g (4½oz) butter, softened, plus extra for greasing (optional)
125g (4½oz) soft light brown sugar
2 eggs
1 tbsp coffee essence (ideally Camp or Irel)
125g (4½oz) plain flour
1 tsp baking powder
150ml (5fl oz) double or regular cream, softly whipped, to serve

For the sauce
125g (4½oz) caster sugar
150ml (5fl oz) double or regular cream
50ml (2fl oz) whiskey (ideally Irish)

Four small ovenproof teacups and their saucers or four 6cm (2½in) diameter ramekins

Preheat the oven to 180°C (350°F), Gas mark 4, and butter the insides of the cups if you intend to tip the cakes out of them to serve. Cream the butter until soft in a large bowl or in an electric food mixer. Add the sugar and beat until the mixture is light and fluffy.

Whisk the eggs together with the coffee essence in a small bowl for just a few seconds until mixed, then gradually add the eggs to the creamed butter mixture, beating all the time. Sift in the flour and baking powder and fold in gently to combine.

Divide the mixture between the teacups or ramekins and place these in a deep-sided ovenproof dish or roasting tin. Pour boiling water into the dish so it comes to halfway up the sides of the cups, then bake for 25–30 minutes or until the centre of each cake is springy to the touch.

While the cakes are cooking, make the sauce. Place the sugar in a saucepan with 75ml (3fl oz) of water and bring to the boil, stirring to dissolve the sugar as the mixture heats up. Turn the heat up to high and continue to boil – but without stirring – until the syrup goes a deep golden caramel colour. Cook the sauce just to the point when it starts smoking. (If it's not cooked enough you won't get a strong enough caramel flavour, but overcooked it will taste slightly bitter.) You may need to swirl the pan, rather than stirring the mixture, towards the end of caramelising to ensure it cooks evenly.

Turn down the heat and immediately stir in the cream and whiskey, taking care as it may bubble and spit, then set aside. You may need to whisk it for a few seconds on a low heat to help the caramel dissolve.

When the cakes are ready, remove from the oven and allow to cool for a couple of minutes. Place on saucers (if using cups), or tip them out onto warm plates. Serve with the warm whiskey sauce and a spoonful of whipped cream.

Chocolate and orange torte with caramelised oranges

This rich thick torte has a smooth texture, similar to a baked chocolate mousse, as it contains no ground almonds or flour. Chocolate and orange are a favourite combination of mine, the orange zest in the torte complemented by the caramelised oranges (see page 162), which are optional but make a wonderful accompaniment to this dish.

Prep time: **25 minutes**
Baking time: **20–25 minutes**
Ready in: **1 hour 30 minutes**
Serves: **6–8**

150g (5oz) butter, plus extra
    for greasing
300g (11oz) dark chocolate, in drops
    or broken into pieces
5 eggs, separated
50g (2oz) golden caster sugar
Finely grated zest of 2 small oranges
Double or regular cream, whipped,
    fresh orange slices or caramelised
    oranges (see overleaf), to serve

20cm (8in) diameter spring-form or
    loose-bottomed cake tin with 6cm
    (2½in) sides (see page 336)

Preheat the oven to 180°C (350°F), Gas mark 4, then butter the base and sides of the cake tin. If you're using a spring-form tin, make sure the base is upside down, so there's no lip and the cake can slide off easily when cooked.

Place the butter and chocolate in a heatproof bowl and place over a pan of simmering water, Leave just until melted, stirring occasionally, then remove from the heat.

Using an electric hand-held beater or an electric food mixer, whisk together the egg yolks and half the sugar until pale and thick. Fold in the melted chocolate and the orange zest and mix together to combine.

Using the hand-held beater or food mixer (and a spotlessly clean bowl in either case), whisk the egg whites together with the remaining sugar until they are stiff and glossy. Gently fold this into the chocolate mixture, then tip into the prepared cake tin and bake for 20–25 minutes or until puffed up and slightly cracked around the edges.

Allow to sit in the tin for 20 minutes, then use a small, sharp knife to loosen the edges and remove the sides of the tin before carefully transferring to a serving plate (see page 336).

Serve with whipped cream or fresh orange slices or with caramelised oranges (see page 162).

Spicy chocolate torte

For a different, spicy twist to this dish, you could replace the orange zest with half a teaspoon each of ground cinnamon and ground cardamom, serving the torte with crème fraîche or softly whipped cream instead of the caramelised oranges.
Recipe continued overleaf

Caramelised oranges

Prep time: **10 minutes**
Cooking time: **5–8 minutes**
Ready in: **45 minutes**

4 oranges
125g (4½oz) caster sugar

Using a small, sharp knife and working over a bowl to catch the juices, peel all the oranges. First cut the ends off each orange, then carefully cut away the peel and pith in a spiral until you have a fully peeled orange with only flesh and no pith.

Squeeze all the juice from the orange trimmings into the bowl, then cut the peeled oranges crossways into slices 5mm (¼in) thick and add these to the orange juice.

Place the sugar and 75ml (3fl oz) of water in a saucepan and set over a medium heat. Stir the mixture to dissolve the sugar, then increase the heat and bring to the boil. Without stirring the mixture, continue to boil, uncovered, for about 5–8 minutes or until you have a deep whiskey-coloured caramel. As the mixture caramelises you can swirl the pan to ensure it browns evenly.

Pour in a further 75ml (3fl oz) of water and swirl the pan over a low heat to dissolve the caramel. Remove from the heat, then tip the orange slices and any juice into the caramel and allow to cool.

Transfer to a bowl and serve with the Chocolate and orange torte (see previous page), with or without some lightly whipped cream.

Cherry marzipan cake

Cherries and marzipan are a divine combination, the almonds complementing the fruit in much the same way as raspberries in a Bakewell tart. When fresh cherries are in season, replace half the dried cherries with pitted fresh ones. (If you use all fresh, the mixture will be too wet.)

Prep time: 15 minutes
Baking time: 1 hour 10 minutes–1 hour 20 minutes
Ready in: 2 hours 15 minutes
Serves: 4–6

100ml (3½ fl oz) sunflower oil, plus extra for greasing
4 eggs
150g (5oz) caster sugar
75ml (3fl oz) milk
1 tsp vanilla extract
225g (8oz) plain flour
2 tsp baking powder
150g (5oz) dried cherries
Icing sugar, for dusting

For the topping
225g (8oz) marzipan (to make it yourself, see page 51)
1 tsp ground cinnamon
1 egg, beaten
25g (1oz) caster sugar
1 tbsp plain flour

20cm (8in) diameter spring-form or loose-bottomed cake tin (see page 336)

Preheat the oven to 180°C (350°F), Gas mark 4, then grease the sides and base of the cake tin with a little sunflower oil. If you're using a spring-form tin, make sure the base is upside down, so there's no lip and the cake can slide off easily when cooked.

Place the sunflower oil in a large bowl with the eggs, sugar, milk and vanilla extract and whisk together until smooth. Sift in the flour and baking powder and add the cherries, folding these in to combine. Tip the batter into the prepared tin, using a spatula to smooth the top.

Next make the topping. Crumble the marzipan into another bowl and add the remaining ingredients. Beat the mixture together just until blended, then spoon on top of the cake batter, spreading it out to cover the cake in an even layer. In cooking, some of the marzipan will sink to the bottom. Don't worry about this, however, as it creates a lovely effect.

Bake for between 1 hour and 10 minutes and 1 hour and 20 minutes or until a skewer inserted into the centre of the cake comes out clean. Allow to cool for 10 minutes, then use a small, sharp knife to loosen the edges before removing the sides of the tin and carefully transferring the cake to a plate (see page 336).

Dust with icing sugar and cut into slices to serve.

After dinner mint cake

Using after dinner mints in a cake is a smart and fast way to infuse it with that cooling combination of mint and chocolate. It does make a nice evening's treat, but really you could eat this at any time of the day. The icing uses fresh mint, which gives a lovely green colour as well as a deliciously fresh flavour. You could add chocolate-covered mint leaves (see page 341) for an impressive, finishing touch, either using them to decorate this cake or serving them on their own with coffee after supper as your own version of after dinner mints.

Prep time: 25 minutes
Baking time: 40–45 minutes
Ready in: 1 hour 45 minutes
Serves: 6–9

125g (4½oz) dark chocolate, in drops or broken into pieces
50ml (2fl oz) milk
150g (5oz) butter, softened, plus extra for greasing
150g (5oz) caster sugar
3 eggs
200g (7oz) plain flour, sifted
2 tsp baking powder
100g (3½oz) after dinner mints (such as After Eight Mints), cut or broken into quarters
Chocolate mint leaves (see page 341), to decorate (optional)

For the icing
15g (½oz) mint leaves, finely chopped
250g (9oz) icing sugar, sifted
A few drops of green food colouring (optional)
100g (3½oz) butter, softened
1 tbsp lemon juice
A few drops of mint essence (optional)

20cm (8in) square cake tin with 5cm (2in) sides (see page 334)

Preheat the oven to 180°C (350°F), Gas mark 4. If the tin has a removable base, butter the sides of the cake tin and line the base with a square of baking parchment, otherwise line the base and sides of the tin.

Place the chocolate and milk in a heatproof bowl and set over a pan of simmering water. Leave just until melted, stirring occasionally, then remove from the heat and set aside.

Cream the butter until soft in a large bowl or in an electric food mixer. Add the sugar and beat until the mixture is light and fluffy. Continuing to beat, pour in the melted chocolate, then add the eggs, one at time, beating continuously. Add the flour, baking powder and mints and gently fold in just until mixed. (You may find that some of the mints sink to the bottom of the cake during cooking, but this won't matter.)

Tip the mixture into the prepared tin and bake for 40–45 minutes or until a skewer inserted into the centre of the cake comes out with no batter sticking to it (although there may still be traces of mint or chocolate).

Remove from the oven and allow to cool for 10 minutes in the tin before carefully removing the cake and leaving on a wire rack to cool down completely (see page 334).

Meanwhile, make the icing. Place the chopped mint in a food processor with 2 tablespoons of the icing sugar and the food colouring and whiz until combined. Alternatively, you could beat these ingredients together in a bowl with a wooden spoon.

Add the butter, followed by the rest of the icing sugar and the lemon juice, and including some mint essence if you'd like to enhance the mint flavour, then whiz again until all the ingredients are combined and the mixture is smooth. Use a palette knife to spread the icing over the top of the cake, then decorate with the chocolate mint leaves (see page 341), if using.

Swedish apple cake

Sweden is famous for its baked goods (see also the Swedish almond cake on page 30) and variations of this basic cake are to be found all over the country – buttery apples mixed with the fragrant cinnamon they love so much. Serve this cake on its own with a cup of coffee or as a dessert with softly whipped cream.

Prep time: **15 minutes**
Baking time: **50 minutes**
Ready in: **1 hour 45 minutes**
Serves: **8–10**

3 cooking apples (such as Bramleys)
250g (9oz) plain flour
2 tsp baking powder
1 tsp ground cinnamon
150g (5oz) caster sugar
150g (5oz) butter, melted, plus extra
    for greasing
3 eggs, beaten

For the glaze
25g (1oz) butter
3 tbsp caster sugar
1 tsp ground cinnamon

25cm (10in) diameter cake tin with 6cm
    (2½in) sides (see page 334)

Preheat the oven to 180°C (350°F), Gas mark 4, then butter the sides of the cake tin and line the base with a disc of baking parchment.

Peel the apples, then cut two into 1cm (½in) dice and one into thin slices/wedges about 5mm (¼in) thick.

Sift the flour, baking powder and cinnamon into a large bowl or into the bowl of an electric mixer, then add the sugar and mix together. Add the two diced apples, then the melted butter and the eggs, and mix all the ingredients together until combined.

Tip the batter into the prepared tin, then lay the apple slices on top, so that they fan out around the edge of the cake. Bake for about 50 minutes or until golden brown and a skewer inserted into the centre of the cake comes out clean.

While the cake is in the oven, make the glaze. Melt the butter in a pan over a medium heat, then add the sugar, stirring until it dissolves. Stir in the cinnamon, then remove from the heat and set aside.

When the cake has finished cooking, remove from the oven and allow to cool for 10 minutes. Loosen around the edges using a small, sharp knife and carefully remove the cake from the tin before transferring to a serving plate (see page 334).

Reheat the glaze, then pour over the cake and allow to cool completely while soaking up the spicy syrup.

Sticky toffee date cakes

Similar to sticky toffee pudding, these cakes are so much faster to make. The rich toffee sauce is absolutely not optional – its thick buttery sweetness is what transforms the cakes into a fabulous dessert. It would be perfect for a dinner party, as both the cakes and the sauce can be made ahead and just reheated.

Prep time: **15 minutes**
Baking time: **20–25 minutes**
Ready in: **1 hour**
Makes: **12 cakes**

150g (5oz) pitted dates, roughly chopped

1 tsp bicarbonate of soda, sifted

75g (3oz) butter, softened

100g (3½oz) caster sugar

2 eggs

150g (5oz) self-raising flour

For the sauce

125g (4½oz) butter

125g (4½oz) soft dark brown sugar

75ml (3fl oz) double or regular cream

12-cup muffin tray and 12 muffin cases (see page 336)

Preheat the oven to 180°C (350°F), Gas mark 4, and line the muffin tray with the paper cases.

Place the pitted dates in a saucepan with 200ml (7fl oz) of water and bring to the boil, then remove from the heat and mix in the bicarbonate of soda.

Cream the butter until soft in a large bowl or in an electric food mixer. Add the sugar and beat until the mixture is light and fluffy.

Whisk the eggs together in a small bowl for a few seconds or just until mixed, then gradually add these to the creamed butter and sugar, beating all the time. Sift in the flour, then add the cooked dates and any water in the pan and carefully fold in until combined.

Divide the cake mixture between the muffin cases, filling each three-quarters full, then bake for 20–25 minutes or until well risen and deep golden in colour.

While the cakes are cooking, mix together the sauce ingredients in a saucepan and bring to the boil, stirring to dissolve the sugar. Boil for 2 minutes until thickened, then remove from the heat.

To serve, remove the paper cases from the muffins, place one (or two) on warmed plates and spoon over the warm sauce.

Tip Any of the sauce that you don't use can be stored in the fridge in an airtight container for up to six months.

Dulce de leche cake

This is a divine cake. It uses one of my favourite ingredients, dulce de leche, a sweet, thick caramel that I often crave just by itself. Here, ground almonds are added to a light sponge which is filled and iced with a gloriously rich, buttery icing made with the dulce de leche. Served as a dessert, this cake needs no accompaniment.

Prep time: **30 minutes**
Baking time: **25 minutes**
Ready in: **1 hour 30 minutes**
Serves: **8–12**

175g (6oz) butter, softened, plus extra
    for greasing
100g (3½oz) soft light brown sugar
1 tsp vanilla extract
200g (7oz) dulce de leche (see the
    tip below)
2 eggs
100g (3½oz) ground almonds
175g (6oz) self-raising flour
25g (1oz) flaked almonds, toasted
    (see the tip on page 125), to
    decorate (optional)

For the filling and icing
50g (2oz) butter, softened
175g (6oz) dulce de leche
    (see the tip below)
1 tsp vanilla extract
150g (5oz) icing sugar, sifted

Two 18cm (7in) diameter cake tins
    (see page 334)

Preheat the oven to 180°C (350°F), Gas mark 4, then butter the sides of each cake tin and line the base with a disc of baking parchment.

Cream the butter until soft in a large bowl or in an electric food mixer. Add the sugar, vanilla extract and dulce de leche and beat the mixture for a good few minutes until the mixture is smooth and light.

Whisk the eggs together in a small bowl for a few seconds or just until mixed, then gradually add these to the creamed butter mixture, beating all the time. Tip in the ground almonds, then sift in the flour, gently folding in until combined.

Divide the mixture between the tins and bake for about 25 minutes or until a skewer inserted into the centre of each cake comes out almost clean. Remove from the oven and allow to cool in the tins for 10 minutes, then loosen round the edges of each tin using a small, sharp knife and carefully remove the cake before leaving on a wire rack to cool down completely (see page 334).

To make the filling and icing for the cake, beat the butter with the dulce de leche and vanilla extract until very soft, then gradually add the icing sugar and beat until smooth.

Place one cake upside down on a serving plate, then spread over a third of the icing. Place the second cake on top, right side up, then spread the rest of the icing over the top. Decorate with toasted flaked almonds, if you wish.

Tip Dulce de leche is boiled condensed milk. You can buy ready-boiled condensed milk, which is sold as dulce de leche or caramel. If you want to make your own, boil unopened tins of condensed milk for 2 hours and let the tins cool *completely* before opening. I like to prepare a few tins at a time and store them in the cupboard, where they'll keep for months.

Raspberry frangipane cake

A frangipane is a rich buttery almond sponge that goes superbly well with raspberries. All this cake needs is a dollop of lightly whipped cream to make a delicious dessert. While not exactly virtuous, this cake has the advantage of being gluten free.

Prep time: 10 minutes
Baking time: 35–40 minutes
Ready in: 1 hour 10 minutes
Serves: 6–10

200g (7oz) butter, plus extra for greasing
200g (7oz) caster sugar
4 large eggs
Finely grated zest of 1 lemon
200g (7oz) ground almonds
25g (1oz) cornflour
200g (7oz) fresh raspberries
Icing sugar, for dusting

20cm (8in) square cake tin with 5cm (2in) sides (see page 334)

Preheat the oven to 180°C (350°F), Gas mark 4. If the cake tin has a removable base, butter the sides and line the base with a square of baking parchment, otherwise line the base and sides of the tin.

Cream the butter until soft in a large bowl or in an electric food mixer. Add the sugar and beat until the mixture is light and fluffy.

Whisk the eggs together in a small bowl for a few seconds or just until mixed, then gradually add the eggs to the creamed butter mixture, beating all the time. Beat in the lemon zest, then add the ground almonds and cornflour and mix to combine.

Tip the batter into the prepared tin, smoothing the surface with a palette knife or spatula. Scatter half the raspberries evenly over the top and lightly push them into the batter. Bake for around 35–40 minutes or until the top is golden and a skewer inserted into the centre of the cake comes out clean.

Remove from the oven and allow to cool in the tin for 15 minutes before carefully removing the cake and leaving on a wire rack to cool down fully (see page 334).

Scatter the remaining raspberries over the top and dust with icing sugar, then cut into squares to serve.

Caramelised orange upside-down cake

Peeled slices of orange look lovely atop this upside-down cake, infusing it with their tangy citrus flavour. The batter combines the zest of the oranges and olive oil for a distinctive-tasting sponge. I like to serve this for dessert with a little custard or orange crème anglaise (see page 157).

Prep time: 15 minutes
Baking time: 30–35 minutes
Ready in: 1 hour
Serves: 6–8

25g (1oz) butter, softened
75g (3oz) soft light brown sugar
3–4 oranges
175g (6oz) plain flour
1½ tsp baking powder
½ tsp salt
125g (4½oz) caster sugar
100ml (3½fl oz) milk
100ml (3½fl oz) extra-virgin olive oil
2 large eggs
Custard or orange crème anglaise
  (see page 157), to serve

26cm (10½in) diameter ovenproof frying
  pan (measured across the top)

Preheat the oven to 180°C (350°F), Gas mark 4.

Spread the butter out in the frying pan and sprinkle evenly with the brown sugar. Finely grate the zest of 2 oranges and set aside.

Using a small, sharp knife and working over a bowl to catch the juices, peel all the oranges. First cut the ends off each orange, then carefully cut away the peel and pith in a spiral until you have a fully peeled orange with only flesh and no pith. Cut each peeled orange crossways into slices about 1cm (½in) thick. Arrange these in a single layer over the sugar in the pan.

Sift the flour, baking powder and salt into a large bowl and stir in the caster sugar. In a separate bowl, whisk together the milk, olive oil and eggs with the orange zest and the reserved juices. Tip this mixture into the dry ingredients and whisk together until well combined.

Pour the batter over the orange slices, taking care not to disturb them, then bake for 30–35 minutes or until a skewer inserted into the centre of the cake comes out clean. Remove from the oven and allow to sit for just 5 minutes before placing a plate over the top and then carefully (but quickly!) flipping the cake over and turning it out onto the plate.

Delicious served on its own or with custard or orange crème anglaise (see page 157).

Rhubarb and custard Swiss roll

Rhubarb is such a great spring ingredient, coming into the shops at a time when there's little else growing locally and hardly any fresh fruit. In this dish, the natural sharpness of the rhubarb is tempered with sugar. It combines extraordinarily well with custard and when rolled up in a light, vanilla-scented sponge makes for a truly special cake.

Prep time: 25 minutes
Baking time: 12–15 minutes
Ready in: 1 hour 15 minutes
Serves: 6

Butter, melted, for greasing
4 eggs
125g (4½oz) caster sugar, plus
    3 tbsp for sprinkling
2 tbsp warm water
1 tsp vanilla extract
125g (4½oz) plain flour, plus extra
    for dusting

For the filling
200g (7oz) rhubarb (about 2 stalks,
    trimmed), cut into 5mm (¼in) slices
125g (4½oz) caster sugar
200ml (7fl oz) milk
1 vanilla pod, split lengthways,
    or 2 tsp vanilla extract
3 egg yolks
15g (½oz) cornflour
100ml (3½fl oz) whipped double
    or regular cream (measured when
    whipped)

25 x 38cm (10 x 15in) Swiss roll tin

Preheat the oven to 190°C (375°F), Gas mark 5. Line the base of the Swiss roll tin with baking parchment, brush the base and sides of the tin with melted butter and dust with flour.

Using a hand-held electric beater or an electric food mixer, whisk together the eggs, caster sugar, water and vanilla extract until light and fluffy. Sift in the flour, about one-third at a time, and fold it into the mixture.

Carefully pour the mixture into the prepared Swiss roll tin and bake in the oven for 12–15 minutes or until the centre of the sponge is slightly springy to the touch and the edges have shrunk a little from the sides of the tin.

Take a piece of baking parchment slightly larger in size than the tin and spread out on a work surface. Sprinkle the paper evenly with caster sugar (this is to stop the cake sticking to the paper). Quickly flip the Swiss roll tin over onto the sugared paper, then carefully remove the tin and baking parchment from the bottom of the cake.

Place a clean, slightly damp tea towel over the cake while it cools – this will prevent it drying out and cracking when you roll it.

Meanwhile, make the filling. Place the rhubarb in a saucepan with 75g (3oz) of the caster sugar and 25ml (1fl oz) of water and place on a medium heat, stirring to dissolve the sugar. Bring to the boil and allow to boil, uncovered and stirring regularly, for 10–15 minutes or until the rhubarb is completely soft and the mixture is quite thick. Tip out onto a plate and allow to cool.

Recipe continued overleaf

Next make the custard. Place the milk and the split vanilla pod (if using) in another pan and bring to the boil. Whisk the egg yolks (and vanilla extract, if using) with the remaining sugar (I like to use a hand-held electric beater for this) for a few minutes or until pale and light. Then briefly whisk in the cornflour.

Pour the hot milk and vanilla pod (if using) onto the egg mixture, whisking as you pour, then tip it all back into the saucepan and cook, stirring all the time, over a low heat for a few minutes or until it forms a thick custard.

Pour it into a bowl and allow to cool, remove the vanilla pod, then fold in the cooled rhubarb and the whipped cream – you can leave it slightly marbled (not fully mixed) if you prefer.

When the sponge is completely cold, spread over the rhubarb and custard mixture, then, with one of the short sides facing you, roll up the Swiss roll away from you and carefully transfer to a serving plate.

Sprinkle with a little extra caster sugar to finish, and cut into slices about 2cm (¾in) thick to serve.

Blueberry and coconut cake with lemon cream

Full of antioxidants and seriously healthy, blueberries are often hailed as a superfood. They are certainly good for you, but let's not overlook the fact that they taste pretty good too! Cooked in this cake, their natural sweetness is brought out, as each berry is a burst of fresh flavour within the soft sponge. The lemon zest and lemon curd cut through the sweet berries and the rich cream, providing a contrasting sharpness. This cake is divine as a dessert or served at teatime, eaten outside or at least with the sun shining through the windows.

Prep time: 30 minutes
Baking time: 20 minutes
Ready in: 1 hour 30 minutes
Serves: 6–8

225g (8oz) butter, softened, plus extra for greasing
225g (8oz) caster sugar
4 eggs, beaten
Finely grated zest of 1 lemon
200g (7oz) plain flour, sifted
2 tsp baking powder
25g (1oz) desiccated coconut
150g (5oz) fresh or frozen (and defrosted) blueberries

For the lemon cream
200ml (7fl oz) double or regular cream
100g (3½oz) lemon curd (to make it yourself, see page 27)
75g (3oz) fresh blueberries

Two 18cm (7in) diameter cake tins (see page 334)

Preheat the oven to 180°C (350°F), Gas mark 4, then butter the sides of each cake tin and line the base with a disc of baking parchment.

Cream the butter until soft in a large bowl or in an electric food mixer. Add the sugar and beat until the mixture is light and fluffy.

Gradually add the eggs to the creamed butter mixture, beating all the time. Add the lemon zest, flour, baking powder and coconut, carefully folding them into the batter until fully incorporated, then fold in the blueberries.

Divide the mixture between the prepared cake tins, then bake for 20 minutes or until well risen and golden or until a skewer inserted into the centre of each cake comes out clean. Remove from the oven and place on a wire rack for 5 minutes, then loosen round the edges of each tin using a small, sharp knife and carefully remove each cake before leaving on a wire rack to cool down fully (see page 334).

As the cakes cool, prepare the lemon cream. In a bowl, whip the cream until it forms firm peaks, then whip in the lemon curd until just stiff.

Place one cake, upside down, on a serving plate, then spread over half the lemon cream mixture. Add the other cake, right side up, on top, then spread over the remaining lemon cream and scatter with the blueberries.

Flourless fig, pine nut and ricotta cake

This festive, flourless concoction is quite a sophisticated dish, the pine nuts providing a savoury contrast to the sweetness of the dried fruit. This cake is moist enough to serve without the icing, but the fresh, tangy taste of the ricotta complements it really well.

Prep time: **30 minutes**
Baking time: **45 minutes**
Ready in: **2 hours**
Serves: **10–12**

250g (9oz) butter, plus extra
   for greasing
250g (9oz) caster sugar
150g (5oz) ricotta cheese
Finely grated zest of 2 lemons
4 eggs
150g (5oz) pine nuts, lightly toasted
   (see the tip below)
100g (3½oz) pitted dates, chopped
200g (7oz) dried figs, chopped
75g (3oz) ground almonds, plus
   1 tbsp for sprinkling

For the icing
100g (3½oz) ricotta cheese
200g (7oz) icing sugar, sifted
Juice of ½ lemon

23cm (9in) diameter cake tin
   (see page 334)

Preheat the oven to 180°C (350°F), Gas mark 4, then butter the sides and line the base of the cake tin with a disc of baking parchment.

Cream the butter until soft in a large bowl or in an electric food mixer. Add the sugar, ricotta and lemon zest and beat until the mixture is light and fluffy.

Whisk the eggs together in a small bowl for just a few seconds until mixed, then gradually add them to the creamed butter mixture, beating all the time. Add 50g (2oz) of the toasted pine nuts, together with the remaining ingredients, and fold into the batter until well mixed in.

Tip the mixture into the prepared cake tin and bake for about 45 minutes or until a skewer inserted into the centre of the cake comes out moist but clean. Remove from the oven and allow to sit for 10 minutes, then loosen around the edges using a small, sharp knife. Scatter a tablespoon of ground almonds over the top of the cake, then place a plate on top and carefully turn the cake upside down and out onto the plate (the almonds will help stop the cake sticking to the plate you're turning with). Then transfer the cake to a serving plate and leave to cool down completely (see page 334).

While the cake is cooling, make the icing by beating together all the ingredients until smooth. Once the cake is cool, drizzle over the icing and sprinkle with the remaining pine nuts.

Tip To toast pine nuts, scatter them over a baking tray in a single layer and toast them in the oven (preheated to 180°C/350°F/Gas mark 4) for 4–5 minutes or until golden brown, or place them in a frying pan and toast over a medium-low heat for a similar length of time. In either case, shake the nuts every so often to prevent them burning on one side.

Caramelised pear upside-down cake

Upside-down cakes are such a comforting dessert and they're supremely simple to put together. This dish includes whole pieces of pear, which caramelise on the bottom of the tin during baking, as well as the grated flesh of the fruit, which is stirred into the cake batter. The effect is to infuse the sponge with moisture and that perfect pear flavour. A little whipped cream is the only accompaniment this cake needs.

Prep time: 10 minutes
Baking time: 40 minutes
Ready in: 1 hour
Serves: 8

75g (3oz) butter
125g (4½oz) brown sugar
4 pears (about 375g/13oz)
150g (5oz) plain flour
2 tsp ground cinnamon
1 tsp bicarbonate of soda
½ tsp salt
175g (6oz) caster sugar
4 eggs
100ml (3½fl oz) sunflower oil
1 tsp finely grated orange zest
Double or regular cream, whipped,
    to serve (optional)

26cm (10½in) diameter ovenproof
    frying pan (measured across the top)

Preheat the oven to 180°C (350°F), Gas mark 4.

Put the butter into the frying pan and melt over a low heat, then remove from the hob and sprinkle over the brown sugar.

Grate one pear, including the skin (but avoiding the pips and core), and set aside. Peel the remaining three pears, slice each into quarters and cut away the core. Arrange the pear quarters, cut side down, in a spiral pattern in the bottom of the pan.

Sift the flour, cinnamon, bicarbonate of soda and salt into a bowl and mix in the caster sugar. In a separate bowl, whisk together the eggs, sunflower oil, orange zest and grated pear, then mix this into the dry ingredients, whisking to combine.

Pour the batter into the frying pan, taking care not to disturb the spiral pattern, then bake for about 40 minutes or until a skewer inserted into the centre of the cake comes out clean. Allow to cool on a wire rack for just 5 minutes, then place a plate on top and carefully turn the cake upside down (the right way up, in other words) and out onto the plate.

Serve while warm or at room temperature, with a little softly whipped cream if you wish.

Petits gâteaux

I adore these neat little cakes. Each square looks so pretty: covered in icing with four tidy corners, they're quite Parisian in appearance. I've given a few variations – just choose whichever flavours or colours you prefer. The colourful berry buttercream cakes (see page 187) would be lovely to hand round at a particularly special teatime such as a baby shower, while the hazelnut praline variation (see page 184) would be perfect served as an after-dinner treat.

Prep time: **20 minutes**
(excluding the icing)
Baking time: **25–30 minutes**
Ready in: **1 hour 30 minutes**
Makes: **16 squares**

175g (6oz) butter, softened
175g (6oz) caster sugar
3 eggs
175g (6oz) plain flour
2 tsp baking powder

20cm (8in) square cake tin with 5cm (2in) sides (see page 334)

Preheat the oven to 180°C (350°F), Gas mark 4. If the cake tin has a removable base, butter the sides and line the base with a square of baking parchment, otherwise line the base and sides of the tin.

Cream the butter until soft in a large bowl or in an electric food mixer. Add the sugar and beat until the mixture is light and fluffy.

Whisk the eggs together in a small bowl for a few seconds or just until mixed, then gradually add them to the creamed butter mixture, beating all the time. Sift in the flour and baking powder and fold in gently to combine.

Tip the batter into the prepared cake tin and bake for 25–30 minutes or until a skewer inserted into the centre of the cake comes out clean.

Remove from the oven and allow to cool in the tin for 10 minutes before carefully removing the cake and transferring to a wire rack to finish cooling (see page 334).

Meanwhile, make one of the buttercream icings of your choice (see pages 184–87).

When the cake has cooled down, transfer to a chopping board and use a sharp, serrated knife to cut it into 16 equal-sized squares.

Use a palette knife to ice the top and sides of each of the 16 squares. If you'd like an especially neat look, fill a jug or bowl with boiling water and keep dipping the palette knife into the hot water before you apply it to the buttercream so that you can carefully level off the edges.

Recipe continued overleaf

Chocolate petits gâteaux

For a chocolate version of these squares, add 25g (1oz) of cocoa powder to the sponge mixture along with the flour and ice with chocolate buttercream icing, drizzling with white chocolate icing to decorate (see page 186).

Peanut butter petits gâteaux

Add 50g (2oz) of smooth or crunchy peanut butter to the cake mixture along with the sugar and then ice with peanut buttercream icing (see page 185).

Praline buttercream icing

Prep time: **20 minutes**
Cooking time: **6–8 minutes**
Ready in: **45 minutes**
Makes: **enough for 16 sponge squares**

450g (1lb) butter, softened
2 tsp vanilla extract
600g (1lb 5oz) icing sugar
6 tbsp milk

For the hazelnut praline
200g (7oz) caster sugar
200g (7oz) hazelnuts

First make the praline. Line a baking tray with baking parchment and set aside, then place the sugar in a frying pan and scatter the hazelnuts over the sugar.

Place the pan over a medium heat to allow the sugar to caramelise, not stirring but swirling the pan every so often to ensure it caramelises evenly. Cook for about 6–8 minutes or until the sugar has completely melted and is a deep golden colour, swirling the pan again so that the hazelnuts are coated in the caramel.

Transfer the coated nuts to the prepared baking tray and spread apart with a fork. Once cool, break up the praline using your hands, then place in a food processor and whiz until it resembles slightly coarse breadcrumbs. Alternatively, place in a plastic bag and crush using a rolling pin.

Next make the buttercream icing. Beat together the butter and vanilla extract until very soft in a large bowl using a hand-held electric beater or in the bowl of an electric mixer. Gradually sift in the icing sugar, beating all the time, until it is fully incorporated. Pour the milk in, a little at a time, and continue to beat. Add just enough so the mixture is softly spreadable, then whisk until it is light and fluffy.

Spread the buttercream over the sponge squares (see the main recipe on page 183), then sprinkle the praline all over the iced cakes.

Peanut buttercream icing

Prep time: 10 minutes

Makes: enough for 16 sponge squares

250g (9oz) smooth or crunchy peanut
butter

200g (7oz) butter, softened

250g (9oz) cream cheese

2 tsp vanilla extract

750g (1lb 10oz) icing sugar

2–3 tbsp milk

Cream together the peanut butter, butter, cream cheese and vanilla extract in a large bowl using a wooden spoon, hand-held electric beater or in an electric food mixer. Gradually sift in the icing sugar and continue beating until fully incorporated, then add the milk and mix in to combine. If you'd like it especially fluffy and you are using a food mixer, continue to beat for a few minutes, then spread over the sponge squares (see the main recipe on page 183).

Recipe continued overleaf

Chocolate buttercream and white chocolate drizzle icing

Prep time: **15 minutes**
Makes: **enough for 16 sponge squares**

250g (9oz) milk chocolate, in drops
   or broken into pieces.
450g (1lb) butter, softened
900g (2lb) icing sugar
50g (2oz) cocoa powder, sifted

For the drizzle icing
75g (3oz) white chocolate, in drops
   or broken into pieces
75g (3oz) butter, softened
100g (3½oz) icing sugar, sifted

Piping bag with a 1 or 2mm (⅟₁₆in) nozzle
   or a freezer bag with 1 or 2mm (⅟₁₆in)
   cut from one corner

To make the buttercream, place the milk chocolate in a heatproof bowl and set over a saucepan of gently simmering water. Leave just until melted, stirring occasionally, then remove from the heat and set aside.

Cream the butter until very soft in a large bowl using a hand-held electric beater or in the bowl of an electric food mixer. Sift in the icing sugar and cocoa powder and continue to mix. Then add the melted chocolate and beat in until fully incorporated.

Spread the buttercream over the sponge squares (see the main recipe on page 183), then make the white chocolate drizzle icing.

Place the white chocolate in a clean heatproof bowl and set over a saucepan of simmering water. Leave just until melted, stirring occasionally, then remove from the heat.

Add the butter and icing sugar to the bowl and beat together until well mixed. Add the icing to the piping bag or freezer bag and carefully pipe a simple design, such as a zigzag pattern or spirals, onto each square (see Decorating ideas on page 340).

Berry buttercream icing

Prep time: **10 minutes**
Makes: **enough for 16 sponge squares**

225g (8oz) hulled strawberries or
    raspberries, plus 16 strawberry halves
    or 16 raspberries, to decorate
1½ tbsp lemon juice
275g (10oz) butter, softened
900g (2lb) icing sugar

Place the strawberries or raspberries and lemon juice in a food processor and whiz for about a minute to purée. Push through a sieve into a large bowl then set aside.

Cream the butter until very soft in a large bowl using a hand-held electric beater or in the bowl of an electric mixer. Gradually sift in the icing sugar, beating all the time, until it is fully incorporated, then pour in the fruit purée, a little at a time and beating continuously.

Spread the buttercream over the sponge squares (see the main recipe on page 183), then place a strawberry half or a raspberry on top of each cake to decorate.

Variation

For a pale purple icing instead of a pink one, make the buttercream as above, replacing the puréed strawberries or raspberries with the same quantity of blackberries or blueberries.

Intensely chocolatey beetroot brownies

It might seem strange adding beetroot to a brownie, but surely no stranger than adding carrot to a cake? The beetroot gives sweetness and moisture while the flavour only enhances the intense chocolate flavour. You can cook the beetroot from scratch for this recipe, or use leftover cooked beetroot, if you have any. Do make sure to let these cakes cool before serving as they are too soft when warm, though if you have to try one straight from the oven, who can blame you? If you're serving them for dessert, they are heavenly with a dollop of softly whipped cream.

Prep time: 15 minutes (excluding cooking the beetroot)
Baking time: 30–35 minutes
Ready in: 1 hour 15 minutes
Makes: 16 brownies

275g (10oz) beetroot, leaves removed
250g (9oz) dark chocolate, in drops or broken into pieces
250g (9oz) butter, softened, plus extra for greasing
300g (11oz) caster sugar
3 eggs
75g (3oz) plain flour
50g (2oz) cocoa powder
½ tsp baking powder
Pinch of salt

20cm (8in) square cake tin with 5cm (2in) sides (see page 334)

Prepare the beetroot by trimming the stalks to about 2cm (¾ in) from the end, then wash carefully under a cold tap. Do not scrub them – simply rub off any dirt with your fingers. You don't want to damage the skin or tails otherwise the beetroot will 'bleed' while cooking.

Place the beetroot in a saucepan and cover with cold water. Bring to a simmer, then cover with a lid and continue to simmer for between 30 minutes and 1 hour, depending on the size and age of the beetroot. They are cooked when their skins rub off easily and a knife can easily be inserted into the centre of each beetroot.

When they are cooked, rub off the skins and discard, then cut into chunks. Place in a food processor and whiz for a few minutes to form a smooth purée, then set aside.

Preheat the oven to 180°C (350°F), Gas mark 4. If the cake tin has a removable base, butter the sides and line the base with a square of baking parchment, otherwise line the base and sides of the tin.

Place the chocolate in a heatproof bowl and set over a saucepan of simmering water. Leave just until melted, stirring occasionally, then remove from the heat and set aside.

Cream the butter until soft in a large bowl or in an electric food mixer. Add the sugar and beat until the mixture is light and fluffy.

Whisk the eggs together in a small bowl for just a few seconds until mixed, then gradually add these to the creamed butter mixture, beating all the time. Beat in the puréed beetroot and melted chocolate, then sift in the remaining ingredients, folding these in until fully combined.

Tip the batter into the prepared cake tin, smoothing the top with a palette knife or spatula. Bake in the oven for 30–35 minutes or until the centre of the cake is almost set but still wobbles when you gently shake the tin. Remove from the oven and place on a wire rack to cool. Allow to cool completely in the tin before carefully removing the cake (see page 334) and cutting into squares to serve. If you can resist them for that long, these will keep in an airtight container for a few days.

Raspberry and white chocolate cheesecake

With nearly a kilogram of cream cheese and a lot of Oreo cookies, this cheesecake is uncompromisingly full on. This is not a cake for a weekday lunchtime – it demands an occasion or celebration as a valid excuse for such outrageous decadence. But should you have any of this left over after the celebration, it is sure to brighten up a more ordinary day!

Prep time: **30 minutes**
Baking time: **1 hour 30 minutes**
Ready in: **4 hours**
Serves: **10–14**

175g (6oz) white chocolate,
   finely chopped
350g (12oz) fresh or frozen
   (and defrosted) raspberries
900g (2lb) cream cheese
300g (11oz) caster sugar
25g (1oz) plain flour, sifted
4 eggs
2 tbsp single or regular cream
2 tsp vanilla extract
Icing sugar, for dusting

For the biscuit base
250g (9oz) Oreo cookies,
   coarsely broken
75g (3oz) butter, melted, plus extra
   for greasing

23cm (9in) diameter spring-form
   cake tin with 6cm (2½in) sides
   (see page 336)

Preheat the oven to 170°C (325°F), Gas mark 3, and butter the base and sides of the cake tin. Make sure the base is upside down, so there's no lip and the cake can slide off easily when cooked.

First make the biscuit base. Place the cookies in a food processor and whiz until they form coarse crumbs. Add the melted butter and whiz together until mixed. Alternatively, place the cookies in a plastic bag and crush them using a rolling pin, then add to the pan with the melted butter and mix together to combine.

Tip the crumb mixture into the prepared cake tin, spreading it out evenly to cover the bottom of the tin and pressing it down firmly.

Next make the cheesecake topping. Place the white chocolate in a heatproof bowl and set this over a pan of just simmering water, stirring occasionally until melted.

While the chocolate is melting, purée the raspberries in the food processor (having first cleaned the bowl), or simply mash them with a fork, then push them through a sieve, discarding the seeds.

Using a hand-held electric beater or an electric food mixer, mix the cream cheese and sugar together until smooth and fluffy. Beat in the flour, followed by the eggs, one at a time, then beat in the cream, vanilla extract, puréed raspberries and melted white chocolate.

Pour the mixture into the prepared tin, spreading it evenly over the biscuit base, then bake on the lowest shelf in the oven for about 1 hour 30 minutes or until the cheesecake is softly set in the middle. It should wobble a little when you gently shake the tin and the top will be slightly cracked.

Allow to cool down fully in the tin, then place in the fridge and leave to set for 2 hours.

To serve, loosen around the edges using a small, sharp knife, then unclip and remove the sides of the tin. Use a palette knife or metal fish slice to loosen the bottom of the cake from the base and ease the cake onto a plate (see page 336). (If you don't feel brave enough to slide the cheesecake off the base of the tin, just leave it on and place it like this on the serving plate.) Dust with icing sugar to serve.

To a child, the birthday cake can be the most important part of their party. Yet to the baker, it can cause the most amount of stress. It really doesn't need to be stressful though, and I've devoted this chapter to showing you how to make children's party cakes that are simple and don't take too much time. There are also some more elaborate recipes for novelty cakes, and as long as you carefully follow each step these cakes are not difficult to make. I have specially created the recipes so that you don't need specific shaped tins, but can use cake tins that you probably have in your cupboard anyway. Children's cakes are such fun to decorate so you can let your imagination take over. Minimalism is certainly not the aim here, and you can adapt the cakes using your own ideas. Whether it is because of their inventive decoration or their layers of sponge and ice cream, these cakes are sure to impress your children and their friends.

07/ Children's

Arctic roll

This nostalgia-drenched dessert will always be a retro classic, but it has seen a recent revival. My amazing assistant Josh Heller, to whom this recipe is dedicated, has particularly fond memories of it. As he says, 'To an eight-year-old boy it's probably the pinnacle of all desserts.' It's very simple to make and will be appreciated by both the adults who remember it from their youth and the youth who are eating it for the first time! It may miss the point a little, but it's delicious served with some fresh raspberries. Once made, it will keep in a container in the freezer for up to a month, though it's best eaten on the day when the sponge is still fresh.

Prep time: **30 minutes**
Baking time: **15 minutes**
Ready in: **1 hour**
Serves: **6–8**

1 litre (1¾ pints) vanilla ice cream

Butter, for greasing

100g (3½oz) caster sugar, plus
    extra for dusting

4 eggs

100g (3½oz) plain flour

1 tsp baking powder

200g (7oz) raspberry jam

23 x 30cm (9 x 12in) Swiss roll tin

Remove the ice cream from the freezer and allow to soften for 10 minutes until mouldable but not melting. If your kitchen is very warm, put the ice cream in the fridge and leave for about half an hour instead. Scoop the ice cream out in blobs to form a line on a large sheet of baking parchment and use the paper to roll it into a sausage 23cm (9in) long and 5cm (2in) in diameter. Roll up the ice cream in the paper, twist the ends of the baking parchment to close and quickly return to the freezer, leaving it there to freeze until solid (30 minutes at least).

Meanwhile, preheat the oven to 180°C (350°F), Gas mark 4, then butter the sides of the Swiss roll tin and line the base with baking parchment.

Place the sugar and eggs in a large bowl or an electric food mixer and whisk together for several minutes until light, thickened and tripled in size. Sift the flour and baking powder over the mixture, then fold in just until combined.

Tip into the prepared tin and smooth the top using a spatula or palette knife, then bake for 10–14 minutes or until it is just springy to the touch in the centre. Remove from the oven and leave the tin to cool down on a wire rack for 5 minutes.

Recipe continued overleaf

Dust the sponge with caster sugar, then place a sheet of baking parchment slightly larger than the tin on top of the sponge. Quickly, but carefully, flip the sponge over onto the paper, remove the tin and baking parchment from the base of the sponge and place on the wire rack to finish cooling.

To assemble the Arctic roll, lift the cooled sponge together with the baking parchment on to your work surface and spread the raspberry jam all over the sponge.

Take the ice-cream cylinder from the freezer and unwrap the paper from around it, then place on the sponge, aligning with the short edge 2cm from the end. Carefully roll up the ice cream in the sponge. Dust with more caster sugar and cut into slices to serve. If you're not eating the Arctic roll immediately, it can be kept in the freezer and slightly defrosted in your kitchen for about 20 minutes before eating.

Hot chocolate fairy cakes

My children love these little chocolate cakes. A hot chocolate in a bun complete with creamy icing and mini marshmallows. You could scatter with chocolate sprinkles rather than dusting with cocoa powder, if you'd prefer.

Prep time: 15 minutes
Baking time: 15–20 minutes
Ready in: 50 minutes
Makes: 12 fairy cakes

125g (4½oz) butter, softened
125g (4½oz) caster sugar
2 eggs
125g (4½oz) plain flour
1½ tsp baking powder
2 tbsp cocoa powder
2 tbsp milk

For the icing
75g (3oz) butter, softened
300g (11oz) icing sugar, sifted
1 tbsp boiling water

To decorate
36 mini marshmallows
1 tsp cocoa powder, sifted, for dusting

12-cup bun tray and 12 bun cases
    (see page 336)
Piping bag with a 4 or 5mm (¼in)
    plain or star-shaped nozzle or a freezer
    bag with 4 or 5mm (¼in) cut from
    one corner (optional)

Preheat the oven to 180°C (350°F), Gas mark 4, and line the bun tray with the paper cases.

Cream the butter until soft in a large bowl or in an electric food mixer. Add the sugar and beat until the mixture is light and fluffy.

Whisk the eggs together in a small bowl for a few seconds or just until mixed, then gradually add these to the creamed butter mixture, beating all the time. Sift in the flour, baking powder and cocoa powder, pour in the milk and fold in gently to combine.

Divide the mixture between the paper cases, filling each about two-thirds full, then bake for 15–20 minutes or until well risen and lightly springy to the touch. Remove from the oven and allow to cool for 5 minutes before removing from the tin and transferring to a wire rack to finish cooling.

As the cakes cook or cool, make the icing. Beat together all the ingredients for a couple of minutes or until light and fluffy.

Place a heaped tablespoon of icing on each cake or use the piping bag or freezer bag to a pipe a rosette of icing onto the cake (see Cake essentials on page 339). Add three mini marshmallows to the centre of each cake, then dust with cocoa powder.

Chocolate and toffee ice-cream cake

Two layers of mocha sponge sandwich a layer of vanilla ice cream with swirls of caramel. The effect of the ice-cream layer inside the cake is impressive to party guests, be they eight or eighty. This cake is definitely best served on the day of eating, though it will keep in the freezer for up to a month. If you're serving it from the freezer, make sure to take it out about 15 minutes before eating just so the cake softens slightly. If you have time, chocolate curls (see Decorating ideas on page 340) make a gorgeous decoration for this cake.

Prep time: 20 minutes
Baking time: 25–30 minutes
Ready in: 1 hour 30 minutes
Serves: 6–8

100g (3½oz) dark chocolate, in drops or chopped into pieces
175g (6oz) butter, softened, plus extra for greasing
175g (6oz) caster sugar
3 eggs
1 tsp coffee essence (ideally Camp or Irel)
175g (6oz) plain flour
2 tsp baking powder
400ml (14fl oz) good-quality vanilla ice cream
200g (7oz) dulce de leche (see the tip on page 168)
Cocoa powder, sifted, for dusting (optional) or Chocolate curls (see page 342), to decorate

Two 18cm (7in) diameter cake tins (see page 334)

Preheat the oven to 180°C (350°F), Gas mark 4, then butter the sides of the cake tins and line the base of each tin with a disc of baking parchment.

Place the chocolate in a large heatproof bowl and set over a saucepan of gently simmering water. Stir occasionally until melted, then set aside.

Cream the butter until soft in a large bowl or in an electric food mixer. Add the sugar and beat until the mixture is light and fluffy. Whisk the eggs together in a small bowl for a few seconds or just until mixed, then gradually add these to the creamed butter mixture, beating all the time. Next beat in the coffee essence and melted chocolate, then sift in the flour and baking powder, folding it in just to combine.

Divide the mixture between the prepared tins, then bake for 25–30 minutes or until springy to the touch and a skewer inserted into the centre of each cake comes out clean. Remove from the oven and allow to cool on a wire rack for 10 minutes, then loosen around the edges with a small, sharp knife and carefully remove each cake from its tin before leaving on a wire rack to cool down completely (see page 334).

Wash one of the tins, then line completely with a double layer of cling film. Fill with the ice cream and use a spoon to swirl in the dulce de leche, then cover the top with another layer of cling film and place in the freezer for about 30 minutes or until completely frozen.

To serve, place one cake upside down on a stand or cake plate. Carefully remove the ice-cream cake from the tin, peeling away all the cling film. Place on top as the next layer, then place the remaining cake over this. Dust with cocoa powder or top with chocolate curls (see Decorating ideas on page 340) and serve before the ice cream has a chance to melt!

Layered chocolate and caramel cake

One of my guilty pleasures is a tin of boiled condensed milk, or actually condensed milk in any shape or form. Once boiled, the sugars in the milk caramelise to make a thick toffee-like sauce. It's perfect for cooking or eating straight from the tin (with or without a spoon!). It's also possible to buy ready-boiled condensed milk, which is sold in tins or jars as dulce de leche – or you can make your own (see the tip on page 168). Here the dulce de leche is combined with chocolate in the sponge and the icing for three layers of undiluted pleasure!

Prep time: 45 minutes
Baking time: 25–30 minutes
Ready in: 2 hours
Serves: 8–10

300g (11oz) butter, plus extra for greasing
300g (11oz) caster sugar
6 eggs
1½ tsp vanilla extract
300g (11oz) self-raising flour
2 tsp baking powder
1 x 397g tin of dulce de leche (to make it yourself, see the tip on page 168)
2 tbsp cocoa powder

For the icing
350g (12oz) milk chocolate, in drops or broken into pieces
150ml (5fl oz) double or regular cream
Pinch of salt

Three 20cm (8in) diameter cake tins (see page 334)

Preheat the oven to 180°C (350°F), Gas mark 4, then butter the sides of the cake tins and line each base with a disc of baking parchment.

Cream the butter until soft in a large bowl or in an electric food mixer. Add the sugar and beat until the mixture is light and fluffy.

Whisk the eggs and vanilla extract together in a separate bowl for a few seconds or just until mixed, then gradually add the eggs to the creamed butter mixture, beating all the time. Sift in the flour and baking powder and fold in gently to combine.

Tip a third of the batter into one of the prepared cake tins and divide the other two-thirds evenly between two separate bowls. Add 4 tablespoons of the dulce de leche to one of the bowls and stir it in, then tip into one of the two empty cake tins. Sift the cocoa powder into the remaining bowl of cake mixture and stir it in, then put the batter into the remaining tin.

Place all three cakes in the preheated oven and bake for 25–30 minutes or until springy to the touch and a skewer inserted into the centre of each sponge comes out clean.

Recipe continued overleaf

Remove from the oven and allow to cool in the tin for 10 minutes, then loosen around the edges of each cake using a small, sharp knife and carefully remove from the tin before leaving on a wire rack to cool down fully (see page 334).

While the sponges are cooking, or while they are cooling down, make the icing. Place the chocolate in a heatproof bowl and set over a saucepan of barely simmering water. Leave just until melted, stirring occasionally, then remove from the heat and stir in the cream and salt. Place in the fridge to chill just until spreadable.

When the sponges have cooled down, place the dulce de leche cake upside down on a cake plate. Spread over half of the dulce de leche left in the tin, then place the chocolate cake on top, right side up. Spread over the rest of the dulce de leche from the tin and add the vanilla cake, right side up, as the final layer. Finally, spread the chocolate icing all over the cake using a palette knife dipped into boiling-hot water for a smooth finish.

Chocolate hedgehog cake

Like the Teddy bear cake (see page 211), this is another creative cake that looks really cute. I've used chocolate fingers for the spikes, though if you prefer you can use chocolate flakes. I've also provided a vanilla and almond variation (see overleaf) for those children who aren't so keen on chocolate (do they exist?).

Prep time: **1 hour**
Baking time: **50–55 minutes**
Ready in: **2 hours 30 minutes**
Serves: **8–12**

175g (6oz) butter, softened, plus extra for greasing
175g (6oz) caster sugar
3 eggs
2 tsp vanilla extract
175g (6oz) plain flour, plus extra for dusting
2 tsp baking powder
25g (1oz) cocoa powder
2 tbsp milk

For the icing
125g (4½oz) milk chocolate, in drops or broken into pieces
225g (8oz) butter, softened
450g (1lb) icing sugar
25g (1oz) cocoa powder

To decorate
2 x 125g packets of chocolate fingers
1 x glacé cherry or 1 red Smartie

2.4 litre (4 pint), 23cm (9in) diameter or similar capacity ovenproof pudding basin/Pyrex bowl (measured across the top)
Large round or oval plate

Preheat the oven to 180°C (350°F), Gas mark 4, then butter the inside of the pudding basin bowl and dust with flour.

Cream the butter until soft in a large bowl or in an electric food mixer. Add the sugar and beat until the mixture is light and fluffy.

Whisk the eggs and vanilla extract together in a small bowl, then gradually add the eggs to the creamed butter mixture, beating all the time. Sift in the flour, baking powder and cocoa powder and fold in gently, then add the milk and mix gently to combine.

Tip the batter into the prepared pudding basin/bowl and bake for 50–55 minutes or until springy to the touch and a skewer inserted into the centre of the cake comes out clean.

Remove from the oven and allow to cool for 5 minutes in the basin bowl. Use a palette knife to loosen the edges of the cake, then place a wire rack upside down over the basin bowl and carefully flip over. Lift off the basin bowl and leave the cake to cool completely on the wire rack.

As the cake is cooking, or while it's cooling down, make the icing. Place the chocolate in a heatproof bowl and set over a saucepan of gently simmering water. Leave just until melted, stirring occasionally, then remove from the heat and set aside.

Cream the butter until soft in a large bowl or in an electric food mixer, then sift in the icing sugar and cocoa powder and continue to mix. Pour in the melted chocolate and beat in until well combined.

Recipe continued overleaf

Place the cake domed side down on a work surface. If the base of the cake is uneven, use a bread knife to level it off. Spread a little of the icing 2–3mm (⅛ in) thick over the base of the cake, then cut the cake in half so that you have two half domes.

Sandwich together the iced sides to form a roughly oval shape, then spread a little icing on the large plate and place the cake on top so it sticks down.

Spread the remaining icing all over the cake, and use a palette knife to shape the face and the snout of the hedgehog (see photograph on previous page). Use a fork to add texture to the snout and the back of the hedgehog, then decorate the iced cake.

Cut the chocolate fingers in half crossways and arrange pointing backwards as the spines of the hedgehog. To make the eyes, cut a chocolate finger in half and insert into the cake with the uncut surfaces pointing outwards. Place the glacé cherry or Smartie at the tip of the snout to make a nose.

Almond hedgehog cake

Prep time: **1 hour**
Baking time: **50–55 minutes**
Ready in: **2 hours 30 minutes**
Serves: **8–12**

For the icing
150g (5oz) butter, softened
2 tbsp milk
2 tsp vanilla extract
200g (7oz) icing sugar

To decorate
100g (3½oz) flaked almonds,
    toasted (see the tip on page 125)
3 x brown Smarties

Mix the cake as in the main recipe on page 202, omitting the cocoa powder and using only 1 tablespoon of milk, then bake.

Meanwhile, make the icing. Using a hand-held electric beater or an electric food mixer, beat together the butter, milk and the vanilla extract until very soft. Then gradually sift in the icing sugar, beating all the time, until it is fully incorporated and light and fluffy.

Assemble and ice the cake as above, then, rather than using chocolate fingers, insert toasted flaked almonds at an angle all over the cake for the spines. Place two of the Smarties on the cake for the eyes and one at the tip of the snout to make a nose.

Strawberry cupcakes

These cupcakes are deceptively simple to make and they taste divine. They are so pretty with the naturally pink icing full of sweet strawberry flavour. If you'd like to make these for a celebration, then you could try decorating them with the crystallised rose petals (see Decorating ideas on page 344).

Prep time: **30 minutes**
Baking time: **20–25 minutes**
Ready in: **1 hour 15 minutes**
Makes: **12 cupcakes**

125g (4½oz) butter, softened
200g (7oz) caster sugar
3 eggs
150ml (5fl oz) milk
1 tsp vanilla extract
300g (11oz) plain flour
3 tsp baking powder
½ tsp salt

For the icing
150g (5oz) fresh or frozen (and
    defrosted) strawberries
1 tbsp lemon juice
175g (6oz) butter, softened
600g (1lb 5oz) icing sugar, sifted
Strawberries, halved, to decorate

12-cup muffin tray and 12 muffin cases
    (see page 336)
Piping bag with a 4 or 5mm (¼in)
    plain or star-shaped nozzle or a
    freezer bag with 4 or 5mm (¼in)
    cut from one corner (optional)

Preheat the oven to 160°C (325°F), Gas mark 3, and line the muffin tray with the paper cases.

Cream the butter until soft in a large bowl or in an electric food mixer. Add the sugar and beat until the mixture is light and fluffy.

Whisk the eggs together in a small bowl for a few seconds just until mixed, then gradually add them to the creamed butter mixture, beating all the time. Beat in the milk, followed by the vanilla extract, then sift in the flour, baking powder and salt and fold in gently to combine.

Divide the mixture between the muffin cases, filling each case about two-thirds full. Bake for 20–25 minutes or until well risen, lightly golden in colour and springy to the touch. Allow to cool for 5 minutes, then remove from the tin and place on a wire rack to cool completely.

While the cupcakes are cooking, or while they are cooling down, make the icing. Place the strawberries and lemon juice in a food processor and whiz for about a minute to purée them. Push through a sieve into a bowl, then set aside.

In a separate bowl, cream together the butter and icing sugar until combined, then gradually add the fruit purée, beating continuously.

Spread the icing onto the cooled cupcakes using a palette knife or the back of a spoon, or pipe the icing onto the cakes (see Cake essentials on page 339) and decorate each cake with half a strawberry.

Variation

Try replacing the strawberries for the icing with the same quantity of raspberries, blackberries or blueberries – which can be either fresh or frozen (and then defrosted). If using blackberries or blueberries the colour will no longer be pink but a lovely purple shade. Decorate each cake with a blackberry, raspberry or blueberry.

Strawberry ice-cream cake with strawberry coulis

This is the recipe to go for when your children (or you!) don't just want ice cream with cake, they want ice-cream cake! With its layers of ice cream and sponge all frozen together, it looks very impressive – especially when served with the strawberry coulis – but is actually quite simple to put together. I've included two further variations on the theme (see pages 209 and 210), but you could create your own versions. As long as you stick to the same basic quantities for the cake and the ice cream, it's really up to you what flavours you choose. While this cake can be made up to a month ahead and kept in the freezer, it is best eaten on the day when the sponge is fresh.

Prep time: **20 minutes**
Baking time: **20 minutes**
Ready in: **4 hours**
Serves: **10–12**

Butter, for greasing
4 eggs
125g (4½oz) caster sugar
125g (4½oz) self-raising flour
400ml (14fl oz) vanilla ice cream
400ml (14fl oz) strawberry ice cream

For the strawberry coulis
250g (9oz) fresh or frozen (and defrosted) strawberries, plus sliced fresh strawberries to decorate
1–2 tbsp caster sugar
Juice of ½ large lemon

Two 18cm (7in) diameter cake tins (see page 334)

Preheat the oven to 180°C (350°F), Gas mark 4, then butter the sides of the cake tins and line the base of each tin with a disc of baking parchment.

Place the eggs and sugar in a large bowl or an electric food mixer. Using a hand-held electric beater or the food mixer, whisk on a high speed for about 3 minutes or until the mixture has roughly tripled in volume, then sift in the flour and fold in gently just until combined.

Divide the mixture between the prepared cake tins, then bake for about 20 minutes or until golden on top and a skewer inserted into the centre of each cake comes out clean.

Remove from the oven and allow to cool in the tins for 10 minutes, then loosen around the edges of each cake using a small, sharp knife and carefully remove from the tin before leaving on a wire rack to cool down fully (see page 334).

Wash and dry both tins, then line completely with a double layer of cling film. Remove the ice cream from the freezer and allow to soften until it is easy to scoop. Fill one of the tins with vanilla ice cream and the other with strawberry. Cover the top with cling film then leave in the freezer for about 30 minutes or until completely frozen.

Meanwhile, make the strawberry coulis. Whiz all the ingredients together in a food processor or blender.

Taste the mixture, adding more sugar or lemon juice if necessary, then push through a sieve. Pour into a serving jug and keep in the fridge (for up to 3–4 days) until you're ready to serve.

To assemble the cake, place one sponge upside down on a work surface or serving plate. Take the vanilla ice cream out of the freezer and remove from the tin, peeling away all the cling film. Place this ice cream layer on top of the sponge, then place the second half of the cake on top, right side up. Next take the strawberry ice-cream layer out of the freezer and remove it from the tin, peeling away the cling film as before. Place on top of the cake and either serve immediately or wrap in cling film and place in the freezer where it will keep for up to a month.

To serve, decorate the top of the cake with sliced strawberries and serve in slices accompanied by the strawberry coulis.

Banana ice-cream cake with butterscotch sauce

Prep time: 20 minutes
Baking time: 25 minutes
Ready in: 4 hours
Serves: 10–12

For the butterscotch sauce
100g (3½oz) butter
250g (9oz) golden syrup
100g (3½oz) soft dark brown sugar
200ml (7fl oz) single or regular cream
1 tsp vanilla extract
¼ tsp salt

To decorate
1 banana, peeled and sliced

Make the cake as in the main recipe opposite, replacing the strawberry ice cream with banana ice cream and decorating the top with slices of banana instead of strawberries.

While the cake tins of ice cream are setting in the freezer, make the butterscotch sauce (to replace the strawberry coulis). Place all the ingredients in a saucepan and set over a medium heat, allowing the butter to melt and the sugar to dissolve. Bring to the boil and continue to boil, stirring regularly, for 3 minutes, then remove from the heat and set aside. The sauce will keep for up to 3 months in the fridge.

Reheat the sauce when ready to serve and pour it warm over slices of the finished ice-cream cake.

Recipe continued overleaf

Chocolate ice-cream cake with chocolate sauce

Prep time: **20 minutes**
Baking time: **25 minutes**
Ready in: **4 hours**
Serves: **10–12**

For the chocolate sauce
150ml (5fl oz) double or regular cream
150g (5oz) dark or milk chocolate,
    or 75g (3oz) of each, in drops or
    broken into pieces, plus extra, grated,
    or chocolate curls (see page 342),
    to decorate
½ tsp vanilla extract (optional)

Make the cake as in the main recipe on page 208, replacing the strawberry ice cream with chocolate ice cream and decorating the top with grated chocolate or chocolate curls instead of sliced strawberries.

While the cake tins of ice cream are setting in the freezer, make the chocolate sauce (to replace the strawberry coulis). Pour the cream into a saucepan and bring to the boil, then remove from the heat. Add the chocolate and stir until it melts, then stir in the vanilla extract, if using. Keep the sauce in the fridge (for up to a week) until you're ready to serve. Reheat gently to serve, pouring it over slices of the finished ice-cream cake.

Teddy bear cake

I love this cake as it looks so impressive and yet doesn't require any special tins, just a few rounds of sponge and a bit of creativity in putting things together. You can be as playful as you'd like with the decorations. You'll see that I've given a couple of alternative versions as well – a chocolate teddy and a snowman, which would be perfect for a winter party. The cake can be prepared up to two days in advance and iced either while fresh or on the day of the party. You'll need to store it somewhere cool but not in the fridge.

Prep time: 1 hour
Baking time: 1 hour 10 minutes
Ready in: 2 hours 45 minutes
Serves: 18–22

400g (14oz) butter, softened, plus extra for greasing
400g (14oz) sugar
8 eggs
400g (14oz) plain flour
4 tsp baking powder

For the icing
450g (1lb) butter, softened
900g (2lb) icing sugar, sifted
A few drops of food colouring, such as pink, red, blue or yellow

To decorate
6–7 small sweets (such as chocolate buttons, Smarties or Jelly Tots) for the eyes, nose and buttons
1 liquorice lace for the mouth

25cm (10in) diameter cake tin and 18cm (7in) diameter cake tin (see page 334)
6-cup muffin tray and 5 muffin cases (see page 336)
Large plate or 40 x 50cm (16 x 20in) cake board

Preheat the oven to 180°C (350°F), Gas mark 4. Butter the sides of the cake tins and line the base of each tin with baking parchment, then line the muffin tray with the paper cases.

Cream the butter until soft in a large bowl or in an electric food mixer. Add the sugar and beat until the mixture is light and fluffy.

Whisk the eggs together in a separate bowl for a few seconds or just until mixed, then gradually add them to the butter mixture, beating all the time. Sift in the flour and baking powder and fold in gently to combine.

Fill the muffin cases and smaller tin three-quarters full with the batter, then put the rest of the mixture into the larger cake tin (it should be about half full).

Bake the muffins and the smaller cake for 20–25 minutes or until they have risen and are golden brown on top. The larger cake will take about 35 minutes.

Remove each cake from the oven when it is ready and allow to cool in the tin for 10 minutes. Then loosen around the edges using a small, sharp knife and carefully remove each cake from its tin before leaving on a wire rack to cool down completely (see page 334). Allow the muffins to cool in the tin for 5 minutes, then remove from the tray and place on a wire rack to cool.

Recipe continued overleaf

Place the large cake right side up on the lower part of the large plate or cake board to make the teddy's body, then place the smaller cake directly above for the head (like a snowman). Arrange four muffins around the body for the arms and legs, then cut the remaining muffin in half vertically and place on top of the head for ears.

To make the icing, beat together all the ingredients for a couple of minutes or until light and fluffy, adding more food colouring if you want a deeper shade.

Using a palette knife or spatula, spread the icing all over the teddy bear. If you want it to look smooth, dip the palette knife regularly into a jug or bowl of boiling-hot water.

Next decorate the cake. Add two sweets (chocolate buttons, Smarties or Jelly Tots) for the eyes and one for the nose. Using the liquorice lace, make a rounded 'W' right under the nose, with the centre of the 'W' elongated to resemble the mouth. Place 3–4 sweets down the front of the body for the teddy's buttons, or cover the whole body in sweets if you like.

Chocolate teddy bear cake

Prep time: **1 hour**
Baking time: **1 hour 10 minutes**
Ready in: **2 hours 45 minutes**
Serves: **18–22**

For adding to the sponge
2 tbsp cocoa powder

For the icing
250g (9oz) milk (or dark) chocolate, in drops or broken into pieces.
450g (1lb) butter, softened
900g (2lb) icing sugar
50g (2oz) cocoa powder

Sift in the cocoa powder to the cake mixture as you add the flour, then make and assemble the uniced cakes into the teddy's body, with the muffins for arms, legs and ears, as in the main recipe above. Then make the chocolate icing.

Place the chocolate in a heatproof bowl and set over a saucepan of gently simmering water. Stir occasionally just until melted and set aside to cool until no warmer than tepid.

Cream the butter until soft in a large bowl or in an electric food mixer. Sift in the icing sugar and cocoa powder and continue to mix. Then add the melted chocolate and beat in until fully incorporated.

Using a palette knife or spatula, spread the icing all over the teddy bear, dipping the knife or spatula into boiling-hot water for a smooth finish.

Decorate in the same way as in the main recipe, though for greater colour contrast you might want to use white chocolate buttons or Smarties for the eyes and nose.

Recipe continued overleaf

Snowman cake

The icing I've suggested here, cream cheese whipped with icing sugar, is very easy to make, but if you're feeling a little more adventurous you could try the American frosting instead (see opposite). If making this cake in advance, it's best to store it in the fridge (because of the cream-cheese icing), but make sure to take it out of the fridge 1–2 hours before serving.

Prep time: 1 hour
Baking time: 1 hour 10 minutes
Ready in: 2 hours 45 minutes
Serves: 18–22

350g (12oz) butter
350g (12oz) caster sugar
7 eggs
350g (12oz) plain flour
3½ tsp baking powder

For the cream-cheese icing
450g (1lb) cream cheese
450g (1lb) icing sugar, sifted

To decorate
10–12 sweets resembling coal
    (such as chocolate buttons
    or chocolate-covered toffees)
    for the eyes and buttons
Baby carrot for the nose (just
    for decoration!)
Chocolate fingers for the arms

Follow the Teddy bear cake method on page 211 but using these sponge quantities. Omit the muffins and just make two round cakes, with one larger as in the main recipe. Place the cooled cakes on the plate or cake board to form the snowman, then make the icing.

In a bowl, beat together the cream cheese and icing sugar until well mixed. Then spread all over the snowman using a palette knife, making little peaks in the icing to resemble snow (see the last step in the American frosting opposite). Alternatively, make up the American frosting (see page 215) and ice the snowman with this.

To decorate the snowman, add the sweets for the eyes and buttons. Insert the baby carrot for the nose and add chocolate fingers for the arms.

American frosting

This delicious soft icing makes a beautiful 'snow' that can be smoothed or peaked, but you'll need to follow the instructions carefully. Quick and accurate decisions are necessary in judging when the icing is ready and it must then be applied to the cake immediately. If the icing is not cooked enough, it will still taste good, but will not dry out properly on the outside. If cooked too much, it will be difficult to spread.

Prep time: 7 minutes
Ready in: 7 minutes
Makes: enough for one large cake

4 large egg whites
250g (9oz) caster sugar
Pinch of salt

Make sure the cakes are ready before you start, as this icing begins to set very quickly. Place all the ingredients in a heatproof bowl, add 2 tablespoons of cold water and set over a saucepan of simmering water. (The bowl should sit snugly over the pan with its base high enough above the water that it does not come into contact with it.)

Whisk slowly using a balloon whisk until the sugar has completely dissolved and the mixture is foamy. Continue to heat and whisk until the mixture reaches 60°C (140°F) when measured with a sugar thermometer – this will take about 4 minutes. If you don't have a thermometer, you can gauge whether the mixture is ready by how it feels and looks: it should be hot to the touch, glossy white in appearance and starting to thicken.

Quickly remove the bowl from the pan and pour the mixture into the bowl of an electric food mixer fitted with the whisk attachment. Alternatively, whisk in the original bowl using a hand-held electric beater. Whisk on a high speed for about 3–5 minutes or until the frosting is very thick, glossy and has cooled.

Spread quickly over the cakes with a palette knife, regularly dipping into a jug of boiling-hot water. The icing sets very quickly at this stage, so speed is essential. If you'd like a 'peaked' snowy look, dip the flat of your palette knife into the icing and quickly lift it away, creating a peak. Continue in this fashion across the cake, if you like.

Princess cake

This is a novelty cake and a half. Every bit of effort you put into making this cake will be so worth it when you see the birthday girl's face light up with delight. The cake can be prepared up to two days in advance and iced either while fresh or on the day of the party. You'll need to store it somewhere cool but not in the fridge.

Prep time: 45 minutes
Baking time: 25–35 minutes
Ready in: 2 hours
Serves: 18–20

400g (14oz) butter, softened, plus
    extra for greasing
400g (14oz) caster sugar
8 eggs, beaten
400g (14oz) plain flour, plus extra
    for dusting
4 tsp baking powder

For the icing (to cover the 'skirt' of
    the doll)
450g (1lb) butter, softened
3 tsp vanilla extract
¼ tsp red or pink food colouring
    (or a colour of your choice)
750g (1lb 10oz) icing sugar, sifted
2 tbsp milk

To decorate
Sprinkles, coloured sugar crystals (to
    make them yourself, see page 233),
    edible glitter, icing flowers or other
    decorations of your choice

Three 18cm (7in) diameter cake tins
    (see page 334)
12cm or 16cm (5in or 6½in) diameter
    ovenproof pudding basin/Pyrex bowl
    (measured across the top)
One doll, clothed from the waist up
One 50cm (20in) long ribbon

Preheat the oven to 180°C (350°F), Gas mark 4. Butter the sides of the cake tins and dust with flour, then line the base of each tin with a disc of baking parchment. Next butter and flour the inside of the pudding basin.

Cream the butter until soft in a large bowl or in an electric food mixer. Add the sugar and beat until the mixture is pale and fluffy, then gradually add the eggs to the creamed butter mixture, beating all the time.

Sift together the flour and baking powder and add to the wet ingredients, folding in just until the mixture comes together. Half fill the pudding basin or bowl with the batter, then divide the rest between the three tins, making a slight hollow in the centre of the cake in the tins so that the cake does not have a peak when cooked, making it easier to assemble the pile of cakes.

Bake in the oven for 25–35 minutes (the cooking time will depend on how evenly you've divided your mixture between the bowl and tins) or until golden on top and a skewer inserted into the centre of each cake comes out clean.

Remove from the oven and leave to cool for 5 minutes, then loosen around the edges of each cake using a small, sharp knife. Place a plate upside down on top of the cake and carefully flip over (see page 334). Remove the basin/bowl or tin and any baking parchment, then transfer to a wire rack and leave to cool down completely.

Recipe continued overleaf

As the cakes cool, wrap the doll from just above her waist down to her toes in cling film (so you can re-use her later).

Make the icing by beating the butter until very soft, then add the vanilla extract, food colouring and half the icing sugar. Continue to beat until light and fluffy, then add the rest of the sugar, followed by the milk, and beat again.

Pile the three cake-tin sponges on top of each other and place the basin/bowl cake (upside down) on top. Then, using a long-bladed knife, cut out a hole about 2cm (¾ in) wide through the centre of the cakes, going from the top of the basin/bowl cake down through to the bottom of the third cake-tin sponge. (You could use the discarded cake for the Cake pops on page 220, if you wish.) This will be the hole that the doll stands in.

Separate the cakes again and place one of the cake-tin sponges on a cake stand or plate. Spread with some of the icing (as if very generously buttering toast), then top with the second cake. Spread with the same amount of icing and add the third cake, then spread with more icing and top with the upturned basin/bowl cake.

Insert the doll into the hole running through the cakes (they should come up to her hips). Fill a jug with boiling water and place a palette knife in it. Now you can start icing all around the cakes and up to the doll's waist to make a rather voluminous skirt! Spreading it with a palette knife (dipped in the hot water) will help to give a smooth finish.

Decorate with icing flowers, edible glitter, hundreds and thousands, Smarties, or whatever you like (see Children's decorating ideas on page 242), but do it now before the outer layer of the icing begins to dry a little. Tie a ribbon around the doll's waist (where the icing meets her clothes) and serve.

Mini mango cupcakes

These cupcakes are a taste of the tropics with the luscious flavour of mango and the rich crunch of toasted coconut. They are a cute little size, which children will love and parents can eat with coffee after the party.

Prep time: 20 minutes
Baking time: 10–12 minutes
Ready in: 40 minutes
Makes: 24 cupcakes

100g (3½oz) butter, softened
100g (3½oz) caster sugar
2 eggs
100g (3½oz) plain flour
1 tsp baking powder
25g (1oz) desiccated coconut
25g (1oz) coconut flakes, toasted (see the tip on page 15), to decorate

For the icing
50g (2oz) mango
    (about ¼ mango), peeled
200g (7oz) icing sugar, sifted
50g (2oz) butter, softened

24-cup mini bun tray with 24 mini bun cases (see page 336)
Piping bag with a 4 or 5mm (¼in) nozzle or a freezer bag with 4 or 5mm (¼in) cut from one corner (optional)

Preheat the oven to 180°C (350°F), Gas mark 4, and line the bun tray with the paper cases.

Cream the butter until soft in a large bowl or in an electric food mixer. Add the sugar and beat until the mixture is light and fluffy.

Whisk the eggs together in a small bowl for a few seconds or just until mixed, then gradually add them to the creamed butter mixture, beating all the time. Sift in the flour and baking powder and add the desiccated coconut, then fold in gently to incorporate.

Divide the batter between the paper cases, using 2 teaspoons – one to scoop the mixture off the other. Bake for 10–12 minutes or until golden brown and springy to the touch, then allow to cool in the tray for 5 minutes before placing on a wire rack to cool down fully.

As the cakes cool, make the icing. First roughly chop the mango and liquidise using a hand blender or food processor, or simply chop it finely, and push through a sieve to make a thick purée. In a large bowl, beat together the icing sugar, butter and mango purée until fluffy.

Add to the piping bag or freezer bag, if using, then pipe the icing onto the cakes (see Cake essentials on page 339), or apply the icing with a teaspoon if you prefer, and sprinkle over the toasted coconut flakes.

Cake pops

Cake pops are such a great treat for children's parties. They're not hard to make but take a little time between each step. They're absolutely worth it, though, and the young guests will definitely think so! They're also a great way of using any leftover cake – any type of sponge cake would do, in fact. Just having balls of cake on sticks can be fun, but the decoration ideas are really what count here. I've suggested a few variations for icing and decorating your cake pops (see page 222), but be creative and use whatever decorations spring to mind.

Prep time: **45 minutes**
Ready in: **1 hour 30 minutes**
Makes: **12 cake pops**

175g (6oz) milk or white chocolate, in drops or broken into pieces
350g (12oz) Madeira cake (see page 38) or any basic sponge cake, chocolate or plain

For the coloured chocolate coating
400g (14oz) white chocolate, in drops or chopped into pieces
A few drops of your choice of food colouring (optional)

12 lollipop sticks
Polystyrene block into which to insert the cake pops for coating and decorating (optional)

First line a baking sheet with baking parchment.

Place the chocolate in a heatproof bowl and set over a saucepan of simmering water, stirring occasionally just until melted. Crumble the cake into the melted chocolate, and stir until well mixed.

Use your hands to roll the mixture into balls each about as large as a golf ball. Insert a lollipop stick into each ball, place on the lined baking sheet and leave in the fridge for about 30 minutes to firm up.

While the cake pops are in the fridge, make the chocolate coating. Place the chocolate in a heatproof bowl and set over a pan of simmering water, stirring occasionally just until melted. Remove from the heat and stir in the food colouring (if you'd like to colour the white chocolate), adding more or less to obtain the exact shade you'd like.

Remove the cake pops from the fridge, then dip each one into the chocolate coating and either insert upright into the polystyrene block or place back on the lined baking sheet. (Inserting the cake pops in the polystyrene block will ensure they have a perfectly round shape rather than a flat side from lying on the baking parchment.) Place somewhere cool, but not the fridge, and leave for 20–30 minutes or just until the chocolate has set.

Before the coating sets on the cake pops, you can roll them in one of the sprinkle options (see overleaf). Alternatively, once the coating has set, you could decorate with the coloured glacé icing (see overleaf).

Cake pops continued overleaf

Coloured glacé icing

Prep time: **10 minutes**
Makes: **100g (3½oz)**

100g (3½oz) icing sugar, sifted
A few drops of your choice of food
    colouring (in a contrasting colour
    to the chocolate icing)

Piping bag with a 1 or 2mm (1⁄16 in) nozzle
    or a freezer bag with 1 or 2mm (1⁄16 in)
    cut from one corner

When the coloured chocolate coating has set on the cake pops (see the main recipe on page 220), make the glacé icing. In a bowl, mix together the icing sugar and food colouring with just enough water (½–1 tablespoon) to make an icing the consistency of thick double cream.

Spoon the icing into the piping bag or freezer bag, then carefully pipe shapes onto the cake pops – such as spirals, zigzags, faces, or a name or number (see page 340) – before inserting in the polystyrene block, or placing on the lined baking sheet, to set.

Tip For more colours, once you've mixed the icing sugar and water, divide the icing into two or three separate bowls and add different types of food colouring to each, then pipe or drizzle the different icings onto the cake pops for a lovely multi-coloured effect.

Sprinkles

Sugar crystals
100g (3½oz) coloured (or
    multi-coloured) sugar crystals
    (or hundreds and thousands)

Popping candy
100g (3½oz) popping candy

Crushed honeycomb
100g (3½oz) honeycomb (see
    Decorating ideas on page 345),
    crushed into a powder but with
    a few larger chunks remaining

After dipping the cake pops in the coloured chocolate coating, you can roll them in one of these toppings. Sprinkle them onto a plate, then roll each of the cake pops in the mixture before leaving to set.

Cake pops continued overleaf

Peanut butter pops

Prep time: 45 minutes
Ready in: 1 hour 30 minutes
Makes: 12 cake pops

100g (3½oz) milk or dark chocolate,
broken into pieces
100g (3½oz) smooth or crunchy
peanut butter
350g (12oz) Madeira cake (see page
38) or any basic sponge cake

To decorate
400g (14oz) dark, milk or white
chocolate, in drops or broken into
pieces
150g (5oz) salted peanuts, chopped

Put the chocolate and peanut butter into a heatproof bowl and place over a saucepan of simmering water, stirring occasionally just until melted. Crumble the cake into the melted chocolate and peanut butter mixture, and stir until well mixed.

Roll the mixture into balls and insert a lollipop stick into each ball, as in the main recipe on page 220, before chilling in the fridge for 30 minutes.

Meanwhile, melt the chocolate for decorating in a heatproof bowl over a pan of simmering water, stirring occasionally just until melted. Place the chopped peanuts on a plate next to the bowl of chocolate.

Remove the balls from the fridge, then dip each one in the chocolate and roll in the chopped peanuts. Insert either into the polystyrene block or place on the lined baking sheet (see main recipe on page 220) and leave somewhere cool, but not the fridge, for 20–30 minutes or just until the chocolate has set.

Tip Here are some recipes that leave leftover cake – perfect for making into cake pops:
Muscovado Madeira cake (see page 38)
Barbie cake (see page 217)
Butterfly cake (see page 227)
Letter or number cake (see page 230)
Castle cake (see page 236)

Butterfly cake

This pretty cake is so easy to make: it uses just one round cake tin and there's no difficult trimming. You can decorate it however you like, too. I've provided a few ideas; but you can get as creative as you like, playing with different colours and decorations.

Prep time: 45 minutes
Baking time: 30–35 minutes
Ready in: 2 hours
Serves: 10–14

225g (8oz) butter, softened, plus extra for greasing
225g (8oz) caster sugar
4 eggs
225g (8oz) plain flour
2½ tsp baking powder

To decorate

3 chocolate fingers (or 4 chocolate matchsticks) for the body of the butterfly
Edible glitter, hundreds and thousands or coloured sugar (to make it yourself, see page 233) and 2 liquorice wheels for the antennae

23cm (9in) diameter cake tin (see page 334)
Large plate or 40 x 50cm (16 x 20in) cake board

Preheat the oven, 180°C (350°F), Gas mark 4, then butter the sides of the cake tin and line the base with a disc of baking parchment.

Cream the butter until soft in a large bowl or in an electric food mixer. Add the sugar and beat until the mixture is light and fluffy.

Whisk the eggs together in a small bowl for a few seconds or just until mixed, then gradually add them to the creamed butter mixture, beating all the time. Sift in the flour and baking powder and fold in gently to combine. Tip the mixture into the prepared tin and bake for 30–35 minutes or until a skewer inserted into the centre of the cake comes out clean.

Remove from the oven and allow to cool in the tin for 10 minutes, then loosen around the edges using a small, sharp knife and carefully remove the cake before leaving on a wire rack to cool down fully (see page 334). To make the butterfly, cut the cake in half down the middle, then make two cuts at an angle from the centre line, slicing through the cake. This will give you two large and two small wedges. Cut the edges off the circle and turn these around so the edges are facing each other, and angle the four wedges so they look like wings.

Next ice the cake using either the coloured buttercream icing (see page 227), dyed whatever colour you like, or the berry buttercream icing (see page 227) for a lovely shade of pale pink or purple. First place the cake on the plate or cake board, sticking it down with a small blob of icing on each corner, then use a palette knife to ice the cake all over. (Have a bowl or jug of boiling-hot water to hand for dipping your knife into to make it easier to spread.)

Once the cake is iced, place a few chocolate fingers or matchsticks aligned in the centre of the cake to make up the body. You can then use the coloured glacé icing (see page 227) to pipe shapes onto each wing (see Cake essentials on page 339) before carefully shaking over edible glitter, coloured sugar (see page 233) or hundreds and thousands. Place two liquorice wheels at the top of the cake for the butterfly's antennae.

Recipe continued overleaf

Coloured buttercream icing

Prep time: 10 minutes
Makes: 475g (1lb 1oz)

200g (7oz) butter, softened
1–2 tbsp milk
1 tsp vanilla extract
275g (10oz) icing sugar
A good few drops of a food
    colouring of your choice

Using a hand-held electric beater or an electric food mixer, beat together the butter, milk and vanilla extract until very soft. Then gradually sift in the icing sugar, beating all the time, until it is fully incorporated. Continue to beat until very soft – if beating in the food mixer, continue whisking the mixture until it is light and fluffy – then whisk in just enough food colouring to give your desired shade for the icing.

Berry buttercream icing

Prep time: 10 minutes
Makes: 900g (2lb)

150g (5oz) fresh or frozen (and
    defrosted) strawberries or raspberries
1 tbsp lemon juice
175g (6oz) butter, softened
600g (1lb 5oz) icing sugar, sifted

Place the strawberries or raspberries and lemon juice in a food processor and whiz for about a minute to purée. Push through a sieve into a large bowl, then set aside. In a separate bowl, cream together the butter and icing sugar until combined, then gradually add the fruit purée, beating continuously.

Coloured glacé icing

Prep time: 5 minutes
Makes: 250g (9oz)

250g (9oz) icing sugar, sifted
A drop or two of food colouring (in a
    contrasting colour to the main icing)

Piping bag with a 1 or 2mm ($\frac{1}{16}$ in) nozzle
    or a freezer bag with 1 or 2mm ($\frac{1}{16}$ in)
    cut from one corner

In a bowl, mix together the icing sugar and food colouring with just enough water ($\frac{1}{2}$–1 tablespoon) to make an icing that you can use to drizzle over the cake (the consistency of thick double cream).

Use this to fill the piping bag or freezer bag and decorate the cake with swirls or stripes (see Decorating ideas on page 340). It looks lovely if you use the icing to draw the outline of the wings to accentuate them. If you'd rather not use a piping bag, you could use a teaspoon instead. Place the bowl of icing next to the cake and dip your spoon into it, then lift the spoon out and drizzle on stripes or swirls. For a lovely multi-coloured effect, see the tip on page 222.

Letter or number cake

There's something so lovely about having a cake created just for you. Whether it gives the age of the child or the first initial of their name, it is a unique creation that will make them feel really special. Of course, this cake isn't just for children, it's perfect for adults celebrating a big birthday, or even retirement. The basic cake is a simple sponge baked in a roasting tin, which gives a nice large rectangle from which you can cut out any number or letter you like. This does result in quite a lot of trimmings, but these can be put to good to use in Cake pops (see page 220)!

Prep time: **20 minutes**

Baking time: **35–45 minutes**

Ready in: **2 hours**

Serves: **8–14 (depending on the number/letter)**

350g (12oz) butter, softened, plus extra for greasing

350g (12oz) caster sugar

6 eggs

350g (12oz) plain flour

3½ tsp baking powder

To decorate

Sprinkles, hundreds and thousands, edible glitter (optional)

25 x 35cm (10 x 14in) roasting tin with 5cm (2in) sides (approximate size)

Large plate or 40 x 50cm (16 x 20in) cake board

Preheat the oven to 180°C (350°F), Gas mark 4, then butter the roasting tin and line the base and sides with baking parchment.

Cream the butter until soft in a large bowl or in an electric food mixer. Add the sugar and beat until the mixture is light and fluffy. Whisk the eggs together in a bowl for a few seconds or just until mixed, then gradually add them to the creamed butter mixture, beating all the time. Sift in the flour and baking powder and fold in gently until mixed.

Tip the batter into the prepared roasting tin and bake on the lower shelf in the oven for 35–45 minutes (depending on the size of the tin) or until a skewer inserted into the centre of the cake comes out clean.

Remove from the oven and allow to cool in the tin for 10 minutes, then loosen around the edges using a small, sharp knife. Place a large wire rack upside down on top of the cake and carefully turn over. Remove the tin and baking parchment and leave to finish cooling on the wire rack.

When the cake has cooled, transfer to a chopping board. Draw a template of your letter or number on a piece of paper and cut this out. Place on top of the cake and use a sharp knife to cut around the template.

Now you can ice the cake. The amount of icing you need may vary slightly depending on the letter or number (a number '8' will need more icing than the figure '1', for instance). Select one of the coloured icings (see page 232) or, if you prefer, use the icing from the chocolate or peanut butter versions of this cake (see page 234). First add a little of the icing to the base of the cake – a small blob on each corner to hold it in place – before placing it on the plate or board. Spread the icing all over the cake using a palette knife, dipping regularly into a jug or bowl of boiling-hot water for a smooth effect.

Recipe continued overleaf

Once your cake is covered in icing, you can decorate it, playing with colours and designs. You could scatter over sprinkles, for instance, or hundreds and thousands. Another option would be to sift over some coloured sugar (see page 233 – ideally in a contrasting colour to the icing). I like to cut out dots, stars or stripes with paper, lay them on the cake, then sprinkle over the coloured sugar or edible glitter. This looks great when you take the paper away. Alternatively, use coloured glacé icing (see page 233) to pipe designs onto the iced cake (see Cake essentials on page 339). Or see pages 242–248 for additional ideas.

Coloured buttercream icing

Prep time: 10 minutes
Makes: 700g (1½lb)

200g (7oz) butter, softened
450g (1lb) icing sugar, sifted
50ml (2fl oz) milk
1 tsp vanilla extract
A few drops of your choice of
    food colouring

Cream the butter and sugar together in a large bowl or in an electric mixer until fluffy and light. Continuing to beat, gradually add the milk with the vanilla extract and food colouring – adding just enough to achieve the desired shade.

Berry buttercream icing

Prep time: 10 minutes
Makes: enough for one large cake

150g (5oz) fresh or frozen (and
    defrosted) strawberries, raspberries,
    blueberries or blackberries
1 tbsp lemon juice
175g (6oz) butter, softened
600g (1lb 5oz) icing sugar, sifted

This is an alternative coloured icing which uses fruit for colour and flavour. Choose strawberries or raspberries for a gorgeous pink colour and blueberries or blackberries for a light purple shade. Place the fruit and lemon juice in a food processor and whiz for about a minute to purée. Push through a sieve into a large bowl and then set aside. In a separate bowl or using an electric food mixer, cream together the butter and icing sugar until combined, then gradually add the fruit purée, beating continuously.

Coloured glacé icing

Prep time: **5 minutes**
Makes: **100g (3½ oz)**

100g (3½ oz) icing sugar, sifted
A few drops of your choice of food
    colouring

Piping bag with a 1 or 2mm (⅟₁₆ in)
    nozzle or a freezer bag with 1 or 2mm
    (⅟₁₆ in) cut from one corner

In a bowl, mix together the icing sugar and food colouring with just enough water (½–1 tablespoon) to make an icing the consistency of thick double cream.

Use this to fill the piping bag or freezer bag and carefully pipe stripes, swirls or even writing onto the iced cake (see Cake essentials on page 339). If you'd rather not use a piping bag, you could use a teaspoon instead. Place the bowl of icing close to the cake and dip your spoon into it, then lift the spoon out and let some icing drip off. Hold the spoon close to the iced surface of the cake as you carefully drizzle on stripes, zigzags or swirls. For a lovely multi-coloured effect, see the tip on page 222.

Coloured sugar

Prep time: **10 minutes**
Makes: **125g (4½ oz)**

125g (4½ oz) icing sugar
3–4 drops of food colouring (ideally in a
    contrasting colour to your choice of icing)

Place the icing sugar and food colouring in a sieve set over a bowl. Push the icing sugar through the sieve into the bowl, then sift it again. Keep doing this maybe three or four times until the food colouring has tinted the sugar. Use this for sifting over the iced cake as suggested in the main recipe on page 232.

Recipe continued overleaf

Chocolate letter or number cake

Prep time: **20 minutes**

Baking time: **35–45 minutes**

Ready in: **2 hours**

Serves: **8–14 (depending on the number/letter)**

For adding to the sponge

2 tbsp cocoa powder

For the icing

125g (4½oz) milk chocolate, in drops or broken into pieces

225g (8oz) butter, softened

450g (1lb) icing sugar

25g (1oz) cocoa powder

To decorate

100g (3½oz) white chocolate, in drops or broken into pieces

Make the cake as in the main recipe on page 230, adding the cocoa powder with the flour.

To make the icing, first place the chocolate in a heatproof bowl and set over a saucepan of gently simmering water. Leave just until melted, stirring occasionally, then remove from the heat.

Cream the butter until very soft in a large bowl using a hand-held electric beater or in an electric food mixer, then sift in the icing sugar and cocoa powder and continue to mix. Pour in the melted chocolate and beat in until well mixed. Use a palette knife to spread the icing all over the cake.

Place the white chocolate in a heatproof bowl and set over a pan of simmering water. Leave just until melted, stirring from time to time, then remove from the heat and place next to the cake. Dip a teaspoon or dessertspoon into the chocolate, then drizzle on stripes, zigzags or swirls.

Peanut butter letter or number cake

Prep time: **20 minutes**

Baking time: **35–45 minutes**

Ready in: **2 hours**

Serves: **8–14**

For adding to the sponge

75g (3oz) smooth or crunchy peanut butter

For the icing

125g (4½oz) smooth or crunchy peanut butter

100g (3½oz) butter, softened

125g (4½oz) cream cheese

1 tsp vanilla extract

375g (13oz) icing sugar

1–2 tbsp milk

Salted peanuts (optional), to decorate

Make the cake as in the main recipe on page 230, adding the peanut butter with the sugar to the creamed butter.

To make the icing, cream together the peanut butter, butter, cream cheese and vanilla extract in a large bowl using a hand-held electric beater or in an electric food mixer. Gradually sift in the icing sugar and continue to beat until all the ingredients are well mixed, then add the milk and beat in to combine. If you'd like it especially fluffy and you are using a food mixer, then continue to beat for a few minutes.

Use a palette knife to spread all over the cake, then decorate with pieces of peanut brittle or chocolate-covered peanuts (see Decorating ideas on page 340–346), or just salted peanuts.

Castle cake

This might just be the dream cake for more than a few children I know. It takes a bit of time and a lot of ingredients, but if you have the time it's definitely worth the effort. I realise this cake uses a lot of sugar and butter, but then it could feed about 40 children. I've provided suggestions for how to decorate it, but let your imagination run wild. You could cover the whole thing with different-coloured sweets, for instance, or even place knights or princesses standing outside! You can make this cake in four batches if you've only one tin, or you can make it in two batches if you have enough tins. These are the instructions for making the cake in two batches; if you're making it in four batches, you need to use a quarter of the quantities listed for the ingredients each time. The photograph opposite is for the chocolate version of this cake (see page 241).

Prep time: 1 hour 30 minutes
(depending on the number of tins)
Baking time: 30 minutes–1 hour
Ready in: 3 hours
Serves: about 40

700g (1½lb) butter, softened, plus
extra for greasing
700g (1½lb) caster sugar
12 eggs
700g (1½lb) self-raising flour

To decorate
Coloured sugar crystals or hundreds
and thousands
5 ice-cream cones for the turrets
Mini marshmallows, sugar cubes or
square Liquorice Allsorts for the
battlements
Wafers, rectangular biscuits, chocolates
(such as Curly Wurlys), thin
matchsticks, for a door and windows
and for edging the sides and liquorice
lace for a drawbridge and ropes

Two 20cm (8in) square cake tins with
5cm (2in) sides (see page 334)
Large plate or a 35cm (14in) square
cake board

Preheat the oven to 180°C (350°F), Gas mark 4, then butter the sides of the cake tins and line the base of each tin with baking parchment.

Cream half the butter until soft in a large bowl or in an electric food mixer. Add half the sugar and beat until the mixture is light and fluffy.

Whisk six eggs together in a bowl for a few seconds or just until mixed, then gradually add them to the butter mixture, beating all the time. Sift in half the flour and fold in gently until mixed.

Tip the batter into the prepared cake tins and bake for 25–30 minutes or until a skewer inserted into the centre of each cake comes out clean.

Remove from the oven and allow to cool in the tins for 10 minutes. Then loosen around the edges of each cake using a small, sharp knife and carefully remove from the tin before leaving on a wire rack to cool down completely (see page 334).

Repeat the process for the next two cakes until you have four square cakes.

Next make the icing, using either the coloured buttercream icing (see page 239) or the berry buttercream (see page 239) for a gorgeous pink or purple icing made using fresh berries. Or if you prefer, use the icing from the chocolate version of this cake (see page 241).

If your cakes are domed or a little uneven on top, use a serrated knife to neaten the tops so they are level. Add a little blob of icing onto the four corners of one of the cakes, then place upside down on the serving plate or cake board (the icing helps hold the cake in place).

Recipe continued overleaf

Next spread the icing onto the cake to about 5mm (¼ in) thick. Add another cake on top and spread that cake with icing, then put a third cake on top.

Take the fourth cake and cut in half then half again to get four equal-sized squares. Spread icing onto one of these smaller squares and place this, icing side down, in the centre of your main cake. Repeat with another two squares so you have another three-layered tier on top of the main cake.

Cut the remaining square of cake into four small squares. Place two of these squares on top of each other in the centre of the main cake, adding icing between each layer so they stick together and on to the main cake. You'll be left with two small squares – feel free to eat these as I think it makes this cake just too tall (and you deserve a treat at this stage!). Or you could otherwise save them for making Cake pops (see page 220).

It's now time to ice the cake. Spread the icing all over the cake using a palette knife, regularly dipping in a bowl of boiling-hot water to make it easier to spread. You won't need all the icing; some should be saved for the ice-cream cones (see below).

Now the cake is iced all over, you can decorate it, starting with the ice-cream cones for the turrets.

Scatter either coloured sugar crystals, hundreds and thousands or sprinkles onto a plate, spreading them out. Spread the icing, not too thickly, on the outside of one ice-cream cone. This is easy to do if you place the cone on two fingers (your forefinger and middle finger) so that they support the cone while you ice it with your other hand. Then, with your two fingers still inside the cone and the forefinger of your other hand supporting the top, roll the cone in the sugar or sprinkles. After the cone is well coated, use the same technique to carefully place on one corner of the bottom tier of the castle. Repeat with the remaining four cones, placing the final cone on the very top of the cake.

Next make the battlements. Using square-shaped sweets such as mini marshmallows or Liquorice Allsorts, space these evenly apart around the middle and top tier of the cake to look like turrets.

After that you can play around with whatever decorations you like. A door is a great touch: I like to use pink wafers if it's a pink cake, or any rectangular biscuits or chocolates otherwise. You could also cut these in half and stick them onto the cake to make windows. You could also 'edge' the sides of the cake with chocolate matchsticks for a neat look.

If you like, you can make a drawbridge by laying Curly Wurlys (cut to size) or white chocolate fingers side by side at the castle entrance, using a little icing to stick them down. If you're feeling adventurous, you can complete the effect by making two ropes for the drawbridge out of thin chocolate matchsticks or liquorice lace, with one end of the 'rope' stuck to the end of the drawbridge and the other to the castle, just above and to one side of the door.

Coloured buttercream icing

Prep time: 15 minutes
Makes: 3kg (6½lb)

1.2kg (2lb 10oz) butter, softened
1 tbsp vanilla extract
1.6kg (3½lb) icing sugar
150–200ml (5–7fl oz) milk
A good few drops of your choice of food colouring

If using a hand-held electric beater, you can make this in one batch in a large mixing bowl. If using an electric food mixer, you will need to do it in 2–3 batches, unless you have a very large mixer.

Using a hand-held electric beater or an electric food mixer, beat together the butter and vanilla extract until very soft. Then gradually sift in the icing sugar, beating all the time, until it is fully incorporated. Gradually pour in the milk while continuing to beat, adding just enough so the mixture is softly spreadable, then whisk until it is light and fluffy. Whisk in just enough food colouring to give your desired shade.

Berry buttercream icing

Prep time: 15 minutes
Makes: 3.75kg (8¼lb)

600g (1lb 5oz) fresh or frozen (and defrosted) strawberries, raspberries, blueberries or blackberries
50ml (2fl oz) lemon juice
700g (1½lb) butter, softened
2.4kg (5lb 5oz) icing sugar, sifted

If using a hand-held electric beater, you can make this in one batch in a large mixing bowl. If using an electric food mixer, you will need to do it in 2–3 batches, unless you have a very large mixer.

Place the fruit and lemon juice in a food processor and whiz for about a minute to purée. Push through a sieve into a large bowl, then set aside. Using a hand-held electric beater or an electric food mixer, cream together the butter and icing sugar until combined, then gradually add the fruit purée, beating continuously.

Recipe continued overleaf

Chocolate castle cake

Prep time: **1 hour 30 minutes**
(depending on the number of tins)
Baking time: **30 minutes–1 hour**
Ready in: **3 hours**
Serves: **about** 40

For adding to the sponge

100g (3½oz) cocoa powder, sifted

For the icing

625g (1lb 6oz) milk chocolate, in drops
or broken into pieces
1.13kg (2½lb) butter, softened
2.25kg (5lb) icing sugar
125g (4½oz) cocoa powder

To decorate

Chocolate sprinkles for the ice-cream
cones
Chocolate-covered toffees for the
battlements
Bourbon biscuits or chocolate fingers
for the door and windows
Thin matchsticks for edging the sides
Chocolate fingers or Curly Wurlys for
a drawbridge and a liquorice lace for
the ropes (optional)

Make the cake as in the main recipe on page 236, decreasing the quantity of self-raising flour to 650g (1lb 7oz) and adding the cocoa powder to the sponge mixture with the flour.

To make the icing (which you may need to do in 2–3 batches, though in the main recipe it can be made in one batch in a large mixing bowl using a hand-held electric beater), first place the chocolate in a heatproof bowl and over a saucepan of gently simmering water. Leave just until melted, stirring occasionally, then remove from the heat.

Cream the butter until soft in a large bowl using a hand-held electric beater or in an electric food mixer, then sift in the icing sugar and cocoa powder and continue to mix. Pour in the melted chocolate and beat until well combined.

Ice the cake as in the main recipe (see pages 236–238), and decorate in the same way, covering the iced ice-cream cones in chocolate sprinkles instead of coloured ones, and using chocolate-covered toffees for the battlements, Bourbon biscuits or chocolate fingers for a door and windows and thin matchsticks for edging the sides. If making a drawbridge, use chocolate fingers or Curly Wurlys for the bridge itself and a cut-up liquorice lace for the ropes.

Tip Should you have any icing left over, store it in the fridge, where it will last for up to a week in an airtight container. The berry buttercream (see page 239) will keep for up to three days in the fridge. You can then use it for buns or sponge cakes – making sure to take it out of the fridge about an hour beforehand to allow it to soften.

Decorating ideas

If you'd like to spend a little more time decorating and want to get really creative, then fondant decorations offer a hugely versatile way of taking your cake to the next level. Sugarcraft, as it's also known, in which intricate structures are created from sugar and coloured with edible dyes, can take hours or even days to create. The ideas included below are much more do-able and simple to achieve, but they look impressive even so.

You can make up the fondant icing recipe I've provided and add food colouring. Alternatively, you can buy pre-coloured fondant icing from supermarkets and specialist shops or online.

Fondant icing

For coloured fondant icing, you can either mix a few drops of food colouring in with the egg white and glucose (as the recipe below), or you can add it to the icing when it's made, kneading it in until the colour is even and the icing is smooth. Any fondant shapes made from this icing should keep for up to two weeks if stored in an airtight box.

Prep time: **10 minutes**
Makes: **450g (1lb)**

1 egg white, whisked
50g (2oz) liquid glucose
¼ tsp vanilla extract
A few drops of your chosen food colouring (optional)
400g (14oz) icing sugar, sifted, plus extra for dusting

In a bowl, mix together the egg white, glucose, vanilla extract and food colouring, if using. Place the icing sugar in a separate bowl or an electric food mixer and gradually add the egg-white mixture, beating continuously until all the ingredients come together.

Place the icing on a spotlessly clean worktop that has been generously dusted with icing sugar and knead the icing for a minute or two or until it is completely smooth on the surface.

Fast fondant flowers

Prep time: **10 minutes**
Makes: **20–30 flowers**

150g (5oz) white fondant icing
Icing sugar, for dusting
A few drops each of 2 different types of food colouring

Flower-shaped cookie cutter or a flower template
(see page 247)

Divide the fondant icing into two pieces, one about a quarter the size of the other. If you would like to use the flower template, trace the shape on page 247 using baking parchment and cut it out.

Dust a work surface with icing sugar, then add a few drops of your chosen colour to the larger piece (this will be for the main part of the flowers) and knead until the colour is even and the icing smooth. Use a rolling pin to roll out to a thickness of about 5mm (¼in), then cut out flowers using a flower-shaped cookie cutter or place the template on the rolled-out icing and cut around it with a sharp knife to make the flowers.

Add a few drops of a different food colouring to the smaller piece of fondant icing (this will be for the centre of your flowers) and knead it in as before.

Next, break off small pieces of this icing and to roll them into little balls (about the size of a lentil) with your hands. Use a little water to moisten the flowers, then press one ball each into the centre of the flowers to stick them on.

Once the flowers are assembled, if you're placing them on top of a cake covered in fondant icing, moisten the bottom first with a little water and then press them down. Alternatively, place on baking parchment and leave in a cool, dry place for a few hours. They can then be placed on top of any iced cake or cupcakes.

Fondant roses

For each rose, you'll need five balls of icing each roughly the size of a hazelnut. The roses in the step-by-step photographs are all the same colour, but you can mix them up, making petals of different colours. I love to have a variety – some white, some pale pink and some a bit darker pink – adding different amounts of pink food colouring to batches of plain fondant icing.

Prep time: **45 minutes**
Makes: **about 25–30 roses**

100g (3½oz) white fondant icing
A few drops of pink food colouring (optional)
Icing sugar, for dusting

You can either leave the fondant icing white or, for pink roses, mix a few drops of food colouring into the icing, or into batches of it for petals in varying shades of pink. Dust your worktop with icing sugar and knead a few drops of food colouring into the icing until the colour is even and the icing smooth.

To make a rose, pinch off five little pieces of the icing, each about the size of a hazelnut, and roll each one into a ball. Place the five small balls, spaced apart, between two sheets of cling film. Press each down with your thumb, flattening it so that it forms an oval shape, slightly thinner on one long side. When you have flattened all five balls like this, remove the top layer of cling film.

To make the centre of a rose, roll one of the pieces into a spiral, with the thin side up. Take another piece and roll it, thin side up, around the centre of the rose, covering the overlap. Take the third piece, thin side up again, and wrap it around the other two pieces, covering the overlap once again. Continue with the last two pieces in the same way, then slightly curve the edges of the petals outwards with your fingertips to make a rose. The rose will probably have quite a long base so pinch this off and remove it. The discarded pieces can be reused to make more roses.

Stick them immediately to the top of your cake by moistening the bottom first with a little water and then pressing them down. Alternatively, you can store them in an airtight box, where they will keep for up to two weeks.

Fondant ghosts

Prep time: 30 minutes
Makes: 6–10 ghosts

200g (7oz) white fondant icing
Icing sugar, for dusting
A couple of drops of black or brown food colouring

Plain-edge 5cm (2in) diameter cookie cutter (optional)

First take six small pieces of fondant icing, each about the size of a walnut in its shell, and use your hands to shape them into balls.

Dust you worktop with icing sugar and roll out the remaining icing to a thickness of about 5mm (¼in), then using the cookie cutter, or a straight-sided glass about 5cm (2in) in diameter, cut out six circles. Drape each circle over one of the balls, then use your fingers to create a few folds.

To make eyes for the ghosts, roll just a tiny amount of fondant icing and add a drop or so of black or brown food colouring. Dust your work surface with icing sugar and knead until the colour is even and the icing smooth. Break off tiny pieces and roll into balls for the eyes. Moisten the balls with a little water and stick a couple onto each ghost.

Stick the ghosts to your cake by moistening the bottom of the ghosts first with a little water and then pressing them down. Alternatively, you can store them in an airtight box, where they will keep for up to two weeks.

Tip These spooky shapes would make a great alternative decoration to the Halloween pumpkin squares on page 296.

Fondant football shirts

Prep time: 20 minutes
Makes: 20–30 shirts

150g (5oz) white fondant icing
A few drops of you chosen food colouring (optional)
Icing sugar, for dusting

For the icing for piping
100g (3½oz) icing sugar, sifted
A few drops of your chosen food colouring

Shirt template (see page 247)
Piping bag with a 1 or 2mm (1/16 in) nozzle or a freezer bag with 1 or 2mm (1/16 in) cut from one corner (see page 339)

First trace around the shirt template on page 247 using baking parchment and cut out the shape. To make a white football shirt, just leave the icing uncoloured, or to colour it add a few drops of food colouring, then dust your work surface with icing sugar and knead until the colour is even and the icing smooth.

Dust the worktop with more icing sugar and roll out the icing to about 5mm (¼in) thick. Place the shirt template on the rolled-out icing and use a knife to cut out shirt shapes, then make up the following icing to draw different colours or patterns for you team on each shirt.

Mix together the icing sugar and a few drops of food colouring in a bowl, adding just enough water (½–1 table-spoon) to make an icing the consistency of thick double cream. Fill the piping bag or freezer bag with the icing and carefully draw stripes or team numbers on each shirt. The shirts will stick on to a freshly iced cake or can be moistened with a little water and pressed lightly down onto the cake.

Tip A crowd-pleasing way of showing off these shirts is to put them on individual iced sponge squares (or cupcakes) and then arrange them on a plate all in one block, like a cake 'team', and then separate the individual 'players' to be eaten!

Fondant butterflies

Prep time: 45 minutes
Makes: 20–30 butterflies

150g (5oz) white fondant icing
A few drops of your chosen food colouring
Icing sugar, for dusting
Cornflour, for dusting

For the icing for piping
100g (3½ oz) icing sugar, sifted
A few drops of your chosen food colouring

Butterfly-shaped cookie cutter or a butterfly template (see page 247) and cardboard for making a few drying 'stands'
Piping bag with a 1 or 2mm (1/16 in) nozzle or a freezer bag with 1 or 2mm (1/16 in) cut from one corner (see page 339)

You can make white butterflies, but if you'd prefer them to be coloured, add a few drops of food colouring to the fondant icing, dust your worktop with icing sugar and knead until the colour is even and the icing smooth. If you would like to use the butterfly template, trace the shape on page 247 using baking parchment and cut it out.

On a work surface dusted with icing sugar, roll out the icing to a thickness of about 5mm (¼in). Cut out the butterflies using a butterfly cutter or alternatively place the paper template on the rolled-out icing and use a sharp knife to cut around it to make the butterflies.

Next, take a small square of cardboard and fold in half, then fold each half over again so you have a 'M' shape if you look at it side on. Dust the cardboard with cornflour, then use a palette knife to transfer each butterfly to a cardboard stand so the middle of its body is in the fold of the 'M' and the wings are angled upwards. Repeat until all the butterflies are on cardboard, with their wings angled upwards, then leave in a cool dry room so they will dry off and stiffen slightly.

To make the icing for the piping, mix together the icing sugar and a few drops of food colouring in a bowl, adding just enough water (½–1 tablespoon) to make an icing the consistency of thick double cream. Fill the piping bag or freezer bag with the icing and carefully draw patterns on your butterflies. The butterflies will stick on to a freshly iced cake or moisten the body of the butterflies with a little water first and then gently press them down on to the cake.

Fondant birds

Prep time: 30 minutes
Makes: about 20 birds

150g (5oz) white fondant icing
A few drops each of 3 different types of food colouring
Icing sugar, for dusting

Bird template (see page 247)

First trace the inner and outer bird templates on page 247 using baking parchment, then cut out the shapes.

Divide the fondant icing into two, then break a small amount off one of the pieces. The largest piece will be for making the bodies of your birds. Add a few drops of your chosen food colouring to this, dust a worktop with icing sugar and knead until you have the colour you desire and the icing is smooth.

The larger of the two remaining pieces of fondant icing will be for the wings. Add a few drops of a different colour and knead again until the colour is even and the icing is smooth. To the final small piece of icing, add, a drop or two of another colour (this will for the beaks), then knead until smooth.

Dust your work surface with a little icing sugar and roll out each piece of icing until about 5mm (¼in) thick. Using a sharp knife and with the body template as guide, cut out the bodies of the birds from the largest piece of rolled-out icing. Next cut out the same number of wings from the larger of the remaining two pieces of icing, and finally cut out the beaks from the third piece of icing.

Moisten a wing piece using your fingertips and a little water, then press this onto a body piece, moist side down, gently rubbing around the icing so the wing sticks. Next moisten the edge of the beak and carefully press it onto the edge of the body so it sticks.

To make an eye, roll just a tiny amount of fondant icing (it could be any colour) and make a tiny ball. Moisten the ball a little and stick down on the body of the bird. Repeat until all the birds have been completed.

Once made, you can either add them straight away to iced cupcakes, or, if you prefer, leave them to dry overnight, then carefully place them flat on to a cake or cakes covered in a thick layer of buttercream.

Fondant snowmen

Prep time: 45 minutes
Makes: 6–10 snowmen

150g (5oz) white fondant icing
A few drops each of orange and black food colouring
Icing sugar, for dusting

Fine paintbrush (optional)
Toothpick (optional)
Snowman template (see page 247) (optional)

To make a snowman, break off a piece of fondant icing about the size of a walnut in its shell, then roll into a ball with your hands – this will be the body. Next break off a slightly smaller piece from the main block of fondant icing and roll again into a ball – this will be the head of the snowman. Moisten the top of the body with a little water and press on the head. (To ensure they stick together, you can push a toothpick through the body and the head, breaking the stick off to make it the correct size if necessary.)

To make a carrot-shaped nose, break off a small piece of fondant icing and add a good few drops of orange food colouring. Dust your work surface with a little icing sugar and knead until the colour is even and the icing smooth. Then break off a tiny piece and roll into a small ball, pinch the ends to form a teardrop shape and roll a little to form a cone. Moisten the end with a little water, then press onto the head to form a nose.

Break off another piece of fondant icing and add a good few drops of black food colouring. Dust your work surface with a little icing sugar and knead the fondant until the colour is even and the icing smooth. Break off several tiny dots (they don't need to be rolled) and moisten these a little before attaching to the snowman as eyes and buttons. Alternatively, dip the very end of your paintbrush into the black food colouring and carefully paint dots on the head for eyes and down the body for buttons.

Repeat the above steps to make the remaining snowmen. Stick the snowmen to your freshly iced cake or you can moisten the bottom of the snowmen first with a little water and then press them gently down on to the cake. You can store them in an airtight box, where they will keep for up to two weeks. Alternatively you can use the snowman template (see opposite) to cut out fondant icing into fun shapes.

Tip These would also work on a Christmas cake (see page 317).

Fondant dinosaurs

Prep time: 40 minutes
Makes: about 12–15 dinosaurs

A few drops of your chosen food colouring
150g (5oz) white fondant icing
Icing sugar, for dusting

For the icing for piping
100g (3½oz) icing sugar, sifted
A few drops of your chosen food colouring

Dinosaur-shaped cookie cutter or a dinosaur template (see page 247)
Piping bag with a 1 or 2mm (1⁄16 in) nozzle or a freezer bag with 1 or 2mm (1⁄16in) cut from one corner (see page 339)

Add a few drops of food colouring to the fondant icing, then dust your worktop with icing sugar and knead until the colour is even and the icing smooth. If you would like to use the dinosaur template, trace the shape opposite using baking parchment and cut it out.

On a work surface dusted with icing sugar, roll out the icing to about 5mm (¼in) thick. Cut out dinosaur shapes using a cookie cutter or place the paper template on the rolled-out icing and use a sharp knife to cut out the dinosaurs.

To make the icing for piping, mix together the icing sugar and a few drops of food colouring in a bowl, adding just enough water (½–1 tablespoon) to make an icing the consistency of thick double cream. Fill the piping bag or freezer bag with the icing and carefully draw stripes, dots or other patterns onto your dinosaurs. They will stick on to a freshly iced cake or you can moisten the bottom of the dinosaurs first and press them gently on to the cake.

Fondant penguins

Prep time: 45 minutes
Makes: 6–10 penguins

200g (7oz) white fondant icing
A few drops each of black and yellow food colouring
Icing sugar, for dusting

Plain-edge approx 2cm (¾in) diameter cookie cutter
    and a very small heart-shaped cutter (optional)
Toothpick (optional)

Break off about a quarter of the fondant icing and from that piece break off another quarter, leaving you with three pieces of icing, decreasing in size.

To the largest piece, add a good few drops (or more) of black food colouring, dust your work surface with a little icing sugar and knead until the colour is even and the icing smooth.

To make a penguin, break off a piece of the black fondant icing about the size of a walnut in its shell, then roll into an oval with your hands – this will be the body. Next break off a smaller piece and roll again into a ball for the penguin's head.

Dust your work surface with a little icing sugar, take the larger piece of white fondant icing and roll out until very thin. Using a cookie cutter or a straight-edged glass roughly the same size in diameter, cut out a circle. Moisten one side of the circle and the body of the penguin with a little water, then press the circle onto the body, rubbing around the icing to firmly attach it. This forms the white 'breast' of the penguin.

To make the penguin's face, use either a very small heart-shaped cutter or a knife to cut out a small heart shape in the icing. Moisten one side of the heart with a little water and press onto the front of the head, rubbing the icing and pressing in with your hands to make sure it sticks on firmly.

Break off another two pieces of black fondant icing for the feet – they should be quite small, each about the size of a cherry stone.

Break off two more pieces of black icing to form the wings – they should be larger than the foot pieces. Use your fingers to form then into flat oval shapes.

Next stick the feet onto the bottom of the penguin's body, moistening with a little water. Then stick the wings to the body, moistening again. Finally stick the head onto the top of the body. (To ensure they stick together, you can push a toothpick through the body and the head, breaking the stick off to make it the correct size if necessary.)

To make the eyes, break off two small pieces of black fondant icing the same size and roll into tiny balls.

To the smaller piece of white fondant, add a few drops of yellow food colouring. Knead until the colour is even and the fondant is smooth. Break off a small piece and roll into a ball the same size as the eyes, then pinch the end a little to form a beak shape. Stick the eyes and beak to the head, moistening with a little water.

Repeat the above steps to make the remaining penguins. Stick the penguin to your freshly iced cake or you can moisten the bottom of the penguin first with a little water and then press them gently down on to the cake. Alternatively, you can store them in an airtight box, where they will keep for up to two weeks.

Tip These cheeky chaps would make an alternative festive decoration to the top of the Christmas cake on page 317.

A celebration can be transformed by cake. Having a cake as a centrepiece to your celebration can make an occasion extra special, whether it is a grand and extravagantly decorated cake, a simple but stunning classic, or a collection of beautiful cupcakes. This chapter has a range of cakes, some of which are relatively quick to put together and some that ask a little more from you in terms of time and effort. While many of these cakes are tailored to certain celebrations such as a wedding or an anniversary, you do not have to be tied down to specifics as you can adapt your cake's decoration to suit your particular celebration, be that a baby shower or a retirement party. Be as inventive as you like with decorations, and I hope you will enjoy making these cakes whatever the event, even if it is just to celebrate a Tuesday afternoon!

08/ Celebration

Hazelnut meringue cake

Half meringue and half cake, this is an elegant dish that uses a few ingredients to impressive effect. It contains no flour but uses ground hazelnuts and egg yolks to give structure and wonderful flavour to a meringue base. Topped, pavlova-style, with softly whipped cream and strawberries or raspberries, this would make a super end to a summer meal.

Prep time: **20 minutes**
Baking time: **45 minutes**
Ready in: **1 hour and 15 minutes**
Serves: **6–10**

Butter, for greasing
225g (8oz) hazelnuts (skin still on), toasted (see the tip on page 125)
6 eggs, separated
200g (7oz) caster sugar

For the topping
350ml (12fl oz) double or regular cream, softly whipped
250g (9oz) fresh raspberries or sliced hulled strawberries or a mixture of the two
A few fresh mint leaves (optional)
Icing sugar, for dusting

23cm (9in) diameter cake spring-form or loose-bottomed tin with 6cm (2½in) sides (see page 336)

Preheat the oven to 170°C (325°F), Gas mark 3, then butter the sides of the cake tin and line the base with a disc of baking parchment. If you're using a spring-form tin, make sure the base is upside down, so there's no lip and the cake can slide off easily when cooked.

Place the toasted hazelnuts in a food processor and whiz for a minute or so until they form a coarse powder with a few larger chunks for texture.

Using a hand-held electric beater or an electric food mixer, whisk the egg yolks and sugar together for 5–7 minutes or until pale, thick and mousse-like, then fold in the hazelnuts.

In a separate, spotlessly clean bowl (and having cleaned the electric beater, if using), whisk the egg whites until they form stiff peaks, then gently fold them into the yolk mixture until incorporated.

Tip the batter into the prepared tin and bake for about 45 minutes or until a skewer inserted into the centre comes out clean and the cake begins to come away slightly from the edges of the tin. Don't worry if it dips slightly in the middle.

Remove from the oven and allow to cool in the tin for 10 minutes. Loosen the sides using a small, sharp knife, then carefully remove the sides of the tin and leave the cake on a wire rack to cool down completely before transferring to a serving plate (see page 336).

Spoon the whipped cream all over the top of the cake, leaving a gap about 1cm (½in) wide around the edge, and scatter the raspberries or strawberries over the cream. Decorate with a few mint leaves, if using, then dust with icing sugar.

Anniversary chocolate mousse layer cake

Four layers of chocolate sponge sandwiched together with a rich chocolate mousse, this is an elegant cake that would be ideal for a wedding anniversary celebration. A couple of tablespoons of rum, brandy or other spirits add to the intensity of the mousse, but if you'd rather not include any alcohol, vanilla extract makes an excellent substitute. The recipe below is based upon one for a classic Genoese cake that calls for browned or clarified butter and requires the eggs and sugar to be whisked over a flame. This version of the recipe omits those steps as I don't feel they're strictly necessary: the resulting cake is still very light and it tastes fabulous.

Prep time: **45 minutes**
Baking time: **30–35 minutes**
Ready in: **2 hours**
Serves: **8–12**

100g (3½oz) butter, plus extra
    for greasing
8 eggs
300g (11oz) caster sugar
200g (7oz) plain flour, plus extra
    for dusting
75g (3oz) cocoa powder
3 tsp baking powder
¼ tsp salt
1 tsp vanilla extract

For the mousse
275g (10oz) dark chocolate, in drops
    or broken into pieces
6 eggs, separated
175g (6oz) butter, softened
2 tbsp rum, brandy, whiskey or orange
    liqueur, or 1 tsp vanilla extract

Ingredients cont. overleaf

Preheat the oven to 180°C (350°F), Gas mark 4. Butter the sides of the cake tins and dust with flour, then line the base of each tin with a disc of baking parchment.

To make the sponge, first melt the butter and set aside for 5–10 minutes to cool until tepid.

Place the eggs and sugar in a large bowl or an electric food mixer. Using an electric hand-held beater or the food mixer, whisk for 6–8 minutes or until the mixture is light and thick. To test if it's thick enough, lift the whisk out of the mixture and draw a figure of eight in the bowl with the batter that's left on the whisk: the '8' should remain visible on the surface for a couple of seconds.

Sift in the flour, cocoa powder, baking powder and salt and fold in gently but thoroughly, then pour in the vanilla extract and the melted butter and fold in again.

Quickly divide the batter between the prepared cake tins before it has a chance to lose any volume, then bake for 30–35 minutes or until the mixture springs back when lightly pressed with a finger and a skewer inserted into the centre of each cake comes out clean.

Remove from the oven and allow to cool in the tins for 5 minutes, then loosen around the edges of each tin using a small, sharp knife and carefully remove the cake before transferring to a wire rack to cool down completely (see page 334).

Recipe continued overleaf

To decorate

Chocolate curls (see page 342), made using either dark, milk or white chocolate or a mixture

Cocoa powder or icing sugar, for dusting (optional)

Two 23cm (9in) diameter cake tins with 6cm (2 ½in) (minimum) sides (see page 334)

While the cakes are cooling, make the chocolate mousse. Place the chocolate in a heatproof bowl and set over a saucepan of simmering water. Leave just until melted, stirring occasionally, then remove from the heat.

Beat in the egg yolks one at a time, then beat in the butter, spirits or orange liqueur or vanilla extract and keep beating until smooth. Set aside to cool while you whisk the egg whites.

In a spotlessly clean bowl or using the food mixer (having cleaned the bowl and whisk), whisk the egg whites until they form stiff peaks. Fold in a quarter of the chocolate mixture, then carefully fold in the rest just until mixed. Set aside and leave to cool at room temperature – not in the fridge, otherwise the mousse will harden and become difficult to spread.

To assemble the cake, first use a bread knife to carefully slice each cake in half horizontally. Place the bottom half of one of the cakes, cut side up, on a plate or cake stand. Spread over some of the mousse in a layer about 5mm (¼in) thick, then sandwich with the other half of the cake, placing it cut side down. Spread over more of the mousse, just as thickly, then sandwich with the bottom half of the second cake, cut side up. Repeat for the next layer until you have four layers of cake sandwiched together with three layers of mousse. Cover the top and sides of the assembled cake with the remaining mousse, smoothing it over with a palette knife.

Decorate the top with chocolate curls, if using, or dust with cocoa powder or icing sugar.

Strawberry white chocolate cake

This recipe uses a lot of fresh strawberries. They're sliced and mixed into the cake, making it extremely moist and really bursting with that summery strawberry flavour. The cake has a slightly rustic and uneven top, but that's part of its charm. Moist as it is, this cake needs no accompaniment (other than a blob of softly whipped cream, if you wish).

Prep time: 10 minutes
Baking time: 50–60 minutes
Ready in: 1 hour 45 minutes
Serves: 6–10

175g (6oz) butter, softened, plus extra for greasing
175g (6oz) caster sugar
2 eggs
175g (6oz) self-raising flour, sifted
100g (3½oz) ground almonds
75g (3oz) white chocolate, in chips or chopped into pieces
450g (1lb) fresh strawberries, hulled and sliced

23cm (9in) diameter spring-form or loose-bottomed cake tin with 6cm (2½in) sides (see page 336)

Preheat the oven to 180°C (350°F), Gas mark 4, then butter the base and sides of the cake tin. If you're using a spring-form tin make sure the base is upside down, so there's no lip and the cake can slide off easily when cooked.

Cream the butter until soft in a large bowl or in an electric food mixer. Add the sugar and beat until the mixture is light and fluffy.

Whisk the eggs together in a small bowl for a few seconds or just until mixed. Gradually add the eggs to the creamed butter mixture, beating all the time. Add the flour and ground almonds and fold in to combine, then fold in the chocolate chips and the strawberries.

Tip the mixture into the prepared tin and bake for 50–60 minutes or until well risen and golden on top and a skewer inserted into the centre of the cake comes out clean.

Remove from the oven and allow to cool in the tin for 20 minutes. Loosen around the edges using a small, sharp knife and remove the sides of the tin before carefully transferring to a serving plate and leaving to cool down completely (see page 336).

Chocolate cupcakes

Cupcakes have become incredibly popular in recent years. One of the reasons for this is their versatility. With a huge range of flavours, styles and toppings, the only limit is your imagination. Here are four different ways of topping a delicious basic cupcake recipe.

Prep time: **10 minutes**
Baking time: **20–25 minutes**
Ready in: **1 hour**
Makes: **12 cupcakes**

For the basic cupcakes
100g (3½oz) butter, softened
150g (5oz) caster sugar
2 eggs
125ml (4½fl oz) milk
175g (6oz) plain flour
25g (1oz) cocoa powder
2 tsp baking powder
Pinch of salt

12-cup muffin tray and 12 muffin cases (see page 336)

Preheat the oven to 180°C (350°F), Gas mark 4, and line the muffin tray with the paper cases.

Cream the butter until soft in a large bowl or in an electric food mixer. Add the sugar and beat until the mixture is light and fluffy.

Whisk the eggs together in a small bowl for a few seconds or just until mixed, then gradually add them to the butter mixture, beating all the time. Pour in the milk and beat until mixed. Sift in the flour, cocoa powder, baking powder and salt and mix gently to combine.

Divide the mixture between the muffin cases, filling each case two-thirds full. Bake for 20–25 minutes or until well risen and lightly springy to the touch. Allow to cool for 5 minutes, then remove from the tray and place on a wire rack to finish cooling down.

While the cupcakes are cooling, you could select one of the options on pages 260–63 for topping them, depending on what feels right for the occasion.

Cupcakes continued overleaf

Chocolate meringue frosting

Prep time: **7 minutes**
Makes: **enough to cover 12 cupcakes**

4 large egg whites
250g (9oz) caster sugar
Pinch of salt
25g (1oz) cocoa powder

Piping bag with a 4 or 5mm (¼in) plain or
   star-shaped nozzle or a freezer bag with 4 or 5mm
   (¼in) cut from one corner (optional)

Make sure the cupcakes are ready before you
start, as this icing begins to set very quickly. Place
all the ingredients, except the cocoa powder, in a
heatproof bowl, add 2 tablespoons of cold water
and set over a saucepan of simmering water.
(The bowl should sit snugly over the pan with its
base high enough above the water that it does not
come into contact with it.)

Whisk slowly, using a balloon whisk, until the sugar
has completely dissolved and the mixture

is foamy. Continue to heat and whisk until the mixture
reaches 60°C (140°F) when measured with a
sugar thermometer – this will take about 4 minutes.
If you don't have a thermometer, you can gauge
whether the mixture is ready by how it feels and
looks: it should be hot to the touch, glossy white in
appearance and starting to thicken.

Quickly remove the bowl from the pan and pour the
mixture into the bowl of an electric food mixer fitted
with the whisk attachment. Alternatively, whisk in
the original bowl using a hand-held electric beater.
Whisk on a high speed for about 3–5 minutes or
until the frosting is very thick, glossy and has cooled.
Sift in the cocoa powder and continue to whisk just
until mixed.

Spread quickly over the cupcakes with a palette
knife and use the back of a teaspoon to shape them,
regularly dipping the spoon into a jug of boiling-hot
water. Alternatively, the icing could be quickly placed
in the piping bag or freezer bag and piped over the
cupcakes (see Cake essentials on page 339).

Chocolate honeycomb topping

Prep time: 10 minutes
Makes: enough to cover 12 cupcakes

150g (5oz) butter, softened
2 tbsp double or regular cream
2 tsp vanilla extract
350g (12oz) icing sugar
2 tbsp cocoa powder
About 12 tbsp honeycomb pieces
(see page 345), to decorate

Piping bag with a 4 or 5mm (¼in) plain or
    star-shaped nozzle or a freezer bag with 4 or 5mm
    (¼in) cut from one corner (optional)

Using a hand-held electric beater or an electric food mixer, beat together the butter, cream and vanilla extract until very soft. Then gradually sift in the icing sugar and the cocoa powder, beating all the time, until fully incorporated. Continue to beat until very soft, then (if using a food mixer) whisk the mixture until it is light and fluffy.

Pipe (see Cake essentials on page 339) or spread the icing (using a palette knife or the back of a spoon) onto the cooled cupcakes. Then sprinkle over the honeycomb pieces (see Decorating ideas on page 345), allowing about a tablespoon per cupcake. I like to try and include a mixture of small and large chunks.

Cupcakes continued overleaf

Peanut butter topping

Prep time: **15 minutes**
Makes: **enough to cover 12 cupcakes**

125g (4½oz) smooth or crunchy peanut butter
100g (3½oz) butter, softened
125g (4½oz) cream cheese
1 tsp vanilla extract
375g (13oz) icing sugar
1–2 tbsp milk
125g (4½oz) salted peanuts, roughly chopped, to decorate

Piping bag with a 4 or 5mm (¼in) plain or
star-shaped nozzle or a freezer bag with 4 or 5mm
(¼in) cut from one corner (optional)

Place the peanut butter, butter, cream cheese and vanilla extract in a large bowl or in an electric food mixer and cream together until well mixed. Sift in the icing sugar a little at a time and beat in to combine, then add the milk and mix in well. If you're using a food mixer, you could continue to beat for a few minutes until the mixture is very fluffy.

When the cupcakes are cool, either pipe the icing onto them (see Cake essentials on page 339) or spread it using a palette knife or the back of a teaspoon. Sprinkle a few chopped peanuts over each cupcake.

Easter nests

Prep time: **20 minutes**
Makes: **enough for 12 cupcakes**

For the icing
100g (3½oz) butter, softened
225g (8oz) icing sugar, sifted
25ml (1fl oz) milk
1 tsp vanilla extract
A few drops of green food colouring (optional)

For the nests
100g (3½oz) dark or milk chocolate, in drops
  or broken into pieces
4 Shredded Wheat
36 sugar-coated mini chocolate eggs

To make the nests, first line a baking tray with baking parchment. Then place the chocolate in a heatproof bowl over a pan of simmering water. Leave just until melted, stirring occasionally, then remove from the heat.

Crumble the Shredded Wheat and add these to the melted chocolate, mixing in until well coated. Working quickly, add about 2 teaspoons of the mixture to form a small mound on the baking parchment. Use your fingers to press down the centre to form a rough nest shape, then add 3 mini eggs, pressing them down into the nest. Repeat with the rest of the mixture and eggs until you have 12 nests, then leave on the tray to cool and set.

Meanwhile, make the icing. Place the butter and sugar in a large bowl or in an electric food mixer and cream together until fluffy and light. Gradually add the milk with the vanilla extract and food colouring (if using) and continue beating the mixture until smooth. When the cupcakes are cool, ice them using a palette knife or the back of a teaspoon. Place a nest on top of each cake, pressing carefully but firmly into the icing.

Rose-water pistachio cupcakes

Rose water makes a fantastic addition to cakes. Its fragrance is quite intense so you don't need to use too much to get a really lovely effect. Pistachios complement the flavour really well, while the green colour of the nuts looks gorgeous against the pale icing covering the cupcakes in this recipe. I've used a simple rose-water icing here, but you could spread the cakes with the pistachio and rose-water buttercream icing (see page 266) if you prefer. Decorated with crystallised pink rose petals (see Decorating ideas on page 344), these look truly pretty and celebratory. The cakes can be made a day ahead and would be fabulous at a wedding as an alternative to one large cake.

Prep time: **15 minutes**
Baking time: **20–25 minutes**
Ready in: **1 hour**
Makes: **12 cupcakes**

150g (5oz) butter, softened
150g (5oz) caster sugar
2 eggs
1 tbsp rose water
200ml (7fl oz) buttermilk
225g (8oz) self-raising flour
25g (1oz) unsalted shelled pistachios, chopped, to decorate
Crystallised rose petals (see page 344), to decorate

For the icing
250g (9oz) icing sugar, sifted
1 tbsp rose water

12-cup muffin tray and 12 muffin cases (see page 336)

Preheat the oven to 180°C (350°F), Gas mark 4, and line the muffin tray with the paper cases.

Cream the butter until soft in a large bowl or in an electric food mixer. Add the sugar and beat until the mixture is light and fluffy.

Whisk the eggs together with the rose water in a small bowl for a few seconds or just until mixed, then gradually add this to the creamed butter mixture, beating all the time. Next beat in the buttermilk, then sift in the flour and fold in gently to combine.

Divide the mixture between the muffin cases, filling each three-quarters full, then bake for 20–25 minutes or until golden on top and lightly springy to the touch. Allow to cool for 5 minutes before removing from the muffin tin and placing on a wire rack to cool down completely.

Meanwhile make the icing. Mix together the icing sugar and rose water with 1 tablespoon of water until you have a thick icing, adding a tiny extra splash of rose water or water if it seems too thick to spread. Spread the icing using the back of a teaspoon or with a palette knife dipped into hot water – or drizzle over the icing – and sprinkle with the chopped pistachios. Alternatively, you could ice the cakes with the pistachio and rose-water buttercream icing (see page 266).

Transfer to a serving plate and scatter with crystallised rose petals (see Decorating ideas on page 344), if using, to finish.

Recipe continued overleaf

Pistachio and rose-water buttercream icing

Prep time: **10 minutes**

Makes: **enough to cover 12 cupcakes**

50g (2oz) unsalted shelled pistachios

250g (9oz) icing sugar, sifted

125g (4½oz) butter, softened

1 tbsp rose water

Place the pistachios in a food processor and whiz for a good few minutes to form a fine powder, then add the icing sugar and pulse just to mix.

Cream the butter until soft in a large bowl or in an electric food mixer. Add the pistachio and sugar mixture a little at a time until combined, then add the rose water and continue to beat until the mixture is light and fluffy.

Orange and almond syrup cake

Dense, moist and richly orange-flavoured, this is an impressive cake even before it's covered in the chocolate icing. You can omit the icing if you like – the cake is delicious without it – but I love the extra intensity that the dark chocolate brings, especially if it's flavoured with a little orange liqueur. Adding crystallised orange peel (see Decorating ideas on page 344) would give a beautiful and really impressive finish to this cake, making it perfect for a proper celebration.

Prep time: **25 minutes**
Baking time: **45–50 minutes**
Ready in: **2 hours**
Serves: **6–8**

200g (7oz) butter, softened,
    plus extra for greasing
300g (11oz) caster sugar
Finely grated zest of 2 oranges
200g (7oz) ground almonds
4 eggs, beaten
100g (3½oz) plain flour, sifted
1 tsp baking powder
Pinch of salt
Crystallised orange peel (see page 344),
    to decorate

For the syrup
Juice of 2 oranges
100g (3½oz) caster sugar

For the icing
75g (3oz) butter, softened
100g (3½oz) dark chocolate,
    in drops or broken into pieces
1 tbsp orange liqueur or orange juice

20cm (8in) diameter cake tin with 6cm
    (2½in) sides (see page 334)

Preheat the oven to 160°C (325°F), Gas mark 3, then butter the sides of the cake tin and line the base with a disc of baking parchment.

Place the butter, sugar and orange zest in a large bowl and beat together until soft and creamy. Add half the ground almonds and continue to mix, then add the eggs, a little at a time, making sure they're well mixed in. Sift in the flour, baking powder and salt and add the rest of the almonds, folding these in until combined.

Tip the cake batter into the prepared tin, spreading it out and levelling the top with a spatula or palette knife. Bake for 45–50 minutes or until a skewer inserted into the centre comes out with just a small amount of moisture sticking to it.

While the cake is cooking, make the syrup. Place the orange juice and sugar in a saucepan. Stir until mixed and bring to the boil. Allow to boil for just 1 minute, then remove from the heat and set aside.

When the cake is cooked, take it out of the oven and let it sit in the tin for just 5 minutes. Loosening around the edges using a small, sharp knife, carefully remove the cake from the tin and transfer to a serving plate (see page 334).

Straight away pour the hot syrup over the cake (reheating the syrup if it has had a chance to cool down) and leave to cool completely while soaking up the syrup.

To make the icing, place the butter in a heatproof bowl with the chocolate and orange liqueur or orange juice and set over a saucepan of simmering water. Leave just until melted, stirring occasionally, then pour the icing over the cake. (This is a wet icing so don't worry if it drips down the sides of the cake.)

Let the icing set and then decorate with pieces of crystallised orange peel (see Decorating ideas on page 344), if you wish.

Pistachio cake

Pistachios and oranges are both redolent of sunnier climes, where pistachios arrive at the market in giant sacks, not tiny plastic packets, and oranges are sold by the boxload. This recipe combines both those flavours, as the sponge is made using ground pistachios and orange zest and the finished cake is drenched in a tangy orange glaze.

Prep time: 15 minutes
Baking time: 30–40 minutes
Ready in: 1 hour 30 minutes
Serves: 6–10

150g (5oz) unsalted shelled pistachios
225g (8oz) plain flour
2 tsp baking powder
100g (3½oz) butter, softened, plus extra for greasing
225g (8oz) caster sugar
4 eggs
100ml (3½fl oz) milk
Finely grated zest of 2 oranges
Double or regular cream, whipped, or Greek yoghurt, to serve

For the glaze
Juice of 1 orange
100g (3½oz) soft light brown sugar

23cm (9in) diameter cake tin (see page 334)

Preheat the oven to 180°C (350°F), Gas mark 4, then butter the sides of the cake tin and line the base with a disc of baking parchment.

Place 100g (3½oz) of the pistachios in a food processor and pulse a good few times until coarsely ground. Tip into a large bowl and sift in the flour and the baking powder, mixing together to combine.

Cream the butter until soft in a separate bowl or in an electric food mixer. Add the sugar and beat until the mixture is light and fluffy.

Whisk the eggs together in a small bowl for a few seconds or just until mixed, then gradually add these to the creamed butter mixture, beating all the time. Next beat in the milk and orange zest, then tip in the ground pistachios and flour and fold gently to combine.

Tip the mixture into the prepared tin and smooth the surface with a spatula. Bake for 30–40 minutes or until a skewer inserted into the centre of the cake comes out clean.

While the cake is in the oven, make the glaze. Place the orange juice and sugar in a saucepan and set over a medium heat. Stir until the sugar is dissolved, then bring to the boil and immediately remove from the heat.

When the cake is cooked, take it out of the oven and let it sit in the tin for just 5 minutes. Loosening around the edges using a small, sharp knife, carefully remove the cake from the tin and transfer to a serving plate (see page 334).

Straight away pour the hot glaze over the cake (reheating it if it has had a chance to cool down), chop the remaining pistachios and scatter over the cake to decorate, then allow to cool completely while soaking up the glaze.

Serve with a spoonful of softly whipped cream or natural Greek yoghurt.

Hazelnut praline triple-layered cake

A triple-layered praline cake makes a fabulous birthday treat. The three layers of sponge are lightened with a good amount of whisked egg whites. For the filling, praline crumbs are mixed into a divinely rich custard cream. The cake is topped in a thick, snowy-white American frosting, crisp on the outside and fluffy and marshmallow-like beneath. As it's covered in icing, the cake will keep for 3–4 days in an airtight container. If you don't have an airtight box big enough, you can use a large mixing bowl upturned over the cake.

Prep time: **1 hour 30 minutes**
Baking time: **30 minutes**
Ready in: **3 hours**
Serves: **14–18**

375g (13oz) plain flour
4 tsp baking powder
1 tsp salt
225g (8oz) butter, softened,
    plus extra for greasing
675g (1½lb) caster sugar
325ml (11½fl oz) milk
2 tsp vanilla extract
9 egg whites (about 250ml/9fl oz)

For the praline
100g (3½oz) caster sugar
100g (3½oz) hazelnuts (skin still on)

Ingredients cont. overleaf

Preheat the oven to 180°C (350°F), Gas mark 4, then butter the sides of the cake tins and line the bases with a disc of baking parchment.

First make the sponge. Sift the flour, baking powder and salt into a bowl. Cream the butter until soft in a large bowl or in an electric food mixer. Add 450g (1lb) of the sugar and beat until the mixture is light and fluffy. Add about a third of the sifted flour along with about a third of the milk and continue to mix gently, in thirds, until all of the flour and milk is well mixed in, then stir in the vanilla extract.

In the bowl of an electric mixer, whisk together the egg whites until foamy, then add the remaining sugar and whisk until the meringue holds stiff glossy peaks. Mix in a quarter of the meringue to the cake mixture, then carefully fold in the rest until fully incorporated.

Tip the mixture into the prepared cake tins and bake for 30 minutes or until a skewer inserted into the centre of each cake comes out clean. Remove from the oven and allow to cool for 10 minutes, then loosen the sides of each tin with a small, sharp knife and carefully remove the cakes from the tins before placing on a wire rack to cool completely (see page 334). (The sponge can be made up to a day in advance and kept in an airtight container.)

To make the praline, first line a baking tray with baking parchment and set aside. Place the sugar in a frying pan and scatter the hazelnuts over the sugar. Place the pan over a medium heat to allow the sugar to caramelise, swirling the pan every so often to ensure it caramelises evenly. Cook until the sugar has completely melted and is a deep golden colour and the hazelnuts are coated evenly.

Transfer the coated nuts to the prepared baking tray. Before the caramel has a chance to harden, set apart about 10 hazelnut clusters (with 4–5 hazelnuts in each cluster) for decorating (see photograph). Using two forks, spread apart

Recipe continued overleaf

For the custard cream
25g (1oz) caster sugar
3 egg yolks
175ml (6fl oz) milk
15g (½oz) cornflour
1 tsp vanilla extract
100ml (3½fl oz) double or
    regular cream

For the frosting
4 large egg whites
250g (9oz) caster sugar
Pinch of salt

Three 20cm (8in) diameter cake tins
    (see page 334)

the remaining hazelnuts and leave the praline to cool completely. Once cool break up the praline using your hands, then place the pieces (but not the reserved clusters) in a food processor and whiz until it resembles slightly coarse breadcrumbs.

To make the custard cream, place the sugar in a saucepan with the egg yolks, milk, cornflour and vanilla extract and whisking all the time bring just to the boil, then reduce the heat to low. Then cook, continuing to whisk, until thickened. Immediately remove from the heat before transferring to a bowl to cool completely. In a separate bowl, whip the cream just until it holds stiff peaks. Add the praline to the cooled custard and mix in, then carefully fold in the whipped cream. Cover the praline custard cream and place in the fridge until you are ready to use it.

You can now assemble the cake. Place one of the cakes on a cake stand or plate. Spread with half of the praline custard, then cover with a second cake. Spread the other half of the custard cream over the cake, then top with the third cake. Use a pastry brush to brush off any excess crumbs from the cake.

Next make the frosting. First place a palette knife in a jug or bowl and put the kettle on. It makes it really easy to frost this cake if you can use a palette knife that has been dipped in hot water. Place all the frosting ingredients in a heatproof bowl, add 2 tablespoons of cold water and set over a saucepan of simmering water. (The bowl should sit snugly over the pan, with its base high enough above the water that it does not come into contact with it.)

Whisk slowly by hand until the sugar has completely dissolved and the mixture is foamy. Continue to heat and whisk until the mixture reaches 60°C (140°F) when measured with a sugar thermometer – this will take about 4 minutes. If you don't have a thermometer, you can gauge whether the mixture is ready by how it feels and looks: it should be hot to the touch, glossy white in appearance and starting to thicken.

Quickly remove the bowl from the pan and pour the mixture into the bowl of an electric food mixer fitted with the whisk attachment. Alternatively, whisk in the original bowl using a hand-held electric beater. Whisk on a high speed for about 3–5 minutes or until the frosting is very thick, glossy and has cooled.

Pour boiling water into the jug or bowl holding the palette knife. Before the frosting has a chance to cool and therefore set, spread it with the hot, wet palette knife over the top and all around the sides of the cake, covering it as evenly as possible. You can go for a smooth appearance or a slightly peaked look by tapping the flat side of the palette knife over the frosting. As you pull it up, it should create little peaks (see Cake essentials on page 339). Do this all over the cake.

Decorate around the top edge of the iced cake with the reserved hazelnut praline clusters.

White chocolate macadamia nut cake

Macadamia nuts hail all the way from Australia. With a higher oil content than almost any other nut, they are perhaps the most decadent, their rich buttery flavour combining wonderfully with the sweet vanilla flavour of white chocolate. Being so rich means that a few macadamias go a long way, which is fortunate as they can be expensive. If you can't find them or would prefer not to use them, walnuts or pecans would do very well instead.

Prep time: **15 minutes**
Baking time: **45–50 minutes**
Ready in: **1 hour 45 minutes**
Serves: **6–8**

200g (7oz) butter, softened,
    plus extra for greasing
200g (7oz) caster sugar
4 eggs
150ml (5fl oz) sour cream
200g (7oz) plain flour, sifted
2 tsp baking powder
100g (3½oz) white chocolate,
    as chips or finely chopped
150g (5oz) macadamia nuts (or walnuts
    or pecans), toasted (see the tip
    on page 41) and roughly chopped

For the icing
150g (5oz) white chocolate, in drops
    or broken into pieces
50ml (2fl oz) sour cream

20cm (8in) diameter cake tin with 6cm
    (2½in) sides (see page 334)

Preheat the oven to 180°C (350°F), Gas mark 4, then butter the sides of the cake tin and line the base with a disc of baking parchment.

Cream the butter until soft in a large bowl or in an electric food mixer until soft. Add the sugar and beat until the mixture is light and fluffy.

Whisk the eggs together in a small bowl for a few seconds or just until mixed, then gradually add them to the butter mixture, beating all the time. Next beat in the sour cream and then fold in the flour, baking powder and chocolate chips, along with 100g (3½oz) of the toasted nuts.

Tip the cake batter into the prepared tin and bake for 45–50 minutes or until a skewer inserted into the centre comes out clean.

Remove from the oven and allow to cool for 10 minutes. Loosening round the edges using a small, sharp knife, carefully remove the cake from the tin and leave on a wire rack to finish cooling before transferring to a serving plate or cake stand (see page 334).

While the cake is cooking, or while it's cooling down, make the icing. Place the chocolate in a heatproof bowl and set over a pan of simmering water. Leave just until melted, then remove from the heat and whisk in the sour cream until smooth.

Drizzle the icing over the cake and sprinkle over the remaining nuts to finish.

Mini wedding fruitcakes

If you'd like an alternative to one large wedding cake, this recipe is worth considering. I love the idea of each guest being given their own mini cake rather than just a slice of a big cake. You could decorate these with roses, bows or something to fit your wedding theme. These mini cakes will keep for a week or two in an airtight container, so you can make them well ahead of time. The recipe can be doubled if you have a large enough bowl or electric food mixer, or alternatively you can make them in as many batches as you need.

Prep time: **1 hour (including the fondant roses)**
Baking time: **40–45 minutes**
Ready in: **2 hours**
Makes: **12 cakes**

125g (4½oz) butter, softened, plus extra for greasing
125g (4½oz) soft dark brown sugar
3 eggs
300g (11oz) mixed fruit
50g (2oz) chopped mixed candied peel
25g (1oz) ground almonds
125g (4½oz) plain flour, plus extra for dusting
1 tsp mixed spice

For the fondant icing
1 egg white, whisked
50g (2oz) liquid glucose
¼ tsp vanilla extract
400g (14oz) icing sugar, sifted, plus extra for dusting

To decorate
250g (9oz) marzipan (to make it yourself, see page 51)
25g (1oz) apricot jam

12-cup muffin tray (see page 336)

Preheat the oven to 150°C (300°F), Gas mark 2, then butter the cups of the muffin tray and dust them with flour.

Cream the butter until soft in a large bowl or in an electric food mixer. Add the sugar and beat until the mixture is light and fluffy.

Whisk the eggs together in a small bowl for a few seconds just until mixed, then gradually add these to the creamed butter mixture, beating all the time. Add the dried fruit and peel and ground almonds and sift in the flour and mixed spice, then fold in to incorporate.

Divide between the 12 muffin cups and bake for 40–45 minutes or until a skewer comes out clean and the cakes feel springy to the touch. Remove from the oven and allow to cool for 5 minutes, then use a small, sharp knife to help release the cakes from the tray and place on a wire rack to cool down fully while you make the fondant icing.

In a bowl, mix together the egg white, glucose and vanilla extract. Place the icing sugar in a separate bowl or an electric food mixer and gradually add the egg white mixture, beating continuously until all the ingredients come together. Place the icing on a spotlessly clean worktop that has been generously dusted with icing sugar and knead for a minute or two until it is completely smooth on the surface, then cover with an upturned bowl or cling film and set aside.

Recipe continued overleaf

Roll out the marzipan to 5mm (¼ in) thick and cut out 12 circles, each 6cm (2½ in) in diameter. Then do the same with 250g (9oz) of the fondant icing. Brush the top of each cooled cake with apricot jam, place a circle of marzipan on top of each, then brush the top of that with apricot jam. Add a circle of icing on top of each.

Use the remaining fondant icing to make fondant roses (see Children's decorating ideas on page 243) for the top of each cake.

Use a small amount of apricot jam to stick the roses to the centre of the cakes, then repeat for each cake.

Variation

If you like, you could use coloured fondant icing for decorating the cakes (adding a few drops of food colouring to the egg white and glucose mixture before combining with the icing sugar), rolling it out and cutting out shapes using a shaped cutter or even with a template cut out of paper. You can make whatever you like to fit with your theme – bows, shoes or hearts, for example.

Vanilla wedding cake

The grand effect of this cake belies its relative simplicity to make. When it's cut into slices, guests may be pleasantly surprised to discover that each beautifully iced tier contains not a heavy fruitcake but a soft, moist sponge. The two things this recipe needs are time and equipment – a number of different tins (listed on page 283). It's well worth the effort, though – a beautiful centrepiece to that special day and a delicious cake that everyone will adore. Unless your oven is very large (or you have a double oven) and your mixing bowl is more than about 35cm (14in) in diameter, you will need to make the sponge for the cake in two batches. The instructions given below are based upon making the cake in this way.

Prep time: **40 minutes**
Baking time: **1 hour 30 minutes**
Ready in: **3 hours**
Serves: **32–40**

800g (1¾lb) butter, softened, plus extra for greasing
800g (1¾lb) caster sugar
800g (1¾lb) plain flour
8 tsp baking powder
16 eggs, beaten

For the icing
1kg (2lb 3oz) caster sugar
20 egg yolks
1kg (2lb 3oz) butter, softened
1 tbsp vanilla extract

Ingredients cont. overleaf

Preheat the oven to 180°C (350°F), Gas mark 4, then butter the sides and line the base of each cake tin with baking parchment.

Cream half the butter until soft in a large bowl or in an electric food mixer. Add half the sugar and beat until the mixture is light and fluffy. Meanwhile sift together half the flour with 4 teaspoons of the baking powder.

Crack eight of the eggs into a separate bowl and whisk together just until mixed, then gradually add them to the creamed butter mixture, beating all the time. Add the sifted flour and baking powder, folding in to combine. Tip the batter into the 30cm (12in) cake tin and bake for 50 minutes or until a skewer inserted into the centre comes out clean.

As the large cake bakes, repeat the last two steps above for the remaining ingredients and divide between the prepared tins, filling each to a depth of 2–3cm (¾–1¼in). Wait until the large cake has finished cooking and you've removed it from the oven before you mix the flour and baking powder into the wet ingredients to complete the second batch of batter.

Bake the cakes for 25–35 minutes or until well risen and golden and a skewer inserted into the centre of each cake comes out clean. They will all probably be ready at different times, so you'll need to keep a close eye on them. When each cake is ready, remove it from the oven and allow to cool in the tin for 10 minutes, then loosen around the edges using a small, sharp knife and carefully remove from the tin before transferring to a wire rack to cool down completely (see page 334).

Recipe continued overleaf

Fresh flowers, such as rosebuds, lilies
    or lavender; edible flowers, such as
    primroses, violets, lavender, borage
    flowers, mint leaves, lemon verbena
    leaves or sweet cicely; crystallised
    flowers or petals (see page 344)

Four round cake tins: one 30cm (12in)
    in diameter; one 25cm (10in) diameter;
    one 18cm (7in) in diameter; one 12cm
    (5in) in diameter (see page 334)
Large plate or 40cm (16in) square
    cake board

To make the buttercream icing, first make a sugar syrup. Place the sugar in a saucepan with 400ml (14fl oz) of water and set over a medium heat, stirring very regularly to dissolve the sugar. Once the sugar is dissolved, turn up the heat and bring to the boil. Continue to boil for 8–12 minutes or until a sugar thermometer reads 110°–115°C (230°–235°F), then remove from the heat. If you don't have a thermometer, this is the 'thread stage'. The mixture will be thick and syrupy and the last couple of drops that fall from a spoon will form a thread.

While the syrup is boiling, whisk together the egg yolks for 2–3 minutes in the cleaned bowl of the food mixer until pale and fluffy, then turn the speed to slow and add the hot syrup in a steady stream. Once the syrup has been incorporated, turn the speed back to high and continue to whisk until the mixture has cooled down. This will take about 15 minutes: you may want to cover the food mixer with a tea towel to avoid too much mess, as the contents of the bowl may splash during mixing. Continue whisking until the mixture is stiff and mousse-like. To test if it's thick enough, pull the whisk out of the mixture and draw a figure of 8 into the bowl with the mixture that's left on the whisk; the '8' should remain visible for a couple of seconds.

In a separate bowl (you may want to use the food mixer for this too, having first decanted the mousse mixture from the bowl), beat the butter until very soft. Then add the vanilla extract and the mousse mixture, adding a large spoonful of this at a time, and keep mixing until fully combined.

To assemble the cake, first slice each cake horizontally in half with a bread knife. Place one half of the 30cm (12in) cake on the cake plate or board, securing it to the plate or board with a few blobs of icing. Spread the top with a layer of icing about 3mm (⅛in) thick, then sandwich with the second half. Spread the top with more icing, then add one half of the 25cm (10in) cake. Continue with the rest of the layers, from the largest to the smallest, until you have a tiered cake, then carefully spread the rest of the icing all over the cake using a palette knife. To ensure that each 'step' of the cake looks well defined, it's best have a jug or bowl of boiling-hot water to hand in which to dip your palette knife before using it to smooth over the surface of the icing.

Decorate the finished cake with fresh or crystallised flowers or petals (see Decorating ideas on page 344). (Photographs on page 285.)

Recipe continued overleaf

Lemon or orange wedding cake

Add the finely grated zest of four lemons or oranges and 50ml (2fl oz) of lemon or orange juice to the cake with the eggs and bake and assemble as in the main recipe on pages 280–83. Replace the 1 tablespoon of vanilla extract in the icing with 2 tablespoons of lemon or orange juice and decorate the iced cake with either Candied or Crisp lemon or orange slices (see Decorating ideas on pages 340 and 341).

Coffee wedding cake

Add 100ml (3½fl oz) coffee essence (ideally Camp or Irel) to the cake mixture along with the eggs, then cook and assemble the cake as on pages 280–83. To the icing, add 2 tablespoons of coffee essence to replace the vanilla extract. When the cake is iced, carefully place about 225g (8oz) toasted skinned hazelnuts (see page 125 for how to toast them) in a band at the base of each tier. In the centre of the top tier you could add a large flower or perhaps miniature models of a bride and groom.

Tip The cake can be made up to three days in advance if kept covered. Probably, you won't have an airtight box big enough to store this cake. In which case, the best thing to do is to keep the cake on a surface and cover it with a large upturned mixing bowl or a large plastic storage box upturned. If you don't have a box or bowl big enough, place wine bottles around the cake (making sure the bottles are taller than the cake), and drape cling film, tin foil or even a table cloth over the cake to cover it.

White chocolate anniversary cake

The elegance of this cake makes it ideal for an anniversary celebration. If it's a silver or diamond anniversary, you could decorate the cake with edible silver or diamonds! The cake itself consists of two delicate layers of sponge encased in a luscious white chocolate ganache. The glucose syrup is essential to the ganache, transforming the chocolate and cream into a thick buttery icing that won't set hard.

Prep time: **45 minutes**
Baking time: **25 minutes**
Ready in: **3 hours 30 minutes**
Serves: **8–10**

Butter, softened, for greasing
4 eggs
125g (4½oz) caster sugar
125g (4½oz) plain flour, sifted, plus
    extra for dusting
1½ tsp baking powder
50g (2oz) white chocolate, as chips
    or chopped into pieces
Chocolate curls (see page 342),
    made using either dark, milk or white
    chocolate or a mixture, to decorate

For the ganache
300ml (11fl oz) double or
    regular cream
45g (1½oz) glucose syrup
400g (14oz) white chocolate,
    in drops or broken into pieces
75g (3oz) butter, softened and cut
    into 2cm (¾in) cubes

Two 18cm (7in) diameter cake tins
    (see page 334)

First make the ganache. Place the cream and glucose syrup in a large saucepan and bring to the boil, stirring occasionally, then immediately remove from the heat and stir in the chocolate. Stir to melt the chocolate – you may need to place it back over a low heat, just so all the chocolate is melted. Remove from the heat and allow to cool until tepid.

Add the butter to the melted chocolate, a few cubes at a time, beating the mixture until all the butter has been incorporated. Leave in the fridge for about 2 hours, stirring a couple of times as it cools. It should stiffen but still be spreadable. Make sure to take the ganache out of the fridge at least 30 minutes before icing the cake. It may be necessary to beat the mixture with a wooden spoon to make it spread more easily.

While the ganache is cooling, you can make the cakes. Preheat the oven to 180°C (350°F), Gas mark 4. Butter the sides of the cake tins and dust with flour, then line each base with a disc of baking parchment.

Using a hand-held electric beater or an electric food mixer, whisk the eggs and sugar together on a high speed for several minutes or until light and mousse-like.

In a separate bowl, mix together the flour, baking powder and chocolate pieces, then fold into the egg and sugar mixture. Divide the batter between the prepared tins and bake for about 25 minutes or until golden on top and lightly springy to the touch.

Recipe continued overleaf

Remove from the oven and allow to cool in the tins for 10 minutes, then loosen around the edges using a small, sharp knife and carefully remove each cake before transferring to a wire rack to cool down fully (see page 334).

When the cakes are cool, place one upside down on a cake plate or stand, then spread over some of the ganache to about 4–5mm (¼in) thick. Place the second cake on top the right way up and use the rest of the ganache to cover the cake completely. Using a palette knife or the back of a spoon, lightly flick the ganache to make peaks all over the cake. If you prefer, you can simply smooth the cake with a palette knife, dipping it from time to time into a jug or bowl of boiling-hot water.

Now you can decorate your cake, selecting one of the options below, if you like. You could otherwise leave the cake undecorated, or scatter with chocolate curls (see Decorating ideas on page 342), either in white or contrasting milk or dark chocolate.

Chocolate anniversary cake

Make the cake as above, using milk or dark chocolate instead of white chocolate in both the ganache and sponge. You could then sprinkle over dark chocolate curls (see Decorating ideas on page 342).

Silver/golden wedding anniversary

Use edible silver or gold glitter to scatter over the cake, or make patterns or spell out words using edible silver or gold balls. Another option is to cut out paper stencils for the first initial of each person in the couple. Place the stencils on the cake and sprinkle the glitter on and around them, then carefully lift the paper off the surface of the cake to reveal the two letters marked out in the ganache.

Ruby wedding anniversary

Scatter with crystallised rose petals (see Decorating ideas on page 344), or arrange hulled strawberry halves in a ring around the top of the cake and use red coloured sugar (see Letter or number cake on page 233) for dusting over stencils of the couple's initials.

Diamond wedding anniversary

Use edible diamonds (available from specialist food shops or online) to spell out the initials of the couple or, if you prefer, arrange them in a sparkling 'necklace' around the base of the cake.

Red velvet cupcakes

These red velvet cupcakes are perfect for Valentine's Day. Red velvet is a classic American cake that has become popular on this side of the Atlantic in recent years. The red tint was originally obtained by mixing cocoa powder with an acidic ingredient such as buttermilk or vinegar. It's worth giving it a helping hand with some red food colouring to make the red even more vivid. The velvet refers to the delicate and light crumb, which comes from folding in whisked egg whites. When decorated with the brilliant white American frosting, the striking colour contrast should make them irresistible to your Valentine.

Prep time: 15 minutes
Baking time: 15–20 minutes
Ready in: 1 hour
Makes: 12 cupcakes

100g (3½oz) butter, softened
200g (7oz) caster sugar
1 tsp vanilla extract
2 eggs, separated
175ml (6fl oz) buttermilk
½ tsp red food colouring
175g (6oz) plain flour
25g (1oz) cornflour
¾ tsp baking powder
1 tbsp cocoa powder
Pinch of salt
1 tsp white vinegar
1 tsp bicarbonate of soda, sifted

For the frosting
4 large egg whites
250g (9oz) caster sugar
Pinch of salt

Ingredients cont. overleaf

Preheat the oven to 180°C (350°F), Gas mark 4 and line the muffin tray with the paper cases.

Cream the butter until soft in a large bowl or in an electric food mixer. Add the sugar and beat until the mixture is pale and fluffy, then add the vanilla extract and the egg yolks, and beat again.

Mix the buttermilk together with the food colouring – it should be very red, so add more if you need to. Sift the flour, cornflour, baking powder and cocoa powder into the butter and egg mixture and add the red buttermilk. Fold everything together gently but thoroughly.

Whisk the egg whites and salt in a large, spotlessly clean bowl until stiff peaks form. Add one-quarter to the batter and mix in. Add the remaining egg whites in two stages, folding them in gently with a spatula until just incorporated and retaining as much air in the mixture as possible.

In a small bowl, mix together the vinegar and bicarbonate of soda until the mixture bubbles up, then gently fold this into the batter. Quickly divide between the muffin cases, filling each case two-thirds full, then bake in the oven for 15–20 minutes or until the cupcakes are well risen and springy to the touch.

Leave in the tin for 5 minutes, then remove the cupcakes and place on a wire rack to cool down while you make the frosting.

Make sure the cupcakes are ready before you start, as this icing begins to set very quickly.

Recipe continued overleaf

Crystallised rose petals made using pink
or red roses(see page 344), or red
coloured sugar (see page 277)

12-cup muffin tray and 12 muffin cases
(see page 336)
Piping bag with a 4 or 5mm (¼in)
plain or star-shaped nozzle or a
freezer bag with 4 or 5mm (¼in)
cut from one corner (optional)

Place all the frosting ingredients in a heatproof bowl, add 2
tablespoons of cold water and set over a saucepan of simmering water.
(The bowl should sit snugly over the pan with its base high enough
above the water that it does not come into contact with it.)

Whisk slowly, using a balloon whisk, until the sugar has completely
dissolved and the mixture is foamy. Continue to heat and whisk until
the mixture reaches 60°C (140°F) when measured with a sugar
thermometer – this will take about 4 minutes. If you don't have a
thermometer, you can gauge whether the mixture is ready by how
it feels and looks: it should be hot to the touch, glossy white in
appearance and starting to thicken.

Quickly remove the bowl from the pan and pour the mixture into
the bowl of an electric food mixer fitted with the whisk attachment.
Alternatively, whisk in the original bowl using a hand-held electric
beater. Whisk on a high speed for about 3–5 minutes or until the
frosting is very thick, glossy and has cooled.

Use immediately to spread quickly over the cupcakes with a palette
knife and use the back of a teaspoon to shape them, regularly dipping
the spoon into a bowl of boiling-hot water. Or the icing could be
quickly placed in the piping bag or freezer bag, if you prefer, and piped
over the cupcakes (see Cake essentials on page 339). The icing sets
very quickly at this stage, so speed is essential.

Once the icing has set, you can then decorate with the crystallised rose
petals, using either one large petal or three small petals per cake, or sift
a little red sugar over each cake.

Cream-cheese frosting

For a much easier and much faster icing, beat together 300g (11oz)
of cream cheese and 300g (11oz) of icing sugar until smooth and then
pipe or spoon this onto the cupcakes, using the back of a teaspoon to
shape the icing on each cake.

Perfect Peanut butter cake

Peanut butter is simply sublime in cakes and puddings. A jar of it can always be found in our house, as the whole family adores its creamy, crunchy goodness. This cake uses dulce de leche (a type of caramel – see the note on page 168) and chocolate for a three-pronged attack of deliciousness! I make this cake for my children but can never resist cutting myself the biggest slice.

Prep time: 15 minutes
Baking time: 30 minutes
Ready in: 1 hour
Serves: 8–12

200g (7oz) butter, softened, plus extra for greasing

75g (3oz) crunchy or smooth peanut butter

200g (7oz) caster sugar

4 eggs

200g (7oz) plain flour

2 tsp baking powder

For the filling and icing

100g (3½oz) milk chocolate, in drops or broken into pieces

3 tbsp double or regular cream

50g (2oz) crunchy or smooth peanut butter

100g (3½oz) dulce de leche

To decorate

50g (2oz) salted peanuts, roughly chopped

1 tbsp icing sugar, for dusting

Two 20cm (8in) diameter cake tins (see page 334)

Preheat the oven to 180°C (350°F), Gas mark 4, then butter the sides of the cake tins and line with a disc of baking parchment.

Cream together the butter and the peanut butter until soft in a large bowl or in an electric food mixer. Add the sugar and beat until the mixture is light and fluffy.

Whisk the eggs together in a small bowl for a few seconds or just until mixed, then gradually add them to the butter mixture, beating all the time. Sift in the flour and baking powder and fold in gently.

Divide the mixture between the prepared tins and bake in the oven for about 30 minutes until golden on top and a skewer inserted into the centre comes out clean. Remove from the oven and allow to cool in the tins for 5 minutes, then loosen around the edges using a small, sharp knife and carefully remove each cake from its tin (see page 334) and leave on a wire rack to cool down completely.

To make the icing, place the chocolate in a heatproof bowl and set over a saucepan of simmering water. Leave just until melted, stirring occasionally, then remove from the heat and beat in the cream, peanut butter and dulce de leche.

Place one cake upside down on a cake plate or stand, then spread over half the icing. Sandwich the second cake on top, sitting the right way up, and spread the rest of the icing over the top.

To decorate the iced cake, scatter over the peanuts and dust with icing sugar. Alternatively, you could scatter over peanut brittle or a handful of chocolate-covered peanuts (see Decorating ideas on page 340).

Across the world cake plays a fundamental part in cultural and religious festivities. Food is woven into the fabric of every important festival and cake will almost always make an appearance at some point in the festivities. This chapter includes seasonal classics, such as the festive cakes made to celebrate Christmas, but there are also less familiar recipes from other countries, such as Vínarterta from Iceland and Italy's panforte, both of which are traditionally made in the winter. I have also included some of my own recipes for marking other festivals such as Halloween and Bonfire Night. There is a great range of divine recipes here, from spicy and fruity to delicate and light, and any of them will make cake the most delicious part of your festivities.

09/ Festive

Halloween pumpkin squares

These pumpkin squares are perfect fare for Halloween. The pumpkin makes the sponge very moist, while the gentle spiciness of the cake is offset by the zesty cream-cheese icing. I like to use black icing to draw spiders and webs on the squares, but they taste just as good unadorned, of course – in which case you could make and eat them at any time of the year!

Prep time: **30 minutes** (excluding cooking the pumpkin)
Baking time: **1 hour**
Ready in: **2 hours**
Makes: **20 squares**

450g (1lb) peeled butternut squash or pumpkin, chopped into 1cm (½in) cubes, or 1 x 425g tin of good-quality cooked pumpkin (such as Libby's)
200g (7oz) butter, softened
300g (11oz) soft brown sugar
4 eggs
300g (11oz) self-raising flour
2 tsp bicarbonate of soda
1 tsp ground cinnamon
½ tsp ground nutmeg
1 tsp ground ginger
1 tsp salt
150g (5oz) sultanas
Juice and finely grated zest of 1 orange

Ingredients cont. overleaf

To cook the fresh butternut squash or pumpkin, if using, place in a saucepan and add 500ml (18fl oz) of water. Bring to the boil and then reduce the heat and simmer, uncovered, for 20–25 minutes or until completely tender. Drain the water and leave to cool, then set aside 425g (15oz) of the cooked squash or pumpkin to use in the cake batter.

Preheat the oven to 180°C (350°F), Gas mark 4, then line the sides and base of the tin with baking parchment, with the paper coming just above the sides of the tin to enable the cake to be lifted out easily.

Cream the butter until soft in a large bowl or in an electric food mixer. Add the sugar and beat until the mixture is light and fluffy. Mash the cooked squash or pumpkin with a fork, then add this or the tinned pumpkin to the cake mixture, beating all the time.

Whisk the eggs together in a small bowl for a few seconds or just until mixed, then gradually add these to the mixture, beating all the time. (It may look slightly curdled at this point, but don't worry.) Sift in the flour, bicarbonate of soda, spices and salt, add the remaining ingredients and fold in gently to combine.

Tip the batter into the prepared roasting tin and bake on the lowest shelf in the oven for about 1 hour or until a skewer inserted into the centre of the cake comes out clean. Remove from the oven and leave to cool for 10 minutes in the tin, then lift it out of the tin with the lining paper, peel away the baking parchment and leave on a wire rack to cool down completely.

Recipe continued overleaf

For the cream-cheese icing
400g (14oz) cream cheese
100g (3½oz) butter, softened
200g (7oz) icing sugar, sifted
Juice and finely grated zest of 1 orange

For the black icing
100g (3½oz) icing sugar, sifted
½–1 tbsp orange juice or water
A few drops of black food colouring

20 x 28cm (8 x 11in) roasting tin
Piping bag with a 4 or 5mm (¼in)
    plain or star-shaped nozzle or a
    freezer bag with 4 or 5mm (¼in)
    cut from one corner (optional)

As the cake cools, make the cream-cheese icing, beating together all the ingredients until well mixed and fluffy. When the cake is cool, spread the top with the icing, using a palette knife to smooth the surface. If you like, you can tap the icing all over using the flat side of the palette knife to create little peaks. Once the cake is iced, you can cut it into squares before making the black icing for decorating each cake.

Put the icing sugar and food colouring into a bowl and mix with just enough orange juice or water to make an icing the consistency of thick double cream. Fill the piping bag or freezer bag with the icing and carefully pipe a spider or web onto each of the iced squares (see page 297).

Jack o' lantern cake

Make the cake mixture as in the main recipe on page 296, but bake it in a 25cm (10in) diameter round cake tin instead. Prepare one and a half times the quantity of the cream-cheese icing, adding a few drops of orange food colouring to the mixture, and cover the whole cake using a palette knife dipped in hot water for a smooth finish. Use a knife to mark the ridges of the pumpkin and, with the black icing, pipe on three triangles, two for the eyes and one for the nose, and an evil toothy grin (see photograph on page 297) and fill in the piped shapes with sugar sprinkles.

Barmbrack or Báirín breac

Barmbrack is a traditional Irish sweetened bread not dissimilar to the Welsh bara brith. In Gaelic it's known as báirín breac or 'speckled loaf', due to the way the dough is dotted with raisins or sultanas. When barmbrack was baked for Halloween, the tradition was to add to the cake mixture a pea, a stick, a piece of cloth, a coin and a ring. Each item had a special significance for the person who discovered it in their slice of cake. The person who received the pea wouldn't marry that year; the stick meant an unhappy marriage, the cloth indicated poverty and the coin riches, while the person who found the ring would wed within the year. Nowadays it's usually just a ring that's added to the mixture.

Prep time: 30 minutes
Baking time: 45 minutes
Ready in: 1 hour 45 minutes (if using dried yeast); 2 hours 45 minutes (if using fresh yeast)
Serves: 8

225g (8oz) strong white flour, plus extra for dusting
2 tbsp mixed spice
¼ tsp salt
25g (1oz) butter, plus extra for greasing
1 x 7g (¼oz) sachet fast-action dried yeast (or 14g/½oz fresh yeast – see page 300 for method)
50g (2oz) caster sugar
150ml (5fl oz) milk
1 egg, beaten
200g (7oz) mixed dried fruit (either ready-mixed or your own mixture of sultanas, raisins and currants)
25g (1oz) chopped mixed peel

900g (2lb) loaf tin (see page 334)

First butter the sides and base of the loaf tin.

Sift the flour, spice and salt into a large bowl or into an electric food mixer and add the butter, yeast (if using fresh yeast, see page 300 for the method) and sugar. Beat together either in the bowl or with the food mixer using the dough hook attachment.

Warm the milk just until tepid, then add to the flour mixture along with the egg. Mix until the dough comes together and then knead well – for 8 minutes by hand or for 5 minutes in the food mixer. Add the dried fruit and mixed peel and knead for a further 2 minutes to mix them in.

Tip the dough out onto a floured work surface (the mixture will be quite wet, but don't worry as this is fine) and mould into a rough loaf shape. Place in the prepared loaf tin, then cover with a light tea towel or napkin and leave to rise in a warm part of your kitchen (by a radiator, for instance, or a sunny window) for 1 hour or until doubled in size.

Meanwhile, preheat the oven to 180°C (350°F), Gas mark 4.

Remove the tea towel or napkin and bake for 45 minutes or until deep golden brown on top. When you think the loaf is ready, gently loosen the sides with a palette knife and tip it out of the tin. If it's fully cooked, it should sound slightly hollow when you tap it on the base and feel springy when you lightly squeeze the sides. Place it on a wire rack to cool.

Slice up the loaf and serve fresh – or it is delicious toasted and buttered.

Recipe continued overleaf

Barmbrack made with fresh yeast

Mix 14g (½ oz) of fresh yeast in a bowl with the tepid milk and leave for 2 minutes or until creamy. Mix with the beaten egg, then pour into the dry ingredients and knead as on page 299. Place the dough in a large bowl, cover with cling film and leave in a warm part of your kitchen to rise for 1–2 hours or until doubled in size. It's ready when you press your finger into the dough and it does not spring back (the indentation stays put). Remove the cling film, tip onto a floured work surface and knock back the dough – by punching it in and then kneading all the air out of it – for about 2 minutes. Now form the dough into a loaf shape and pop it into the tin before leaving it to rise as in the main recipe on the previous page.

Bonfire Night cupcakes

These cute little cupcakes with their faux fires make a delicious Bonfire Night treat. And they are somewhat kinder to your teeth than a toffee apple!

Prep time: **25 minutes**
Baking time: **15 minutes**
Ready in: **1 hour**
Makes: **12 cupcakes**

125g (4½oz) butter, softened
125g (4½oz) caster sugar
2 eggs, beaten
125g (4½oz) self-raising flour
1 tbsp cocoa powder

For the icing
75g (3oz) white chocolate, in drops
    or broken into pieces
75g (3oz) butter, softened
100g (3½oz) icing sugar, sifted
4 chocolate Flake bars
A few drops of orange food colouring

12-cup bun tray and 12 bun cases
    (see page 336)
Piping bag with a 2 or 3mm (⅛in)
    nozzle or a freezer bag with 2 or
    3mm (⅛in) cut from one corner

Preheat the oven to 180°C (350°F), Gas mark 4, and line the bun tray with the paper cases.

Cream the butter until soft in a large bowl or in an electric food mixer. Add the sugar and beat until the mixture is light and fluffy. Gradually add the eggs to the butter mixture, beating all the time. Sift in the flour and cocoa powder and fold in to combine.

Divide the mixture between the bun cases, filling each case three-quarters full, and bake for about 15 minutes or until well risen and lightly springy when you gently press one or two of the cakes in the middle. Allow to cool for 5 minutes in the tin, then transfer to a wire rack and allow to cool down completely.

Meanwhile, make the icing. Place the white chocolate in a heatproof bowl and set over a saucepan of simmering water. Leave just until melted, stirring occasionally, then remove from the heat and allow to cool until barely tepid.

Add the butter and icing sugar and beat together until smooth, then spread most of the icing on the cupcakes, reserving 2 tablespoonfuls.

Break the Flake bar into shards (these will be the 'logs') and arrange on the top of each iced cupcake in the shape (roughly!) of a bonfire.

Add a few drops of orange food colouring to the remaining icing, then place in the piping bag or freezer bag and pipe small blobs of orange icing (see page 339) on top of the chocolate logs for flames.

Maple pecan cake

Thanksgiving is a festival about food and this maple pecan cake is a traditional dessert that brings together two of my favourite American ingredients. Maple syrup and pecan nuts are the very best of friends. That they both hail from the same continent may be a coincidence, but there is no better sweetener for pecans and no better nut to combine with maple syrup. The sponge here is quite light, with the maple-pecan flavour dispersed throughout. The icing tastes more strongly of the syrup, but this is counterbalanced by a little sharpness from the cream cheese. The pecans make a wonderfully crunchy addition, though you don't need to caramelise them if you'd prefer not to; just toast them instead.

Prep time: **20 minutes**
Baking time: **20–25 minutes**
Ready in: **1 hour**
Serves: **6–10**

200g (7oz) self-raising flour
¼ tsp salt
200g (7oz) soft light brown sugar
125ml (4½fl oz) buttermilk
200g (7oz) butter, melted,
  plus extra for greasing
50ml (2fl oz) maple syrup
2 eggs, beaten
75g (3oz) pecans, finely chopped

For the pecan praline
50g (2oz) caster sugar
50g (2oz) pecans

For the icing
300g (11oz) cream cheese
25ml (1fl oz) maple syrup
200g (7oz) icing sugar, sifted

Two 18cm (7in) diameter cake tins
  (see page 334)

Preheat the oven to 180°C (350°F), Gas mark 4, then butter the sides of the cake tins and line the base of each tin with a disc of baking parchment.

Sift the flour and salt into a large bowl and mix in the sugar. In a separate bowl, whisk the buttermilk with the butter, maple syrup and eggs. Add the wet ingredients to the flour and sugar, mixing together to combine, then fold in the chopped pecans.

Divide the batter between the prepared tins and bake for 20–25 minutes or until golden on top and springy to the touch.

Remove from the oven and allow to cool in the tin for 10 minutes. Loosen around the edges using a small, sharp knife and carefully remove each cake from its tin before transferring to a wire rack to finish cooling down (see page 334).

Meanwhile, make the pecan praline. First line a baking tray with a sheet of baking parchment, then place the sugar in a non-stick frying pan or saucepan and scatter the nuts over the top. Cook over a medium heat until the sugar turns a caramel colour. Do not stir the pan, but carefully 'swirl' it to allow the sugar to caramelise evenly and to coat the nuts in caramel. Alternatively, you could just toast the pecans instead (following the tip on page 125).

Pour the mixture into the paper-lined baking tray. Using two forks, separate the nuts to make sure they don't stick together, then set aside to cool and harden.

To make the icing, whisk together all the ingredients until smooth. Place one cake upside down on a plate and spread over some of the icing, so that it's about 5mm ($\frac{1}{4}$ in) thick. Place the other sponge on top, right side up, then cover the whole cake with the icing, using a palette knife dipped in hot water to smooth the surface.

Decorate with the caramelised or toasted pecans to finish.

Ballymaloe mincemeat crumble cake

This is a lovely Christmas dessert that we make at the Cookery School. A very satisfying cake, full of flavour and texture: the mincemeat keeps it firmly festive, while the layer of sponge is delicate and light and the crumble topping good and crunchy. I've included a recipe for mincemeat (see opposite), but feel free to use your own favourite variety. At other times of the year I like to replace the mincemeat with 300g (11oz) of raspberry jam. This cake is best served warm as a pudding, though if you have any left over it makes an excellent snack with a cup of tea or coffee.

Prep time: 25 minutes (excluding the mincemeat)
Baking time: 45–50 minutes
Ready in: 1 hour 15 minutes
Serves: 8–10

100g (3½oz) butter, softened, plus extra for greasing
100g (3½oz) soft light brown sugar
2 eggs
½ tsp vanilla extract
2 tbsp milk
175g (6oz) self-raising flour
550g (1lb 3oz) mincemeat (to make it yourself, see page 305)
Icing sugar, for dusting
Double or regular cream, whipped, to serve

For the crumble topping
100g (3½oz) self-raising flour, sifted
75g (3oz) caster sugar
75g (3oz) butter, chilled and cut into 1cm (½in) cubes
25g (1oz) flaked almonds

22cm (8½in) diameter spring-form or loose-bottomed cake tin with 6cm (2½in) sides (see page 336)

Preheat the oven to 180°C (350°F), Gas mark 4, and butter the sides and base of the cake tin. If you're using a spring-form tin, make sure the base of the tin is upside down, so there's no lip and the cake can slide off easily when cooked.

First make the crumble topping. Place the flour and caster sugar in a bowl, then add the butter and, using your fingertips, rub it in until the mixture resembles coarse breadcrumbs. Stir in the almonds and set aside.

To make the sponge, first cream the butter until soft in a large bowl or in an electric food mixer. Add the sugar and beat until the mixture is light and fluffy.

Whisk the eggs together in a small bowl with the vanilla extract and milk for a few seconds or just until mixed, then gradually add them to the creamed butter mixture, beating all the time. Sift in the flour and fold in gently to combine.

Tip the mixture into the prepared tin, then spoon in the mincemeat, spreading it evenly over the batter, before sprinkling over the crumble topping.

Place on the lowest shelf in the oven and bake for 45–50 minutes or until golden brown on top and a skewer inserted into the centre of the cake comes out just clean. Remove from the oven and allow to cool in the tin for 20 minutes, then loosen around the edges using a small, sharp knife and remove the sides of the tin before carefully transferring the cake to a serving plate (see page 336).

Dust the cake with lots of icing sugar, then serve warm with softly whipped cream.

Mincemeat

This delicious mincemeat will keep happily in a cool dark place for at least a year. If you are preparing your own suet (the fat that surrounds the beef kidney), make sure that every trace of blood has been removed before you whiz it in the food processor, otherwise it will cause the mincemeat to go off.

Prep time: **20 minutes**
Cooking time: **8–10 minutes**
Ready in: **50 minutes**
Makes: **2.7kg (6lb)**

2 large cooking apples, peeled, cored and cut into large chunks
Juice and finely grated zest of 2 oranges and 2 lemons
250g (9oz) shredded suet, or butter, chilled and grated
275g (10oz) raisins
275g (10oz) sultanas
275g (10oz) currants
125g (4½oz) chopped mixed peel
650g (1lb 7oz) soft dark brown sugar
50g (2oz) nibbed (chopped) almonds, or chopped pecans
2 tsp mixed spice
75ml (3fl oz) Irish whiskey or brandy

Place the apple chunks in a small saucepan with 1 teaspoon of water, cover with a lid and cook over a low heat for 8–10 minutes or until the apples are cooked down to a pulp. Remove from the heat and set aside to cool.

Mix with all the remaining ingredients in a large bowl and place in sterilised jars (for sterilising jars, see the tip on page 27). Leave to mature for at least two weeks, if possible, before using. If properly stored (somewhere cool in sterilised jars), this mincemeat should last for 1–2 years.

Tip To prepare suet properly, first peel off all the papery membrane that surrounds the suet. Next, use a knife to cut away any traces of kidney, blood or any gristle. Then roughly chop the suet and put it into a food processor. Pulse a few times until it is the consistency of rough breadcrumbs. Suet, once prepared, can be frozen.

Chocolate chestnut torte

Chestnuts are a truly festive ingredient. Their beguiling sweetness makes them ideal for adding to stuffing for the Christmas turkey, as well as making into truffles, tarts and tortes. This flourless cake is almost mousse-like, the only solid ingredient being the chestnuts themselves. It must be allowed to cool completely before you remove it from the tin. I like to decorate this torte with marrons glacés – chestnuts candied in sugar syrup – if I can get hold of them. Hugely popular in southern France and northern Italy, they are available either whole or as a purée. (You can buy them in specialist food shops and delis.) The whole ones would look, and taste, fabulous with this cake.

Prep time: **20 minutes**
Baking time: **30 minutes**
Ready in: **1 hour**
Serves: **8–10**

200g (7oz) dark chocolate, in drops or broken into pieces
200g (7oz) butter, plus extra for greasing
200g (7oz) cooked and peeled chestnuts (available vacuum-packed; to roast them yourself, see the tip on page 307)
200ml (7fl oz) milk
3 eggs, separated
125g (4½oz) caster sugar
Pinch of salt

To decorate
Cocoa powder, for dusting (optional)
8–10 marrons glacés (optional)

23cm (9in) diameter spring-form or loose-bottomed cake tin with 6cm (2½in) sides (see page 336)

Preheat the oven to 170°C (325°F), Gas mark 3, then butter the base and sides of the cake tin. If you're using a spring-form tin, make sure the base is upside down, so there's no lip and the cake can slide off easily when cooked.

Place the chocolate and butter in a heatproof bowl and set over a saucepan of simmering water. Leave just until melted, stirring occasionally, then remove from the heat.

Place the chestnuts in a separate saucepan with the milk and bring to the boil, then boil for 3 minutes before removing from the heat. Tip into a food processor and whiz for a few minutes to form a coarse purée.

In a large bowl, whisk together the egg yolks and 100g (3½oz) of the caster sugar for a few minutes or until light-textured and pale in colour. Stir in the melted chocolate along with the chestnut purée and mix in thoroughly.

In a separate, spotlessly clean bowl, whisk together the egg whites and salt until frothy, then add the remaining sugar and continue to whisk until the mixture forms stiff peaks. Fold carefully into the chocolate and chestnut mixture, then tip into the prepared tin.

Bake for about 30 minutes or until just set – a skewer inserted into the centre of the cake will still be slightly sticky. Remove from the oven and place, in the tin, on a wire rack to cool down completely. Loosen around the edges using a small, sharp knife, then remove the sides of the tin before carefully transferring the cake to a serving plate (see page 336).

Dust the top of the cake with cocoa powder or decorate with marrons glacés, if using. You can serve the torte warm, if you prefer, leaving it in the oven (preheated to 130°C/250°F/Gas mark $\frac{1}{2}$) for about 10 minutes to warm through.

Tip If you like, you can roast your own chestnuts over an open fire – the smell and the resulting sweet treats are divine, though it's a little easier to roast them in the oven. For the recipe above, you'll need 300g (11oz) of whole chestnuts. Use a sharp knife to cut a small cross in each nut, then place in a roasting tin and cook in the oven (preheated to 200°C/400°F/Gas mark 6) for about 30 minutes. Allow the nuts to cool before peeling them.

Spiced pear and ginger cheesecake

Cheesecake makes a fabulous alternative for the festive season. This recipe is very Christmassy in fact, as the pears are poached with mulled wine spices before being added to the cheesecake topping. The base contributes even more to the festive mix, with the ginger nuts, ground ginger and mixed spice.

Prep time: 30 minutes

Baking time: 40–45 minutes

Ready in: 3 hours

Serves: 8–10

Butter, for greasing

450g (1lb) cream cheese

150g (5oz) caster sugar

4 eggs, beaten

For the poached pears

50g (2oz) caster sugar

1 cinnamon stick

1 star anise

3 whole cloves

4 pears, peeled, quartered and cored

For the biscuit base

175g (6oz) ginger nut biscuits

1 tsp ground ginger

1 tsp mixed spice

75g (3oz) butter, melted

23cm (9in) diameter spring-form cake tin with 6cm (2½ in) sides (see page 336)

Preheat the oven to 180°C (350°F), Gas mark 4. Butter the sides and base of the cake tin, making sure the base is upside down, so there's no lip and the cake can slide off easily when cooked.

First poach the pears. Place the sugar and spices in a saucepan with 200ml (7fl oz) of water and set over a medium heat. Heat the syrup, stirring until the sugar has dissolved, then raise the heat and bring to the boil. Reduce the heat to a simmer, then add the pears and cover with a disc of baking parchment.

Simmer for 10 minutes or until the pears have softened, then remove from the syrup and place on a plate to cool. Reserve the poaching syrup.

Next make the biscuit base. Place the biscuits and spices in a food processor and whiz for a few minutes or until the mixture resembles coarse breadcrumbs. Add the melted butter and whiz again just until mixed. Alternatively, place the biscuits in a plastic bag and crush them using a rolling pin, then tip into the pan with the melted butter, add the spices and mix together to combine.

Tip the mixture into the prepared cake tin, spreading it out evenly to cover the bottom of the tin and pressing it down firmly.

Next make the cheesecake topping. Pour the pear-poaching syrup into a bowl, using a sieve to catch the whole spices – which you can keep for decorating the cheesecake later. Add the cream cheese, sugar and eggs and whisk together until well mixed and smooth.

Recipe continued overleaf

Arrange the pears in a single layer on the biscuit base, then pour over the cream-cheese mixture. Bake for about 40–45 minutes or just until golden on top – it will be slightly cracked on top and should wobble a little in the middle when you gently shake the tin. Remove from the oven and allow to cool in the tin, then place in the fridge and leave to set for 2 hours.

To serve, loosen around the edges using a small, sharp knife and then unclip and remove the sides of the tin (see page 336). Use a palette knife or metal fish slice to loosen the bottom of the cake from the base and, with the help of the palette knife or fish slice, carefully ease the cake onto a plate. (If you are worried about sliding the cheesecake off the base of the tin, then fear not: you can always serve it from the base. Simply transfer it, base and all, to your serving plate.)

If you like, you can place the reserved whole spices on top of the cheesecake to serve.

Vínarterta

My mum is Icelandic and this is the cake that she remembers most from her childhood; it's a real favourite of both hers and mine. Traditionally made at the start of winter, it's then stored and eaten over the Christmas period as it keeps well. With seven layers, the cake does take some time to make, but it isn't tricky if you take it step by step. After making, the cake should be covered and stored for a week to let it soften and 'mature'. It will keep for a few months and steadily improves, as the flavours are then given the chance to really get to know each other. You will need to cook this recipe in batches, as it's unlikely you'll have enough baking sheets, oven space or wire racks! For that reason, it's worth putting the remaining dough in the fridge while you cook the first or second batch, as it shouldn't really be out of the fridge for more than about 40 minutes before baking because it becomes difficult to roll.

Prep time: 1 hour 15 minutes

Baking time: about 1 hour (depending on the number of baking sheets and amount of oven space)

Ready in: a week!

Serves: 12–14

450g (1lb) plain flour, plus extra for dusting

2 tsp baking powder

½ tsp salt

1 tsp ground cardamom (to grind it yourself, see the tip on page 311)

225g (8oz) butter, softened

225g (8oz) caster sugar

2 eggs

1 tbsp milk

1 tsp vanilla extract

Icing sugar, for dusting

For the filling

975g (2lb 2½oz) pitted prunes

200g (7oz) caster sugar

1 tsp ground cardamom (to grind it yourself, see the tip on page 311)

1 tsp vanilla extract

First make the cake dough. Sift the flour, baking powder and salt into a bowl and mix in the ground cardamom. Cream the butter until soft in a large bowl or in an electric food mixer. Add the sugar and beat until the mixture is light and fluffy.

Whisk the eggs together in a small bowl for a few seconds or just until mixed, then gradually add them to the butter mixture, beating all the time. Mix in the milk and vanilla extract, followed by the dry ingredients, and stir together until combined.

Flatten out slightly to form a thick disc – if it's in a ball, the middle won't chill sufficiently – then wrap in cling film and leave in the fridge to chill for 30 minutes while you make the filling.

Place the prunes and sugar in a saucepan, add 400ml (14fl oz) of water and set over a medium heat. Cover and cook for 15 minutes, stirring regularly, until the prunes are tender, then remove the lid and cook uncovered for another 5 minutes, stirring regularly, until the mixture has thickened.

Remove from the heat and allow to cool for 5 minutes before blending until smooth with the ground cardamom and vanilla extract in a food processor or using a hand-held blender. Set aside and leave to cool down completely.

Recipe continued overleaf

Preheat the oven to 180°C (350°F), Gas mark 4.

Remove the dough from the fridge and divide it into seven equal pieces, each about 135g (4¾ oz) in weight. Shape into balls, then press down with the palm of your hands and place on to floured sheets of baking parchment before rolling out into circles 23cm (9in) in diameter using the base of a cake tin or a plate as a guide. (It's best to roll out the number of circles that will fit into the oven in one batch, keeping the rest of the dough covered in the fridge until you're able to use it.) When rolling out, try and keep the dough in a circle and use the rolling pin to enlarge it, tucking it in with your hands to shape the dough into a disc if it is losing its circular shape. Make sure, too, that it isn't sticking to the parchment by dusting frequently with flour and lifting the dough using a palette knife or metal fish slice. Trim each circle to the right size, if necessary, using a sharp knife and the cake-tin base or plate as a guide.

Transfer each circle to a baking sheet (no need to grease or line the sheet) and place in the oven. Bake for 12–16 minutes or until golden brown around the edges, then allow each cake to cool on its sheet for 2–3 minutes before running a palette knife or metal fish slice underneath and lifting out onto a wire rack to finish cooling. Repeat as necessary until you have seven quite thin, biscuit-like cakes.

To assemble the cakes, place one on your serving plate, then use a knife (a palette knife is ideal) to evenly spread over the filling. It should be spread quite thickly (to about 5mm/¼ in), but if you're concerned that you might be using too much, simply weigh the filling – you need six layers' worth in total, allowing 200g (7oz) for each layer. Cover with another round of cake, then spread over more filling. Keep going until all seven layers of cake are sandwiched together with six layers of prune filling.

Place in an airtight container or cover with cling film and store for a minimum of a few days, ideally a week. After a week, dust generously with icing sugar and cut into slices to serve. This cake will keep for at least a month if stored in an airtight container.

Christmas cake

Christmas cake is a classic for a reason: the strong fruit flavours go so well with the almond paste and sweet white icing. The cake also keeps for months, so you can serve slices whenever people drop by during the Christmas holidays. This recipe is a play on the classic, with the slightly spicy addition of crystallised ginger. There are three icing paths you can take, too. The first, outlined in the main recipe, is to cook the cake again once it's been covered in almond paste – toasting the paste really accentuates the almond flavour, and my mother-in-law, Darina, has been doing it like this for years. The second option is to ice over the almond paste with royal icing (see page 320). Made from whisked egg whites and sugar, this icing will dry to a crisp shell, and can be 'peaked' all over to resemble snow. The third option is to use fondant icing (see page 320), also known as sugar paste, which is rolled out and laid over the almond paste and can be made perfectly smooth. Choose whichever option you prefer.

Prep time: 1 hour 30 minutes
Baking time: 2 hours 30 minutes–
   3 hours 15 minutes
Ready in: 7 hours (or a few days)
Serves: 15–20

275g (10oz) butter, softened,
   plus extra for greasing
275g (10oz) soft light brown sugar
5 eggs
1 tsp finely grated orange zest
75g (3oz) ground almonds
275g (10oz) plain flour
2 tsp mixed spice

For the fruit
225g (8oz) sultanas
225g (8oz) raisins
125g (4½ oz) pitted dates, chopped
50g (2oz) currants
125g (4½ oz) chopped mixed peel
50g (2oz) crystallised ginger,
   finely chopped
125ml (4½ fl oz) brandy or whiskey

Ingredients cont. overleaf

First prepare the fruit for the cake. Place the dried fruit, mixed peel and crystallised ginger in a bowl, pour over the brandy or whiskey and allow to soak for at least 2 hours.

Preheat the oven to 150°C (300°F), Gas mark 2. Line the cake tin with baking parchment and wrap a collar of brown paper or a double layer of baking parchment around the outside to help prevent the cake from drying out as it bakes.

Cream the butter until soft in a large bowl or in an electric food mixer. Add the sugar and beat until the mixture is light and fluffy, then add the eggs, one at a time and beating well between each addition.

Stir in the orange zest and ground almonds, then sift in the flour and mixed spice and fold in gently. Fold in the soaked dried fruit, together with any brandy or whiskey left in the bowl, and transfer the mixture to the prepared cake tin.

Bake in the oven for 2 hours 30 minutes to 3 hours 15 minutes or until a skewer inserted into the centre of the cake comes out clean. Cover the cake, still in the tin, with foil and allow to cool. Once the cake has cooled, carefully tip it out of the tin (see page 334) and wrap in foil until you are ready to cover it with almond paste. (The cake will keep like this for a couple of months.)

Preheat the oven to 220°C (425°F), Gas mark 7.

Recipe continued overleaf

For the almond paste

450g (1lb) ground almonds

450g (1lb) caster sugar

1 egg

2 tbsp brandy or whiskey

A couple of drops (not more than ⅛ tsp) of almond essence or extract

Icing sugar, for dusting

For brushing the cake

1 small egg white, lightly beaten

2 egg yolks, lightly beaten

23cm (9in) diameter cake tin with 6cm (2½in) sides or 20cm (8in) square tin with 5cm (2in) sides (see page 334)

Sugar paste cutters in festive shapes (optional)

Large plate or a 28cm (11in) square cake board

To make the almond paste, first mix the ground almonds and sugar together in a bowl. In another bowl, beat the egg, add the brandy or whiskey and the almond essence or extract, then add to the dry ingredients and mix to a stiff paste. (You may not need to add all the egg mixture.) Sprinkle a work surface with icing sugar, turn the almond paste out of the bowl and gently knead until smooth.

Remove the foil and baking parchment from the cake. Take about half of the almond paste and place it on a work surface dusted with icing sugar. Roll out until it is slightly bigger than the cake itself and about 1cm (½in) thick. Brush the top of the cake with the lightly beaten egg white and turn it upside down onto the almond paste. Cut around the edge of the cake, then carefully turn the cake the right side up with the lid of almond paste attached to the top. (Alternatively, you could cut the almond paste out using the cake tin as a template, and place it on top of the cake.)

Next measure the circumference of the cake with a piece of string. Roll out one long strip of almond paste (or two shorter strips joined together) the same length as the string, and trim both short edges to the same height as the cake. Brush the cake and the almond paste lightly with egg white and press the strip against the sides of the cake, but without overlapping or there will be a bulge. Trim away any overlapping pieces of almond paste, then use a straight-sided tumbler to even the edges and smooth the join, and rub the cake well with your hand to ensure a nice flat surface. (If you would like to ice the cake at this stage, omit the next two steps and follow the recipes for making and applying either royal icing or fondant icing – see page 320.)

Now carefully place the cake on a large, greased baking sheet. Roll out the remainder of the almond paste to about 5mm (¼in) thick and cut out shapes in the paste, such as Santa Claus, using sugar paste cutters, if you like. Brush the whole surface of the cake with the beaten egg yolks and stick the shapes on top and around the sides, if you wish. Brush these with egg yolk as well.

Bake the cake for 10–20 minutes (not too near the top of the oven or it may burn) until it is golden and toasted. Remove from the oven, allow to cool, then carefully – using a palette knife or metal fish knife to ease it off the baking sheet – transfer to a serving plate or cake board.

It can be nice to tie a ribbon around the finished cake (whichever icing option you choose), then decorate the top with a sprig of holly leaves – either fresh or fondant (see page 331) – or whatever festive decorations you like, such as some adorable fondant penguins (see page 248).

Royal icing

Prep time: **10 minutes**
Makes: **725g (1lb 9½oz)**

4 egg whites
675g (1½lb) icing sugar, sifted
1⅓ tsp glycerine

Place the egg whites and icing sugar in a large bowl or in an electric food mixer. Using either a hand-held electric beater or the food mixer, whisk for several minutes or until the icing stands up in stiff peaks, then whisk in the glycerine just for a second or two to combine.

Use a palette knife to spread the icing all over the cake, covering the almond paste, then use the flat of the palette knife to gently lift up the icing in small peaks all over for a 'snow scene' effect.

Fondant icing

Prep time: **10 minutes**
Makes: **675g (1½lb)**

1½ egg whites, whisked
100g (3½oz) liquid glucose
½ tsp vanilla extract
600g (1lb 5oz) icing sugar, sifted, plus extra for dusting

In a bowl, mix together the egg white, glucose and vanilla extract. Place the icing sugar in a separate bowl or an electric food mixer and gradually add the egg-white mixture, beating continuously until all the ingredients come together.

Place the icing on a spotlessly clean worktop that has been generously dusted with icing sugar and knead it for a minute or two or until it is completely smooth on the surface.

Dust your worktop again with icing sugar and roll out the icing into a round about 30cm (12in) in diameter. Make sure that the worktop doesn't get sticky by regularly lifting up the icing with a palette knife or metal fish slice and dusting the work surface beneath it with icing sugar to stop the icing sticking to it.

Brush the almond paste with boiling-hot water so that the fondant icing will stick to it, then carefully lift the round of icing and place over the cake. Press and smooth the icing all over the cake with your hands. Use a straight-sided tumbler to roll all over the cake, then, with a sharp knife, trim away any excess from the 'skirt'. Keep rolling over the cake with the tumbler for a very smooth and neat finish. If making a square cake, press something flat like a hardback book against each side to neaten and flatten the sides.

Miriam's light Christmas pudding

This recipe comes from my friend Miriam Murphy, using a recipe that was handed down from her grandmother, to her mother, to her. Miriam's grandfather could no longer eat Christmas pudding as he found it too heavy, so his wife created this light version of the traditional dish using cider, to enhance the fruitiness of the pudding, and no suet. There are no spices either, keeping things simple, but if you'd like it spicier you could try adding a teaspoon of cinnamon or mixed spice. The brandy cream makes a lovely light alternative to brandy butter, although you can use plain whipped cream if you prefer.

Prep time: **30 minutes**

Baking time: **2 hours–2 hours 30 minutes**

Ready in: **6 hours (but do make at least a week ahead)**

Serves: **10–14**

100g (3½oz) butter, softened
175g (6oz) soft light brown sugar
3 eggs
100g (3½oz) plain flour
75g (3oz) ground almonds
75g (3oz) fresh white breadcrumbs
50ml (2fl oz) brandy

For the fruit
225g (8oz) mixed dried fruit (either ready-mixed or your own mixture of sultanas, raisins, currants and/or cranberries)
75g (3oz) chopped mixed peel
75g (3oz) glacé cherries, halved
1 x 300ml can of cider

For the brandy cream (optional)
200ml (7fl oz) double or regular cream
1–2 tbsp icing sugar, sifted
3 tbsp brandy or rum, or 3 tbsp Cointreau with 1 tsp finely grated orange zest or double or regular cream, whipped, to serve

1.8 litre (3 pint) ovenproof pudding basin

To prepare the fruit for the pudding, place the mixed dried fruit in a bowl with the chopped peel and glacé cherries and pour over the cider. Mix together and leave to soak for at least a few hours or preferably overnight.

When you're ready to make the pudding, preheat the oven to 140°C (275°F), Gas mark 1.

Cream the butter until soft in a large bowl or in an electric food mixer. Add the sugar and beat until the mixture is light and fluffy.

Whisk the eggs together in a small bowl for a few seconds or just until mixed, then gradually add them to the creamed butter mixture, beating all the time. Sift in the flour and tip in the ground almonds and breadcrumbs, followed by the soaked fruit and any remaining cider, then stir everything together until well mixed.

Spoon the mixture into the pudding basin and level the top. Gently bang the bowl on the work surface to release any air bubbles.

Next cut a disc of baking parchment about 6cm (2½in) larger in diameter than the rim of the basin. Place it over the pudding basin and tie with a long piece of string under the lip of the bowl. Place in an ovenproof saucepan a bit bigger than the basin and carefully pour hot water around the bowl to come three-quarters of the way up the sides.

Cover with the saucepan lid and bring to the boil, then immediately transfer to the oven to cook for between 2 hours and 2 hours 30 minutes, checking once or twice during cooking that the water in the saucepan has not evaporated and topping up with water as necessary.

The pudding can also be cooked on the hob, rather than in the oven, for the same amount of time on a low heat. The pudding is ready when a skewer inserted into the centre comes out moist, but with no mixture sticking to it.

Remove the bowl from the water and allow to cool just slightly, then remove the paper lid and pour over the brandy. Either serve immediately or place the baking parchment lid over the top again, then cover with foil and store in a cool place, where it will keep for up to two months.

To serve, reheat (if necessary) by steaming for 1 hour in the same way as above, and make the brandy cream, if using. Whip the cream until almost stiff and fold in the remaining ingredients. When the pudding is ready, turn it out onto a plate and serve with the brandy cream or a dollop of plain, softly whipped cream.

Pecan Yule log with caramel sauce

This retro-style festive treat makes the perfect centrepiece for a Christmas party or dinner. The cake itself is given a nutty flavour and slight crunch by the toasted pecans, which are ground before being mixed into the batter for the sponge. The bark effect for the log is easily achieved by running a fork along the icing. Served with a rich caramel sauce, this cake not only looks fantastic, but tastes as good as it looks!

Prep time: **30 minutes**
Baking time: **15–20 minutes**
Ready in: **2 hours 30 minutes**
Serves: **8–12**

250g (9oz) pecans, toasted
   (see the tip on page 125)
6 eggs, separated
½ tsp salt
125g (4½oz) caster sugar
75g (3oz) butter, melted
25g (1oz) plain flour

For the icing and sauce
275g (10oz) caster sugar
275ml (9½fl oz) double
   or regular cream
100g (3½oz) butter, softened
   and cut into cubes
½ tsp salt
350g (12oz) dark chocolate,
   in drops or broken into pieces

To decorate
Sprig of holly leaves
Icing sugar, for dusting

23 x 30cm (9 x 12in) Swiss roll tin
Large plate or large cake board

Preheat the oven to 180°C (350°F), Gas mark 4, then line the sides and base of the Swiss roll tin with baking parchment, with the paper coming just above the sides of the tin to enable the cake to be lifted out easily.

Place the toasted pecans in a food processor and pulse a good few times until the nuts are finely chopped, but not fully ground.

Place the egg whites and salt in a large, spotlessly clean bowl or in an electric food mixer. Using a hand-held electric beater or the food mixer, whisk until foamy. Tip in 50g (2oz) of the sugar and continue to whisk until stiff and glossy peaks form, then set aside.

In a separate bowl, whisk the egg yolks with the rest of the sugar for a few minutes or until thickened. Add the egg-white mixture and the melted butter and fold in carefully, then sprinkle over the finely chopped pecans and sift in the flour, folding it in to combine.

Tip into the prepared tin, smoothing the batter with a spatula to form an even layer. Bake for 15–20 minutes until it feels lightly springy in the centre, then cover with a clean, slightly damp tea towel and place the cake, still in the tin, on a wire rack to cool.

Next make the caramel. Place the sugar in a saucepan with 50ml (2fl oz) of water and set over a medium heat. Cook, stirring regularly, until the sugar dissolves, then increase the heat and bring to the boil. Once the mixture has come to the boil, remove the spoon and continue to boil – without stirring, though you can swirl the pan every so often to help it cook evenly – for about 10 minutes. The caramel is ready when the mixture has turned a deep golden whiskey colour.

Recipe continued overleaf

Remove the pan from the heat and whisk in the cream followed by the butter a few bits at a time, followed by the salt – the mixture will bubble vigorously. Place the pan over the heat again and stir until all the caramel bits dissolve, then remove from the hob and measure out 225ml (8fl oz) of this sauce, pouring it into a jug for serving later.

To make the icing add the chocolate to the remaining caramel in the saucepan and whisk until smooth. Transfer to a bowl and allow to stand, stirring occasionally, until spreadable. This should take about an hour if left in a cool place, but not the fridge as it will solidify.

When the cake is cool and you're ready to roll it up (though it will sit very well like this for 24 hours), remove the tea towel covering the cake, lift the cake out with the baking parchment still attached and place on a work surface next to your cake board or plate.

Spread some of the icing over the cake as if you were thickly buttering a slice of bread, then, beginning at one short side, and using the baking parchment to help, carefully roll up the cake. It may crack a little, but don't worry about this. Transfer the rolled-up cake from the baking parchment to the serving plate or board, removing the paper. Position the cake so the seam is at the bottom, then carefully tuck in the edges of the roll to neaten it.

Roughly 5cm (2½in) from one end of the log, make a cut running diagonally across the cake, with the other end about 12cm (5in) from the end of the log (see photograph on page 324). Spread a little of the icing on the cut side of the smaller section of cake and then place it about a third of the way down the log to look like a branch, pressing it in on its iced surface.

Now spread the rest of the icing all over the cake to completely cover it. To decorate, use a fork to make lines all along the log and branch to look like bark, making concentric circles at each end. This may get a little messy, so if you like you can neaten the serving plate or board by cleaning around the 'log' with kitchen paper.

Decorate with the holly leaves and lightly dust with icing sugar (to resemble snow). The cake will keep somewhere dry and cool (but not the fridge) for 2–3 days, covered with a large upturned bowl.

When you're ready to serve, cut into slices and pour over the reserved caramel sauce (reheating this if you like).

Clementine cake

Intensely moist and citrusy, this cake will be an expression of whichever fruit you'd prefer to use, with the flavour of its juice and zest. You could use clementines, tangerines, satsumas or even mandarins if you can get hold of them. The syrup in this cake means it will last for up to 10 days if kept in an airtight container.

Prep time: 20 minutes
Baking time: 40–50 minutes
Ready in: 1 hour 45 minutes
Serves: 8–12

200g (7oz) caster sugar
100g (3½oz) ground almonds
50g (2oz) fresh white breadcrumbs
2 tsp baking powder
4 eggs, beaten
175ml (6fl oz) sunflower oil,
   plus extra for greasing
Finely grated zest of 5 clementines

For the syrup
75g (3oz) caster sugar
Juice of 3 clementines

20cm (8in) diameter cake tin
   (see page 334)

Preheat the oven to 180°C (350°F), Gas mark 4, then grease the sides of the cake tin with sunflower oil and line the base with a disc of baking parchment. (It's a good idea to place a baking sheet under the tin before cooking this cake, or line the floor of the oven with a sheet of foil, in case there are any leaks.)

Place the sugar in a bowl and mix together with the ground almonds, breadcrumbs and baking powder. In a separate bowl, whisk together the eggs, sunflower oil and clementine zest. Pour the wet ingredients into the breadcrumb mixture and stir everything together until they are thoroughly mixed, then tip the batter into the prepared tin.

Bake on a lower shelf in the oven for 40–50 minutes or until lightly springy in the centre, golden brown on top and a skewer inserted into the centre of the cake comes out clean.

As the cake cooks, peel two of the clementines and slice crossways into rounds about 5mm (¼in) thick.

Next make the syrup. Place the caster sugar and clementine juice in a saucepan and set over a medium heat, stirring to dissolve the sugar. Bring to the boil and allow the mixture to boil, without stirring it, for 3 minutes or until slightly syrupy. Remove from the heat and set aside.

When the cake is cooked, take it out of the oven and let it sit in the tin for 10 minutes. Loosening around the edges using a small, sharp knife, carefully remove the cake from the tin and transfer to a serving plate (see page 334).

Arrange the clementine slices over the top, then reheat the syrup and pour it over the cake. Allow the cake to cool completely before serving.

Mincemeat muffins with eggnog icing

A fun, festive treat for anyone who's looking for an alternative to mince pies. The eggnog icing isn't strictly necessary but offers another layer of Christmas cheer. Freshly grating the nutmeg yourself will give an even better flavour than using ready ground. The mincemeat recipe here is very quick to make and can be used immediately, but you can of course use ready-made mincemeat if you prefer.

Prep time: 20 minutes (including the mincemeat)
Baking time: 20–25 minutes
Ready in: 1 hour
Makes: 12 muffins

200g (7oz) butter
150g (5oz) caster sugar
4 eggs
200g (7oz) plain flour
2 tsp baking powder

For the quick mincemeat
50g (2oz) mixed dried fruit (either ready-mixed or your own mixture of raisins, sultanas and currants)
50g (2oz) soft dark brown sugar
½ tsp mixed spice
1 cooking apple, peeled, cored and grated
Juice and finely grated zest of 1 orange
1 tbsp brandy or whiskey
or 175g (6oz) ready-made mincemeat (see also page 305)

Ingredients cont. overleaf

Preheat the oven to 180°C (350°F), Gas mark 4, and line the muffin tray with the paper cases.

Place all the mincemeat ingredients in a saucepan and set over a medium heat, allowing it to simmer, uncovered, for 10 minutes or until nearly all the liquid has gone. Remove from the heat and set aside to cool.

Cream the butter until soft in a large bowl or in an electric food mixer. Add the sugar and beat until the mixture is light and fluffy.

Whisk the eggs together in a small bowl for a few seconds or just until mixed, then gradually add them to the creamed butter mixture, beating all the time. Beat in the cooled mincemeat, then sift in the flour and baking powder and fold in gently to combine.

Divide between the muffin cases, filling each three-quarters full, then bake for 20–25 minutes or until well risen, deep golden on top and lightly springy to the touch. Remove from the oven and allow to cool for 5 minutes before removing from the tin and placing on a wire rack to cool down completely.

As the muffins cool, make the icing. Whisk together all the icing ingredients and place in a saucepan. Bring to the boil, stirring continuously, then remove from the heat and transfer to a large bowl or an electric food mixer. Using a hand-held electric beater or the food mixer, whisk continuously for a few minutes until the mixture has cooled and become very thick.

Recipe continued overleaf

For the icing

4 egg yolks

1 tsp cornflour

50g (2oz) caster sugar

25ml (1fl oz) brandy or whiskey

100ml (3½ fl oz) double
  or regular cream

½ tsp finely grated nutmeg,
  plus extra for dusting

12-cup muffin tray and 12 muffin cases
  (see page 336)

Spoon the icing onto the cooled muffins, and sprinkle with extra grated nutmeg for decoration. For an even more festive touch, you could decorate the tops of the muffins with fondant holly leaves (see below), adding one or two to each cake, depending on the size of the leaves.

Fondant holly leaves

Prep time: **30 minutes**

Makes: **about 20–30 holly leaves**

½ egg white, whisked

35g (1¼oz) liquid glucose

¼ tsp vanilla extract

A few drops of green food colouring

200g (7oz) icing sugar, sifted,
  plus extra for dusting

Holly leaf sugar paste cutter

In a bowl, mix together the egg white, glucose, vanilla extract and food colouring. Place the icing sugar in a separate bowl and gradually beat in the egg-white mixture.

Place the icing on a spotlessly clean work surface that has been dusted with icing sugar and knead for a minute or two or until it is completely smooth on the surface.

Dust your worktop again with icing sugar and roll out the icing to about 5mm (¼ in) thick, then use a sugar paste cutter to cut out the holly leaves. Using a sharp knife, score one line along the length of each leaf and add lines radiating out to the spikes to form a leaf shape. Then place the leaves on the cakes, adding one or two per cake, depending on the size.

Tip This recipe uses half an egg white. The easiest way of halving an egg white is to first separate the egg, then whisk the white lightly in a bowl and pour off half.

Tip For additional shapes made out of fondant icing see pages 242–48.

Panforte

Probably the oldest type of cake in this book, panforte dates back to the twelfth century. It hails from the Italian city of Siena, in which you'll find it in numerous guises. Panforte is similar to fruitcake but is made in a very different way: a mixture of honey, butter and sugar is boiled to make a thick syrup, then mixed with the other ingredients before being baked. The result is distinctively chewy and quite crunchy due to all the nuts in the cake. Traditionally eaten at Christmas, panforte is now available all year round. It can be served with tea or coffee, or as a pudding with a glass of sweet dessert wine. Once made, it will last, stored in an airtight container, for a good three months.

Prep time: **25 minutes**
Baking time: **50–55 minutes**
Ready in: **2 hours**
Serves: **10–12**

150g (5oz) hazelnuts, toasted, skinned and coarsely chopped (see the tip on page 125)

150g (5oz) pecan halves, toasted (see the tip on page 125) and coarsely chopped

75g (3oz) pitted dates, coarsely chopped

50g (2oz) candied orange peel, coarsely chopped

75g (3oz) dried cherries or dried cranberries

50g (2oz) dried figs, coarsely chopped

50g (2oz) plain flour, sifted

150g (5oz) honey

150g (5oz) caster sugar

25g (1oz) butter

23cm (9in) diameter cake tin (see page 334)

Preheat the oven to 150°C (300°F), Gas mark 2, and line the sides and base of the cake tin with baking parchment, with the paper coming just above the sides of the tin to enable the cake to be lifted out easily.

In a large bowl, mix the nuts and dried fruit with the flour and set aside.

Place the honey in a saucepan with the sugar and butter and set over a medium–low heat. Stir together, allowing the butter to melt, and continue to heat for 5–10 minutes or until a sugar thermometer reads 110°–115°C (230–235°F). If you don't have a thermometer, this is the 'thread stage'. The mixture will be thick and syrupy and the last couple of drops that fall from a spoon will form a thread. At this stage, immediately remove from the heat and add to the fruit and nuts.

Beat until well mixed: this is quite hard work and may take a while – it is easiest using an electric food mixer. Press the mixture into the prepared tin and bake for 50–55 minutes or until the cake feels firm in the middle.

Remove from the oven and place on a wire rack to cool down completely. When cool, remove from the tin with the lining paper, peel off the baking parchment and place on a serving plate.

Gaff's porter cake

Traditionally made for St Patrick's Day, this cake is flavoured with stout, for which 'porter' is another name. While you can serve it straight from the oven, it is best eaten a few days or even a week later, to give all the flavours a proper chance to get to know each other. This recipe comes from a friend of mine, Gaff, who swears this is the very best porter cake you'll find. You can make it with the stout of your choice, though Gaff prefers to use Murphy's.

Prep time: 15 minutes
Baking time: 1 hour 30 minutes
Ready in: 2 hours 30 minutes
Serves: 8–12

225g (8oz) butter, softened, plus extra for greasing
225g (8oz) soft light brown sugar
3 eggs
225ml (8fl oz) Irish stout (such as Beamish, Murphy's or Guinness)
450g (1lb) plain flour
½ tsp bicarbonate of soda
1 tsp mixed spice
1 tsp ground cinnamon
225g (8oz) sultanas
100g (3½oz) chopped mixed peel
450g (1lb) mixed dried fruit (either ready-mixed or your own mixture of sultanas, raisins and currants)
50g (2oz) almonds (skin still on), chopped, or nibbed (chopped) almonds

23cm (9in) diameter cake tin with 6cm (2½in) sides (see page 334)

Preheat the oven to 150°C (300°F), Gas mark 2. Butter the sides of the cake tin and line the base with a disc of baking parchment, then double wrap the outside of the cake tin with extra baking parchment or with foil.

Cream the butter until soft in a large bowl or in an electric food mixer. Add the sugar and beat until the mixture is light and fluffy.

Whisk the eggs together in a small bowl for a few seconds or just until mixed, then gradually add them to the butter mixture, beating all the time. Pour in the stout and beat it in, then sift in the flour, bicarbonate of soda and spices and fold in with the remaining ingredients until fully incorporated.

Tip the mixture into the prepared tin and bake for 1 hour 30 minutes or until a skewer inserted into the centre of the cake comes out clean. Check the cake halfway through baking and if it is looking a deep golden brown already, cover with baking parchment or foil for the remainder of the cooking time.

Remove from the oven and allow to sit in the tin for 10 minutes, then loosen around the edges using a small, sharp knife and carefully remove the cake from the tin before leaving on a wire rack to cool completely (see page 334).

Cut a slice now, if you like, but for a better flavour, store in an airtight container for a few days before eating.

Cake essentials

Cake making has a real magic to it – a few ingredients mixed together and then transformed behind the oven door – but rather than magic, much of it is pure science. The recipes are formulas that should be followed exactly: ingredients need to be carefully weighed and cake tins measured. There is no secret to cake making however, and you won't go wrong if you follow the steps in the recipe and keep in mind these tips and suggestions:

– Weigh all your ingredients carefully.
– Measure your cake tins, as the baking times in each recipe are specific to the size of the tin called for.
– Don't open the oven door too early or your cake may collapse.
– Make sure your oven is preheated to the correct temperature before placing the cake inside.
– When creaming make sure your butter is softened and cream butter and sugar together thoroughly; when I say light and fluffy, I really mean it.

Mixing the cake

When making the batter for a sponge, sugar is mixed with butter in the creaming process. It's important to do this step really thoroughly. If the mixture isn't light and fluffy, it won't have enough air bubbles and it won't combine properly with the eggs when you add them.

When you do add the eggs, doing so gradually will prevent the mixture from curdling. If it does curdle, add a tablespoon of the flour weighed out for adding after the eggs, and mix together before you add the remaining eggs. If the mixture does curdle a little at this point, don't worry as the cake will be fine when it's cooked.

When adding the flour to your sponge, it's generally folded or mixed in gently. Extended beating will work the gluten in the flour and toughen the batter, resulting in a heavier cake.

Another method for making sponges involves simply putting all the ingredients into a food processor or electric food mixer and whizzing just until combined. This produces a less delicate sponge but it is convenient, if you're short of time.

Some sponges are fat free. Eggs or egg yolks are whisked with sugar to make a light mousse; plain flour is then folded in with baking powder and the resulting sponge is very light.

When is the cake ready?

There are two good ways of checking when a cake is ready:

– A skewer inserted into the centre should come out clean with no raw mixture sticking to it; this shows that the middle of the cake – which takes the longest time to cook – is fully cooked.
– The centre of the cake should feel slightly springy to the touch and not at all wet.

Cake tins

How you remove a cake from its tin depends on the type of tin you're using. Below I've given instructions on the best way of doing this for each type of tin. In every case, the cake is left to cool the right way up, following my own preference. You can leave your cake to cool upside down, of course, but allowing it to cool upright means that there will be no grid marks left in the top of the cake from the wire rack, which can spoil its appearance.

Standard These are cake tins in one piece – they can be round or square – without a removable base. They are easy to use, but to remove a cake from them they must be tipped upside down. Some cakes may be too fragile for this, however, or may have a topping that needs to remain the right way up, in which case a loose-bottomed or spring-form tin would be more appropriate.

To remove a cake from a standard tin, first loosen around the edges using a small, sharp knife. Then place a spare plate upside down on top of the cake and carefully turn the cake over, still in its tin. Remove the tin and peel away any baking parchment, then place a wire rack upside down on top of the cake and carefully turn upright again, leaving the cake on the wire rack to cool down completely.

Loaf Suitable for making loaf-shaped cakes and fruit loaves, these also come in one piece. To remove the cake, follow the same procedure as for a standard tin. Where the tin is fully lined, as specified in some recipes, the cake can alternatively be lifted out with the baking parchment.

Spring-form This is a type of round cake tin with a removable base and sides that are kept together by a clasp, which is ideal if you can't turn the cake upside down and would like to slide

Standard square

Loaf

Spring-form

Sandwich

Bundt

Bun tray

Muffin tray

Madeleine tray

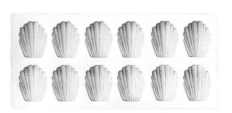

it off the base onto a serving plate. Most spring-form bases have a 'lip', however, and if this is uppermost, you won't be able to slide the cake off easily. In each of the recipes in this book for which a spring-form tin is specified, I have included the instruction to turn the base of the tin over before you fill the tin.

When the cake is cooked, loosen around the edges using a small, sharp knife, then carefully unclasp and remove the sides of the tin. If the cake can be turned over, follow the same procedure as for a standard tin. If it can't be turned over, use a palette knife or metal fish slice to loosen the bottom of the cake from the base of the tin, then slide the palette knife or fish slice under the cake and ease it onto a serving plate.

Loose-bottomed This type of tin – either round or square – consists of two sections: a loose base and a ring or square-sided frame for the sides. The base doesn't have a 'lip', hence the cake can be slid off onto a serving plate or flipped over if the cake isn't too delicate for this.

When the cake is cooked, loosen around the edges using a small, sharp knife. Then place a heavy jar, sturdy glass or small bowl on your work surface and set the cake on top of it, still in its tin. Carefully push down the sides of the tin, then lift away the cake and base from the jar, glass or bowl. If the cake can be turned over, follow the procedure as for a standard tin. If it can't be turned over, use a palette knife or metal fish slice to slide the cake from the base of the tin, as you would for a spring-form tin.

Sandwich This is a round tin generally with a diameter of 18–20cm (7–8in) and relatively shallow sides. Sandwich tins usually come in pairs, as they are used in recipes where two cakes are sandwiched together. They tend not to have removable bases, so cakes baked in them should be removed as for a standard type of cake tin.

Bundt This tin is used for making a ring-shaped cake, which has a ridge design that can be more or less elaborate depending on the tin. The resulting cake looks fantastic and as it's ring-shaped, with a larger surface area than one made in a standard tin, it has a crisper crust. It's especially important to make sure the inside of each ridge is greased with butter or oil before adding the cake mixture so that the cake can be tipped out easily. To remove the cake, first loosen around the edges using a small, sharp knife, then place a wire rack on top of the cake and flip it over. Remove the tin and leave on the rack to cool down fully.

Muffin trays These come in various sizes, but for this book a standard 12-cup tray has been used in every instance, where each hole is 7.5cm (2¾ in) wide, 3cm (1¼ in) deep and has a volume of 100ml (3½ fl oz).

Bun trays Bun trays also come in different sizes, but in this book a 12-cup tray is specified, smaller than the one used for muffins, where each hole is 6cm (2½in) wide, 2cm (¾in) deep and has a volume of 55ml (2fl oz).

Size of tin

All the recipes in this book call for a specific size of tin, hence it's important to measure the tin before you begin, to ensure that you have the correct one for the timings in a particular recipe. If you don't have a tin the right size but you have something similar, you can still bake the cake; you'll just need to adjust the cooking times slightly. If your tin is wider, the cooking time will be less as the cake will be shallower (the same amount of mixture but spread over a larger area). Likewise, if the width of your tin is slightly smaller, the cake will be deeper and will take a little longer to cook.

Lining cake tins

Lining a tin with paper helps to prevent the cake from sticking. I prefer baking parchment to greaseproof paper, as I find it works better. I also use non-stick silicone coated baking parchment as it can be used again and again. I keep discs of silicone baking parchment that I have cut out for each of my cake tins and I simply store them in the tins ready to bake, washing and drying them each time.

To line the base of a round or square cake tin, stand the tin on a piece of baking parchment or silicone baking parchment and draw around the base with a pencil, then cut out the circle or square and place in the base of the tin. To line the base and sides of a square tin or loaf tin, place the tin on a piece of baking parchment and draw around the base. Draw another square or oblong around the tin, larger than the tin itself this time, to mark out the paper that will line the sides of the tin. Cut around this square/oblong and then cut from each corner just to the corner of the smaller square or oblong. Fit the paper inside the tin and fold up the sides, allowing the paper to overlap at the corners and come above the sides of the tin so that the cake can be lifted out easily once baked.

Greasing tins

The sides of cake tins are almost always greased to prevent them from sticking to the cake. I think it's worth greasing even non-stick tins as they often do stick! To grease a tin, apply a little softened butter to the sides using a butter wrapper or a piece of baking parchment, making sure to cover the whole surface. If the recipe uses oil rather than butter, you can grease the tin using the same type of oil specified in the recipe.

When you've finished using a cake or loaf tin and have washed and dried it, place it in the oven while it's still warm from baking the cake to enable it to dry completely. This will help prevent it from rusting, keeping it in good condition so that the next cake you bake doesn't stick.

Timings

The following times appear at the top of each recipe to help you assess how long it will take to prepare and bake the cake in question.

Prep time This is the amount of time – after you've weighed all your ingredients – that you'll spend actually making the cake, whether that's creaming, whisking, mixing or icing.
Baking time This shows the amount of time the cake will be in the oven, allowing you to spend time doing something else.
Ready in This includes the prep time, cooking time and any cooling time.

Ovens

Fan versus conventional

Conventional ovens radiate heat from the top and bottom. The oven temperature varies based on which shelf you use: the bottom shelf is the coolest part of the oven and the top shelf is the hottest. Fan or convection ovens circulate the heated air, so the temperature is roughly the same throughout. The great advantage of this is that you can bake your cake in any part of the oven, or use all of the oven's shelves at the same time if you're cooking more than one cake, without having to move the tins around for even baking.

All the recipes in this book were tested using a conventional oven and baking the cake on the middle shelf (unless other-wise stated), and all oven temperatures are for conventional rather than fan ovens. If you have a fan oven, reduce the temperature by about ten per cent and the cooking time by a few minutes (the latter varying, depending on your oven).

Cooking times

Never take the cooking time as gospel! Oven temperatures will vary and your oven may run hotter or cooler than the thermostat states. For the best results, buy an oven thermometer for checking the temperature.

Preheating the oven is essential when baking. It should be allowed to come up to the correct temperature before you put in your cake. Never put a cake into an oven when it's cold and then switch it on, as the cake won't cook properly.

Similarly, it's important not to open the oven too soon: if you do, there's a risk the cake will collapse. A good general rule is not to open the oven before three-quarters of the cooking time specified in the recipe has elapsed.

Other equipment

You really don't need anything elaborate or specialist to make a cake. A mixing bowl, a wooden spoon and a cake tin are pretty much all you need. Cakes are easily achievable with just those three things, although other equipment can come in handy, as you'll see from the list below:

Mixing bowls It's worth having a few different bowls of varying sizes. Pyrex bowls are especially useful. They are heatproof and are good for gently melting chocolate or heating eggs over simmering water. I also have a large stainless-steel bowl and a plastic one.
Spatula A large spatula is useful for scraping the last of the mixture from the bowl as well as for folding mixtures together.
Palette knife A long, rounded tool, this is useful for spreading icing and, being flat and flexible, for sliding underneath cakes to help manoeuvre them.
Whisk I like to have two different-sized whisks, a small one for whisking just a couple of eggs and a bigger one for whisking larger quantities of eggs or cream.
Rolling pin This isn't just for rolling out dough; it can also be used as a pestle to grind toasted nuts or spices, or for crushing biscuits to make a cheesecake base.

Grater Having a good-quality fine grater to hand makes grating lemon or orange zest so much easier.

Wire rack Metal cooling racks are important as they enable air to circulate round your cake, helping it to cool down quickly.

Pastry brush Used to brush on glazes or syrups or to brush away excess crumbs from your cake before icing it.

Piping bag A piping bag with a range or nozzles in different shapes and sizes is very useful if you like to decorate your cakes quite precisely. (For more on these, see page 339.)

Sugar paste cutters These come in all different shapes and sizes and they're great for quickly cutting out shapes from fondant icing to use as decoration. You can also use cookie cutters to make fondant shapes.

Icing turntable This is like a cake stand but with a plate that revolves. It makes icing easier but is really not essential. Instead, I tend to place a cake on an upturned plate when icing it, so that the 'lip' of the plate doesn't get in the way, making for a neater finish.

Cake board Large cake boards are useful for particularly big cakes and are available at most kitchen shops, but you could of course use a chopping board, large plate or even a tray instead.

Electric food mixer Almost all the cakes in this book can be made without using a free-standing electric food mixer, being achievable with just a large bowl, a wooden spoon and perhaps a whisk. However, a food mixer does take a lot of the work out of cake making, and if you're an avid baker I would really recommend getting one. If you don't have a food mixer then a hand-held electric beater is a good substitute, especially for making meringues – making them using just a hand whisk is a mighty task indeed!

Ingredients

Making self-raising flour

Self-raising flour is essentially plain flour that has been mixed with baking powder. If you don't have any self-raising flour, you can easily make your own by adding 2 level teaspoons of baking powder for every 150g (5oz) of plain flour and mixing or sifting together well before using. Or in case a smaller quantity of flour is needed, you can add 1 level teaspoon of baking powder for every 75g (3oz) of plain flour.

Using eggs

All the eggs used in this book are medium-sized.

When you're whisking egg whites, make sure to use a spotlessly clean, dry bowl and whisk or the egg whites won't properly whisk up into peaks.

To separate an egg, crack the centre of the egg on the side of a bowl, then hold it over the bowl and carefully break the shell into two halves, holding each half upright in each hand, with one half containing the yolk. Pass the yolk back and forth a few times between each half shell, allowing the white to drop down into the bowl until you are left with just the yolk. It is important not to let any of the yolk get into the white and it is a good idea to separate each egg into a smaller bowl before tipping it into a larger one containing the other egg whites, just in case you have an accident and some egg yolk escapes into your egg whites.

Egg yolks can be kept covered for use within two hours (although they are best used immediately). Egg whites can be stored for much longer; kept covered in the fridge, they will remain fresh for a few weeks provided they're used within the 'use by' date. Egg whites can also be frozen – they'll keep like this for up to two months.

Melting chocolate

Chocolate can go from melted to burnt quite quickly, so it should never be melted by being placed straight in a saucepan and set over the heat. Instead, it should be placed, broken into pieces, into a heatproof bowl and then set over a saucepan of simmering water. (The bowl should fit snugly in the pan, its base not touching the water.) This ensures a regular and relatively low heat. If the water is left at a rolling boil for too long, the chocolate will burn. Indeed, if you are unable to keep an eye on the chocolate to ensure it doesn't burn, it's a good idea to take it off the heat once the water comes to the boil. Left like this, it will just melt slowly, with no risk of overheating. Don't place melted chocolate in the fridge to cool, as this causes the fat to 'bloom' on the surface, creating an ugly white-grey mark.

Icing

Glacé icing Glacé icing is made simply by mixing a liquid (usually lemon or orange juice or water) with icing sugar. It can be thick or thin, depending on how much liquid is used.

Fondant icing Also called sugar paste, fondant icing is made from icing sugar, egg white and glucose syrup. It is mouldable and can be rolled out to cover cakes or shaped into anything you like, from roses to bows (see pages 242–48).

American frosting American frosting is made from egg whites and sugar that are whisked together and heated to make a meringue-like mixture which is then spread over the cake. American frosting will dry out on the surface but remain light and almost marshmallowy on the inside.

Buttercream icing There are two types of buttercream icing. The first and most simple kind – frequently used in this book – consists of butter and icing sugar beaten together so they are light and fluffy. Flavourings are also added, such as vanilla extract or lemon zest. The second type of buttercream icing, also known as French buttercream, is more complicated, consisting of a sugar syrup that is boiled and added slowly to whisked egg yolks. Although not as quick to make, it results in an icing that is lighter but still rich and creamy.

Cream-cheese icing A mixture of icing sugar, cream cheese and some additional flavouring, this icing is rich but offset by a slight tang from the cream cheese.

Royal icing Royal icing is a white icing made with egg whites and sugar. It should set quite hard but with the inclusion of a little glycerine, it won't set too hard.

If you'd like a smooth flat icing, keep a bowl of hot water close to the cake and periodically dip your palette knife into it. For a 'snowy' effect with royal icing, use your palette knife (not dipped in hot water) to gently lift small peaks all over the cake.

Piping bags

Piping bags are useful for precise cake decorating. The control you get with one means you can easily create exact shapes such as swirls or zigzags or write letters and spell out names. Different nozzles also allow you to make specific shapes. For example, using a star-shaped nozzle you create rosettes. It's amazing how effective a simple cake can look with a few piped rosettes of whipped cream or buttercream icing dotted around the top. They also look quite pretty as a base for candles to sit in on top of a birthday cake.

Making a piping bag

On those occasions where delicate decoration is needed or something quite precise, then there's no substitute for a piping bag or bottle with a small nozzle attached. Yet often a home-made paper piping bag, or even just a simple plastic sandwich or freezer bag with the corner snipped off, will suffice. A paper piping bag is not as sturdy as one made from plastic, but it still works well for piping something quite soft such as glacé icing, melted chocolate or American frosting.

To make a paper piping bag, cut out a piece of baking parchment, about 25cm (10in) square, then fold it in half to make a triangle. Cut along the fold to give you two triangles, enough for two piping bags. Hold one triangle in front of you with the long end on top (so that the triangle is upside down). If you are right-handed, bring (but do not fold) the top corner on the right down to the bottom, right-angled corner. Twist your hand to turn the paper so that it forms a cone, making sure the two corners are aligned. Using your left thumb and index finger, hold the two aligned corners in place so that the cone is upright with the held-together corners on the far side of the cone. Then with your right hand bring the so far unused corner down and wrap it around so that it is at the back of the cone, aligned with the other two corners. Make sure the point of the cone doesn't have a big hole: if you look down through the cone, you should not be able to see through it. You can secure the edges by either folding them in to hold everything in place, or stapling them together. Now you can fill the paper piping bag with your chosen icing, folding down the top to enclose your filling and using scissors to snip a tiny piece off the end – not too much or the filling will fall out too quickly.

Alternatively, using a plastic sandwich or freezer bag with 1–2mm ($\frac{1}{16}$in) cut out of one corner works very well.

How to fill a piping bag

Hold the bag with one hand upright and fold down the top of the bag with your other hand to form a 'cuff' over the hand holding the bag. Half fill the bag with icing – do not let it get too full or the icing may be forced out of the wrong end.

To close the bag, unfold your 'cuff' and twist the top of the bag closed, forcing the icing down the bag towards the nozzle. Hold the bag with your thumb and forefinger, keeping the twist closed. Place your other hand nearer the nozzle and use your top hand to gently squeeze the bag to push out the icing.

Using a piping bag

To write letters or precise shapes Select a plain nozzle for your bag, then fill with your chosen icing. Holding the bag at a 45° angle from the cake and using gentle but consistent pressure, carefully guide the nozzle to spell out whatever letter or shape you like. This is the method to use to draw on stripes, zigzags or spirals.

To pipe dots Select a plain nozzle for your bag, then fill with your chosen icing. Holding the bag as upright as you can, with the nozzle just above the cake, carefully squeeze out just enough icing to form a dot, then lift off and repeat as desired.

To pipe icing beads Select a plain nozzle for your bag, then fill with your chosen icing. Holding the bag so it is at a 45° angle, place the nozzle just above the cake and gently squeeze until a small dot is formed. Continue squeezing and pull the top down slightly to form a teardrop shape, then stop squeezing, lift off and repeat as desired.

To pipe rosettes Choose a star-shaped nozzle for your bag, then fill with your chosen icing. A liquid type of icing such as melted chocolate or glacé icing, or something that's very stiff like fondant icing, won't be suitable for making rosettes, whereas buttercream icing, American frosting, royal icing or whipped cream are ideal. Holding the bag upright over the cake, about 2cm (¾in) from the surface, squeeze it to make a rosette the size of your choice, pushing more icing through for a larger rosette. Lift off your piping bag and repeat as desired. If you'd rather not use a piping bag, you can use a spoon to drizzle patterns on the cake using glacé icing. Place the bowl of icing close to the cake and dip your spoon into it, then lift the spoon out and let some icing drip off. Hold the spoon close to the cake as you drizzle on stripes, zigzags or swirls.

Decorating ideas

Candied lemon or orange slices

Prep time: **20 minutes**
Cooking time: **30 minutes**
Ready in: **1 hour 30 minutes**
Makes: **enough to cover two 20–25cm (8–10in) diameter cakes**

200g (7oz) caster sugar, plus 4 tbsp for sprinkling
4 lemons or oranges (unpeeled), cut crossways into slices about 5mm (¼in) thick and any pips removed

Line a baking tray with baking parchment and sprinkle over 2 tablespoons of the caster sugar. Place the 200g (7oz) sugar and 500ml (18fl oz) of water in a saucepan or large frying pan and set over a medium heat, then bring to the boil, stirring occasionally. Add the lemon or orange slices and continue to boil for 5 minutes, turning the slices over halfway through.

Reduce the heat to low and keep the syrup simmering for about 30 minutes, turning over the slices occasionally. The syrup will reduce during cooking, but keep an eye on it and don't let it reduce too much. If it does it will caramelise and start to brown and you want to avoid this, otherwise the lemon or orange will caramelise too and harden, whereas you want them to remain soft.

After 30 minutes the lemon or orange slices will have softened and become translucent. Carefully remove them from the pan and place in the baking tray on the sugared baking parchment, spreading the slices out so they're not too close to each other. Allow to cool completely, then sprinkle with another 2 tablespoons of caster sugar. Either decorate your cake with the candied slices or place in an airtight container, where they'll keep for up to two months.

Crisp lemon or orange slices

Prep time: 5 minutes
Cooking time: 6–8 hours
Ready in: 6–8 hours
Makes: enough to cover two 20–25cm (8–10in)
    diameter cakes

4 oranges or lemons (unpeeled), cut into slices as thin
    as you can get them (2–3mm/⅛in if possible)
Icing sugar, for dusting

Preheat the oven to its lowest setting.

Place the citrus slices on a rack in a baking tray and leave
in the oven for 6–8 hours or until completely crisp. When they
are ready, remove from the oven and allow to cool. Dust with
icing sugar and use to decorate your cake. Stored in an airtight
box, these will keep for up to a week undusted, but once
dusted in icing sugar they'll keep for only a day or two.

Chocolate-covered coffee beans

Sweet-tasting with a coffee kick, these work well scattered over
or neatly arranged on top of a coffee or chocolate cake. They
can be made up to a couple of weeks in advance and stored
in a box or jar somewhere cool but not the fridge.

Prep time: 10 minutes
Makes: 100g (3½oz)

75g (3oz) dark, milk or white chocolate, in drops or broken
    into pieces
25g (1oz) coffee beans

First line a baking tray with baking parchment. Place the chocolate in a heatproof bowl set over a pan of simmering water.
Stir occasionally just until melted, then remove from the heat.

When the chocolate has melted, stir in the coffee beans until
they are well coated, then using two forks lift out a few coffee
beans at a time and place them on the baking parchment.
Separate out the beans using the forks so they aren't touching,
then leave somewhere cool to set.

Chocolate-covered mint leaves

Prep time: 15 minutes
Makes: roughly 20 leaves

75g (3oz) dark chocolate, in drops or broken into pieces
A handful of good-quality, large fresh mint leaves

Line a baking tray with baking parchment.

Place the chocolate in a heatproof bowl and set over
a pan of simmering water. Leave just until melted, stirring
occasionally, then remove from the heat.

Holding a mint leaf by the base, or by the stalk if it's still
attached, carefully dip into the melted chocolate. Lift it out
and hold over the bowl to allow any excess to drip off, then
place on the baking parchment to set. (You may find it easier
to hold the mint leaves using tweezers.) Repeat with the rest
of the mint leaves and place somewhere cool to set.

Chocolate-covered peanuts

Prep time: 10 minutes
Makes: 175g (6oz)

75g (3oz) dark or milk chocolate, in drops
    or broken into pieces
100g (3½oz) roasted salted peanuts

Line a baking tray with a sheet of baking parchment.

Place the chocolate in a heatproof bowl and set over a pan
of just simmering water. Leave just until the chocolate has
melted, stirring occasionally, then remove from the heat and
stir in the peanuts.

When the nuts are well coated, tip onto the lined baking
tray and spread out well so they don't cluster or stick
together too much. Allow to cool until set, then add to your
cake to decorate.

Chocolate squares

Wafer thin, these chocolate shapes make an impressive but easy decoration that can be made in advance (up to a couple of weeks) and stored until needed. They can be stuck around the top or sides of a cake, or inserted into piped rosettes of buttercream or whipped cream.

Prep time: **10–15 minutes**
Ready in: **30–45 minutes**
Makes: **about 30 squares**

100g (3½oz) dark, milk or white chocolate, in drops or
   broken into pieces, plus an additional 25g (1oz) (optional,
   using a contrasting type of chocolate to the main variety)

Line a baking sheet with baking parchment (alternatively, you could use the shiny side of a cereal packet, which works just as well).

Place the 100g (3½oz) of chocolate in a heatproof bowl, then set over a saucepan of simmering water and stir occasionally just until melted. Remove from the heat and pour onto the baking sheet or cereal packet, spreading the melted chocolate with a palette knife and carefully evening it out to just 2–3mm (⅛ in) thick.

If you like, you can also melt an additional 25g (1oz) of chocolate, using a contrasting variety to the 100g (3½oz), such as white or milk chocolate if you're using dark chocolate for the squares. When this has melted, drizzle over the thin layer of chocolate and leave as it is or swirl the different types of chocolate together using a small, sharp knife or a cocktail stick.

Leave somewhere cool, but not in the fridge, for 20–30 minutes or until the chocolate has set and is matt in appearance. Transfer to a chopping board, still with the paper attached, and trim with a large knife to straighten the edges.

Next cut the chocolate carefully to make squares or diamonds. You can cut in a grid pattern or, for diamonds, cut in parallel straight lines, then cut another set of parallel lines at an angle to the first ones (as in the photograph opposite). Alternatively, use a cookie cutter to cut hearts, stars or whatever shapes you'd like.

Carefully lift the chocolate pieces off the baking parchment or cereal box, and store in an airtight box, somewhere cool but not in the fridge.

Chocolate curls

Prep time: **15 minutes**
Makes: **enough to cover one 18cm (7in) cake**

300g (11oz) dark, milk or white chocolate,
   in drops or chopped into pieces

Place the chocolate in a heatproof bowl over a saucepan of water on a medium heat and bring to a rolling boil, then turn off the heat. Allow the chocolate to melt slowly, stirring occasionally.

Place a baking tray or roasting tin upside down on your work surface. Once the chocolate has completely melted, pour it over the upside-down tray or tin and, using a palette knife, spread it out so that it's 3–4mm (⅛ in) thick and about the size of an A4 sheet of paper.

Place the chocolate somewhere cool (but not the fridge as this will be too cold – see tip below) and allow it to slowly set. The chocolate is set when it is no longer shiny – it should become matt in appearance.

Using a swivel-bladed vegetable peeler or a cheese slicer, run along the top of the chocolate to shave off curls. Either place the curls directly onto a cake or, if you'd like to make them ahead of time, transfer them onto a plate or into an airtight box and place somewhere cool (but not the fridge). Stored in an airtight container, they will keep for up to two weeks.

Tip It's important that the chocolate is completely set before using it, yet not too cold. If it's too cold, it will not 'curl', but if it's not sufficiently set the curls will collapse.

Crystallised orange peel

Prep time: **10 minutes**
Cooking time: **20 minutes**
Ready in: **1 hour**
Makes: **enough to cover one 20–25cm
(8–10in) diameter cake**

2 oranges
200g (7oz) caster sugar

First line a baking tray with a sheet of baking parchment.

Peel the oranges very thinly with a peeler, being careful not to include the white pith. Cut the peel into thin strips (each as thin as a matchstick), then place in a small saucepan and cover with cold water.

Bring to a simmer and allow to cook for 5 minutes. Drain the peel and return to the saucepan. Cover again with fresh water and simmer for another 5 minutes, then drain once more and set aside.

Next make the syrup. Place 150g (5oz) of the sugar and 150ml (5fl oz) of water in the same saucepan that you used for boiling the zest, and set over a medium heat, stirring to dissolve the sugar. Bring to the boil and allow the syrup to bubble for 2 minutes, without stirring the mixture, then return the zest to the saucepan and simmer gently for 6–8 minutes – covering the pan with a lid if the syrup is thickening – until the strips of peel look glossy and translucent.

Remove from the syrup using a small sieve or slotted spoon and spread the zest out to cool on the paper-lined baking tray, reserving the orange-scented syrup for homemade lemonade or cocktails, or to make more crystallised peel another time.

Once the zest is cool, pour the remaining sugar over it and use your fingertips to coat each piece of orange peel in the sugar grains. Allow the crystallised peel to sit in a dry atmosphere for about 30 minutes or until it has dried slightly, then use straight away or store in an airtight box or jar where it will keep for up to a month.

Crystallised flowers

Prep time: **30 minutes**
Ready in: **about 3 hours**
Makes: **50–60 petals or about 30–40 flowers
(depending on size)**

1 egg white, lightly whisked
About 75g (3oz) caster sugar
Edible flowers, such as primroses, violets or violas, or rose petals

Dip a small paintbrush into the egg white and carefully brush the flowers, using just enough egg white to cover the surface of each flower. Sprinkle the sugar over the petals, being careful to cover every petal.

Gently shake off any excess sugar and arrange carefully on a tray lined with baking parchment. Place somewhere dry (and even slightly warm, such as near a radiator or in an airing cupboard) and leave to dry for a few hours or overnight. Remove from the tray and use to decorate your cake. Stored in an airtight box, these will remain at their best for up to 1–2 weeks, after which time their colour begins to fade.

Tip See page 242 for how to make fondant roses.

Honeycomb

Honeycomb looks seriously impressive but is actually not too tricky to make. It requires glucose syrup, which you can get from some supermarkets, as well as chemists and specialist food shops. It's easier to make if you have a sugar thermometer, but it's not essential as you can check for the 'hard crack' stage instead (see below). The honeycomb can be stored in an airtight container, where it will keep for a couple of weeks. Try crumbling over ice cream or adding to melted chocolate.

Prep time: 15 minutes

Cooking time: 5–10 minutes

Ready in: 45 minutes

Makes: 500g (1lb 2oz)

325g (1½lb) caster sugar
50g (2oz) honey
125g (4½oz) glucose syrup
1 tbsp bicarbonate of soda

Line a large baking tray with baking parchment.

Place the sugar, honey and glucose syrup in a large saucepan and add 50ml (2fl oz) of water. Bring to the boil, stirring until the sugar dissolves, then reduce the heat to medium and simmer without stirring for 5–10 minutes or until the syrup turns a light golden colour and a sugar thermometer dipped into the mixture reads 149°C (300°F). Alternatively, check whether it has reached the 'hard crack' stage. To test for this, use a spoon to drop a small amount of syrup into a bowl of very cold water. If it's reached the right temperature in the pan, the syrup will solidify into hard, brittle threads that immediately break when you bend them. (Bear in mind that the syrup is now very hot and can easily burn; allow it to cool in the water for a few moments before touching it.)

Immediately remove the pan from the heat and quickly whisk in the bicarbonate of soda. The mixture will treble in size very quickly, so be careful it doesn't spill over. Pour onto the baking parchment, swirling the tray to spread the mixture evenly. Leave to cool down fully and harden before breaking into chunks. Cut with a knife or break with your hands into small pieces about the size of rough gravel. Use pieces to decorate your cake, then place the rest in an airtight container where it will keep for a couple of weeks. It is delicious stirred into ice cream or dipped into melted chocolate and allowed to set.

Peanut brittle

Prep time: 5 minutes

Cooking time: 20–25 minutes

Ready in: 30–40 minutes

Makes: 400g (14oz)

225g (8oz) butter, diced
225g (8oz) caster sugar
½ tsp salt
150g (5oz) salted peanuts, roughly chopped

Line a baking tray with baking parchment.

Place all the ingredients, except the peanuts, in a heavy-based saucepan with 50ml (2fl oz) of water and bring slowly to the boil, stirring until the sugar has dissolved. Reduce the heat to low and simmer for 15–20 minutes without stirring until a sugar thermometer dipped into the mixture reads 150°C (302°F). It will be deep golden brown in colour. Below this temperature and the brittle will not set; above and it will taste burnt. If you don't have a sugar thermometer, check that the 'hard crack' stage has been reached: if you drop a teaspoonful of the syrup into a bowl of iced water it will solidify into hard, brittle threads that immediately break when you bend them. (Bear in mind that the syrup is now very hot and can easily burn; allow it to cool in the water for a few moments before touching it.)

Immediately (and taking great care as it is very hot) add the peanuts to the syrup, without stirring the mixture, then pour onto the baking tray and swirl the tray around to spread evenly. It will begin to set almost straight away, so you need to work quickly.

Once the brittle has completely hardened, after 5–10 minutes, slam the baking tray on the counter to break into small pieces. Chop or break up the pieces if they are not small enough.

Scatter some of the peanut brittle over the cake to decorate, placing any remaining pieces in an airtight container where they will keep for 3–4 days.

Tip See the recipe for Hazelnut praline triple-layered cake on page 271 if you would like to make hazelnut praline as a decorative topping for your cake.

Salted peanut praline

Prep time: **5 minutes**
Cooking time: **10 minutes**
Ready in: **45 minutes**
Makes: **200g (7oz)**

100g (3½oz) caster sugar
100g (3½oz) salted peanuts

First line a baking tray with a sheet of baking parchment.

Place the sugar in a frying pan or saucepan and scatter the nuts over the top. Set over a medium heat until the sugar turns a caramel colour. Do not stir, but instead carefully 'swirl' the pan to allow the sugar to caramelise evenly and to coat the nuts in caramel.

Pour the mixture onto the prepared baking tray and, using two forks, separate out the nuts to make sure they don't stick together, then allow to cool and harden. Roughly chop the salted peanut praline and scatter over your cake to decorate.

Stored in a jar or airtight container, this will keep for a couple of weeks.

Elderflower sugar

Prep time: **10 minutes**
Ready in: **2–3 hours**
Makes: **450g (1lb)**

For sprinkling over 1 large cake
2 elderflower heads
Finely grated zest of ½ lemon
50g (2oz) caster sugar

For the store cupboard
About 20 elderflower heads
Finely grated zest of 2 lemons
400g (14oz) caster sugar

Carefully knock or pick just the flowers from the elderflower heads and mix in a bowl along with the lemon zest and sugar. Add half of the mixture to a food processor and whiz for a few minutes, then return to the bowl with the rest of the mixture.

Spread out on a baking tray lined with baking parchment and leave to dry somewhere warm – such as the side of a stove, perched over a radiator or in a sunny window – for a few hours or until the sugar has dried. Stored in a sealed container, the sugar will last for months if you want to make the larger quantity. Try sprinkling it over pancakes or porridge.

Tip See page 277 for how to make decorative coloured sugar.

Index

A

after dinner mint cake 164
almonds: almond hedgehog
   cake 205
   almond paste 318
   almond praline 131
   Bakewell cake 18
   banana, almond and honey
      muffins 140
   chocolate almond
      madeleines 114
   chocolate fudge cake 158
   chocolate, rum and almond
      cake 62–5
   date and almond honey
      cake 76
   dulce de leche cake 168
   Dundee cake 111
   lemon and rosemary
      polenta cake 32
   orange and almond syrup
      cake 268
   orange lamingtons 106
   raspberry and blueberry
      friands 47
   raspberry frangipane
      cake 170
   Toscatårta (Swedish almond
      cake) 30
   see also marzipan
American frosting 215, 339
angel food cake 100–3
anniversary cakes 255–6, 287–8
apples: apple and blackberry
   oat muffins 87
   apple and ginger (or
      cinnamon) muffins 14
   apple and walnut cake 17
   apple, oat and pecan
      bars 52
   mincemeat 305, 328
   Swedish apple cake 166
apricot, pistachio and saffron
   muffins 13
Arctic roll 194–6

B

báirín breac 299–300
baked Alaska 90–3
Bakewell cake 18
baking powder 338
Ballymaloe mincemeat
   crumble cake 304
bananas: banana, almond and
   honey muffins 140
   banana cake 154
   banana ice-cream cake 209
   banoffee blondies 131
   sugar-free banana bread 66
banoffee blondies 131
barmbrack 299–300
Battenberg cake 108–10
beads, piping 340
beer: Gaff's porter cake 333
beetroot brownies, intensely
   chocolatey 188–9
berry buttercream icing 187,
   227, 232, 239
birds, fondant 245
black icing 298
blackberries: apple and
   blackberry oat muffins 87
blondies, banoffee 131
blueberries: blueberry and
   coconut cake 175
   dairy-free blueberry
      crumble cake 75
   raspberry and blueberry
      friands 47
boiled fruitcake 141
Bonfire Night cupcakes 301
bran: 30-day bran and
   pumpkin seed muffins 67
brandy cream 322
Brittany butter cake 123
brownies: cheesecake 128
   double chocolate peanut
      butter 149
   gluten- and dairy-free
      pecan 71
   intensely chocolatey

beetroot 188–9
bundt cakes: cardamom
      yoghurt cake 144
   lemon poppy-seed cake 10
hundt tins 335, 336
bun trays 335, 336
butter: Brittany butter
   cake 123
   mixing cakes 334
buttercream icing 339
   berry 187, 227, 232, 239
   chocolate 186
   coloured 227, 232, 239
   peanut 184
   pistachio and
      rose-water 266
   praline 184
   vanilla 132
butterflies, fondant 245
butterfly cake 225
butternut squash: Halloween
   pumpkin squares 296–8
butterscotch sauce 155, 209

C

cake pops 220–4
cake tins 334–7
   greasing 337
   lining 336
   size of 336
   turning out cakes 334
   types of 334–6
candied lemon or orange
   slices 340
cappuccino squares 132
caramel: almond praline 131
   butterscotch sauce 155, 209
   caramel carrot cake 96
   caramel sauce 325–6
   caramelised orange
      upside-down cake 171
   caramelised oranges 162
   caramelised pear
      upside-down cake 178
   chocolate and toffee

ice-cream cake 198
chocolate honeycomb
   topping 261
dulce de leche cake 168
hazelnut praline
   triple-layered cake 271–2
honeycomb 345
layered chocolate and
   caramel cake 199–201
peanut brittle 345
pecan praline 302
perfect peanut butter
   cake 293
praline buttercream icing 184
salted peanut praline 346
sticky toffee date cakes 167
upside-down peach and
   saffron cake 59
cardamom: cardamom
   yoghurt cake 144
   removing seeds 144
   spicy chocolate torte 160
   Vínarterta 311–12
carrots: caramel carrot cake 96
   carrot cake 94
   ginger carrot cupcakes 96
castle cake 236–41
celebration cakes 250–93
cheese see cream cheese;
   mascarpone; ricotta cheese
cheesecakes: cheesecake
   brownies 128
   chocolate hazelnut 124–5
   raspberry and white
      chocolate 190–1
   spiced pear and ginger
      308–10
cherry marzipan cake 163
chestnuts: chocolate chestnut
   torte 306–7
   roasting 307
chocolate: after dinner
   mint cake 164
   anniversary chocolate
      mousse layer cake 255–6

Thank yous

My huge, heartfelt thanks to Lizzy Gray, Elizabeth Woabank and Hannah
MacDonald and to the amazing team at Collins who brought this book together.
Also thanks to: Martin Topping, Lucy Sykes-Thompson, Heike Schussler, Elen
Jones, Annie Rigg, Polly Webb-Wilson, Phil Webb, Annabel Hornsby, Sam Head,
Helen Cuddigan, Fiona Lindsay and everyone at Limelight, and Darina and Tim
Allen and all at Ballymaloe.

Thanks to Irish designer Lucy Downes of Sphere One (www.sphereone.ie)
whose gorgeous cashmere I wore throughout the photography and filming.
An unbelievably ginormous thank you to Josh Heller.

Lastly, a great big thank you to my family to whom I dedicate this book: Isaac,
Joshua, Lucca and Scarlett Lily.